MUSIC HALL

The business of pleasure

Edited by PETER BAILEY

Open University Press
Milton Keynes · Philadelphia

Open University Press
Open University Educational Enterprises Limited
12 Cofferidge Close
Stony Stratford
Milton Keynes MK11 1BY, England

and

242 Cherry Street
Philadelphia, PA 19106, USA

First Published 1986

British Library Cataloguing in Publication Data

Music hall: the business of pleasure.—
  (Popular music in Britain)
  1. Music-halls (Variety theaters, cabarets,
  etc.) — Great Britain—History
  I. Bailey, Peter, 1937–   II. Series
  792.7'0941   PN1968.G7

ISBN 0 335 15278 3
ISBN 0 335 15129 9 Pbk

Library of Congress Cataloging in Publication Data

Music Hall.
  (Popular music in Britain)
  Companion vol. to: Music hall: performance and style/
  edited by J. S. Bratton. 1986.
  Includes index.
  1. Music, Popular (Songs, etc.) — Great Britain—
History and criticism. 2. Songs, English—Great Britain—
History and criticism. 3. Music-halls (Variety-theaters,
cabarets, etc.) — Great Britain. 4. Musical revue,
comedy, etc.) — Great Britain. 5. Great Britain—popular
culture. 6. Great Britain—Social life and customs.
I. Bailey, Peter, 1937–   II. Series.
ML3650.M9 1986   782.81'00941   86–12837

ISBN 0–335–15278–3
ISBN 0–335–15129–9 (pbk.)

Typeset by S & S Press, Abingdon, Oxfordshire
Printed in Great Britain
at The Alden Press

Contents

Editorial Preface

What *is* British popular music? Does such a thing exist? What makes certain music and songs popular? And who made the musical cultures of these islands? What did Scots, Welsh, Irish and North American people have to do with the process? What part did people in the English regions play — the Geordies, Cockneys, midlanders and all the rest? Where did the Empire fit in? How did European 'high' culture affect what most people played and sang? And how did all these factors vary in significance over time? In the end, just how much do we know about the history of musical culture on these tiny patches of land? The truth is that we know very little, and this realization led to this series.

The history of British people and culture has been dominated by capitalism for centuries; and capitalism helped to polarize people into classes not only economically, but culturally too. Music was never *simply* music: songs were never *simply* songs. Both were produced and used by particular people in particular historical periods for particular reasons, and we have recognized this in the way in which we have put this series together.

Every book in this series aims to exemplify and to foster inter-disciplinary research. Each volume studies not only 'texts' and performances, but institutions and technology as well, and the culture practices and sets of social relationships through which music and songs were produced, disseminated and consumed. Ideas, values, attitudes and what is generally referred to as ideology are taken into account, as are factors such as gender, age, geography and traditions. Nor is our series above the struggle. We do not pretend to have helped produce an objective record. We are, unrepentantly, on the side of the majority, and our main perspective is from 'below', even though the whole musical field needs to be in view. We hope that by clarifying the history of popular musical culture we can help clear the ground for a genuinely democratic musical culture of the future.

Dave Harker and Richard Middleton

Notes on Contributors

Peter Bailey teaches history at the University of Manitoba. Author of *Leisure and Class in Victorian England* and several articles on the popular culture of the period, he is preparing a book on the social history of British music hall.

Jeremy Crump teaches in a comprehensive school in Leicestershire, and completed his doctoral thesis on the history of popular recreation in nineteenth century Leicester, at the Centre for the Study of Social History, University of Warwick in 1985. He has a number of publications in this and related areas.

John Earl is a freelance consultant in theatre conservation and research. As a trained building surveyor he was previously with the GLC's Historic Building Division, and among several publications in the field is author (with John Stanton) of *Canterbury Hall and Theatre of Varieties*, 1982.

Dagmar Höher is completing a doctorate on the social history of the English music hall at the Freie Universität in West Berlin. She has written on women's work in the industrial revolution, and was visiting British Council scholar at St. Antony's College, Oxford, 1983–4.

Susan Pennybacker is Assistant Professor of History at Trinity College, Hartford, Connecticut. She has several pieces on the London County Council under preparation for publication, derived from her Cambridge PhD thesis on the LCC and the labour question, 1889–1919.

Lois Rutherford is taking an MSc in Applied Social Work at Wolfson College, Oxford. She has worked in theatre and light entertainment, and undertook her research into music hall at Girton College, Cambridge.

Chris Waters lectures in History and Literature at Harvard University. Author of several pieces on Victorian popular culture, he is currently revising his Harvard PhD thesis on socialism and the politics of popular culture in Britain, 1884–1914, for publication.

Introduction: Making Sense of Music Hall

PETER BAILEY*

Music hall has become one of the great clichés or passwords in the vocabulary of popular culture and the collective historical memory. The term mobilises a limited but still resonant set of associations that fall into place in a familiar collage of names and images: Marie Lloyd, Dan Leno; the Old Met, Collins's; 'Boiled Beef and Carrots', 'Down at the Old Bull and Bush'; the sing-song and the comic turn. One may offer substitutions or additions to this essentialist catalogue or point to latter-day displacements of the style in film and television, but the commonest location for all theatrical reconstructions of the music hall and its mythic lodgement in the popular mind is in the contrived and secure past of the Good Old Days — a plush and womb-like never never land of Edwardian England. In this persistent sense music hall is as fixed and ahistorical a category as 'folksong', as wishful and misleading a construction as the good old London bobby. Perhaps it is that the characteristic capacity of music hall to deflate and parody the pretentious somehow deters the social historian from applying his/her corrective specificities to such a generalised representation (collapse of stout party?) or the disciple of cultural studies from deconstructing this cultural form, so obviously mythic yet taken for granted; but it is remarkable, given the present configuration of scholarly interests, that this territory is so underworked.

This collection of essays, in conjunction with its companion volume edited by J. S. Bratton, *Music Hall: Performance and Style*, seeks to make good some of this deficiency. Neither makes any claim to be either definitive or encyclopaedic and indeed some of the familiar landmarks and celebrities of music hall history will be found to be 'resting' from these pages. These books are concerned to reconstruct the wider and deeper patterns of operation and performance within which the great halls and their stars worked, to locate the structure and process of music hall as a dominant form of cultural production in the context of a modernising capitalist society, and to relate such

* I wish to thank the Social Sciences and Humanities Research Council of Canada for their generous support of my own research into the history of the halls.

studies to the interpretative debates of recent scholarship in social history and cultural studies. Though the range of enquiry has been substantially extended, there remain some unfortunate but unavoidable limitations in terms of time and space. For the most part contributions do not venture beyond 1914, within a period which we have loosely designated 'Victorian', and though several pieces escape the centrifugal pull of London, we could find no one with work in hand on music hall outside England. These and other deficiencies noted below clearly constitute opportunities for a further collection of studies.

Though scholarly investigation is still only modest in extent and there are many gaps and obscurities in the record, there is a mountain of writing on the music halls, contemporary and otherwise, but before mapping out this daunting mass it may be helpful to provide an elementary outline of the halls' development.[1]

The origins of music hall are to be found in a closely related yet diverse cluster of institutions providing popular entertainment in the rapidly expanding towns and cities of the 1830s and 1840s. By then, the traditional localised amateur entertainment of the pub, the 'free and easy', was becoming a more specialised function catering to a wider public. The back-room get-together gave way to the 'singing saloon' concert with its expanded premises and professional performers. Overlapping in terms of audience and programme was the popular theatre played in the minor or burletta houses (some also sited in pub saloons) or on the road in booths and fit-ups. Here the dramatic episodes were interspersed with other items from the miscellaneous entertainments of the popular tradition; as in the saloons, eating, drinking and smoking continued during the performance. Among various other tributary sources in the formation of the music hall we may note the song and supper rooms or night houses (most notably in London), where a more fashionable and all-male audience took late-night refreshment and indulged its bohemian pretensions with songs from low-life. The pleasure gardens of the period, in the capital and larger provincial cities, were also influential as sites of popular entertainment and public sociability. Though now less patronised by the upper classes they maintained something of the tradition of the easy mingling of the classes at play, and in their varied range of entertainment sustained the popular taste for the spectacular and theatrical (as too did the circus, then enjoying its first great efflorescence).

By the 1850s music hall emerged from the ruck of complementary forms as a distinct institution under the direction of a number of publican entrepreneurs who separated out and commoditised the entertainment function of the pub in purpose-built halls while retaining the former's distinctive ambience. The differentiation of specific territories had been assisted by the Theatres Act 1843 which distinguished between the legitimate drama house (now freed from monopoly) and other premises which were denied the privilege of staging the drama but allowed the running sale and consumption of drink and tobacco in the auditorium. Drink remained a critical element in the economy of the music hall, but its proprietors, who adopted the new title for its associations with high culture, emphasised their concern to improve popular recreations and repeatedly challenged the law by producing dramatic episodes on their bills. This much advertised concern to elevate the popular taste was both a reflection of the proprietors' aspirations to respectability and a defence against the attacks of critics who contested the granting of licences with charges of intemperance and immorality. The one man whom the new industry and subsequent historians represented as embodying both the social ideals of rational recreation for the people and the speculative acumen of the pioneer leisure entrepreneur or 'caterer' was Charles Morton, 'the father of the halls'. Morton's ventures, first with the Canterbury music hall in Lambeth, then in his move to the Oxford in the West End in 1861, are important landmarks in the history of the halls, but his endeavours were matched and in part anticipated by other publican-entrepreneurs, in the provinces as well as in London, who exploited the new market opportunities in commercialised entertainments as marginal but significant gains in wages and free time stimulated popular demand and older recreations were outlawed, embattled or otherwise reduced.

After the take-off in the 1850s music hall enjoyed its first great boom in the 1860s and early 1870s. In London the number of halls more than trebled in a decade and, though growth was less dramatic or assured in the provinces, there was significant expansion there, too; the trade press listed 31 large halls in the capital in 1870, and 384 in the rest of Britain.[2] Growth was registered not only in the number of halls, but in the scale and commercialisation of their operation: capacities increased, amenities grew more sophisticated, programmes were extended, staff were added, and caterers' profits multiplied. Performers became a more or less professionalised labour force, appearing in London at several different halls each night under the intensive turns system, and working the provincial halls in frequent tours that made the medium a prime agent in the construction of a national taste in entertainment. The new glamour and opulence of music hall was advertised by the major stars of the period, George Leybourne and the Great Vance, the swells who celebrated the good life of wine, women and song, while G. H. McDermott made a sensational hit with his great patriotic song 'By Jingo!'. Most of what was sung was now the product of a song-writing industry. Music hall entertainment continued to be diverse and eclectic as determined by its hybrid origins, but there was a tendency to more elaborately staged productions and a taste for the sensational, typically in the aerial acts of Leotard and Blondin. It was, however, the comic singer, male and female, who gave music hall its own distinctive voice.

If the comic singers reinforced the hold of the music hall upon its public, they jeopardised the status and livelihood of its operators by concentrating the hostilities of reform lobbies. Fearful for the renewal of their annual licences, London proprietors sought to pre-empt such attacks by petitioning the Home Secretary in 1879, hoping to secure 'fun without filth' by the appointment of an official censor to protect them against their own incorrigible comics and the strictures of an amateur and capricious magistracy.

Though they solicited control and protection in this quarter, proprietors talked the language of free trade in their campaign to share the right to play the legitimate drama. A Parliamentary Select Committee in 1866 reported in favour of ending the restrictive double jurisdiction though this was not put into law and the conflict of music hall and theatre interests rumbled on for another forty years and produced a further official enquiry in 1892. (In the meantime theatre learned how to exploit its new rival by poaching its stars for pantomime.)

While music hall was thus embattled without, it was also exercised by less visible internal conflicts. In the 1870s came the first organised protest among artists, though their hostility to management was displaced upon the agents, whose proliferation in these years is a ready index to the expanded scale and bureaucratisation of music hall operation and the deepening impress of market values.

After a period of more subdued growth and consolidation in the late 1870s and early 1880s music hall underwent a new burst of innovation and expansion. Conventionally the opening of the restyled London Pavilion in 1885 is celebrated as inaugurating the era of the de-luxe hall or variety theatre, though the trend was discernible earlier. The new appellation reflected the industry's perennial concern to dignify its image but was accurate enough in registering its more complete adoption of the physical apparatus of the theatre in house and stage design. The open and fluid logistics of the earlier halls gradually gave way to fixed stall seating, the more pronounced internal segregation of audiences, and the distancing of the performer. Production facilities became more elaborate. The cost of this greater formalisation was compounded by new municipal safety regulations (most notably those of the London County Council) while the inflation of star performers' salaries also added to the expense of music hall operation. To meet the new demands on capital the industry increasingly went public for its funds and moved into combination, the London Syndicate formed in 1893 of three major West End halls being an early example. But the process was most dramatic and extensive in the provinces, where Moss, Stoll and Thornton (and a number of other carpet-baggers) put together country-wide or regional chains that transformed the music hall business into an oligopoly. A new wave of building ensued, conferring opulent new 'Empires' and 'Palaces' on the big cities, while the new men from the provinces made their mark on the capital with the Hippodrome and the Coliseum as their imperial headquarters. In the late 1890s the combines also began their rapid colonisation of the suburbs.

By most accounts the syndicated operations now dominated the market. This made for greater standardisation of entertainment, though competition between the chains also brought a more reckless search for novelty and exotic production. There remained, however, an extensive undergrowth and feeder system of smaller halls and pub concert rooms. In particular, in the North and parts of the Midlands, the 'free halls', with admission still charged by refreshment ticket exchangeable for drink, constituted their own vigorous and self-sufficient field of operation, though unacknowledged by the music hall establishment, its press and historians. Prior to the 1880s in most boroughs outside London there had been no requirement for a separate entertainment licence to complement the traditional liquor licence dispensed by the magistrates, but from then on local government and public health acts made a music and dancing licence a universal requirement for all public entertainments. The reformed licensing authorities proved particularly severe on the 'smalls' and free halls, being more doubtful of the respectability of back-street operations than of the grand new people's emporia. (Though if physical welfare was as much their concern as morality they might have noted that a free hall in the Yorkshire mining village of Denaby boasted central heating, a Bechstein grand piano and 'excellent lavatories'.)[3]

For all its attempts to present a respectable image and come to some accommodation with the authorities, the music hall business was still subject to attack from moral and social reform lobbies. Foremost in the industry's demonology in the 'battle of the halls' in the late century were Frederick Charrington, the brewer turned zealot, and Mrs Ormiston Chant, an earlier incarnation of Mrs Whitehouse who campaigned against prostitution in the fashionable promenade at the Empire, Leicester Square. The LCC was particularly strict in its controls of the halls and provided some encouragement to protestors; elsewhere reform associations and magistrates continued to exercise their inquisitive vigilance. The most plainly registered change they effected was the prohibition of drink in new halls. Thus of 29 halls operated across the country by Stoll in 1909, only eight held a liquor licence. On another front, proprietors, now more obviously businessmen and bosses than genial father figures, provoked further and more determined resistance from artists against exploitation and restrictive practices. The conflict, which had resurfaced in the mid-1880s, broke out again in protests against the combines, producing a strike by the newly-formed Variety Artists' Federation in 1907, another legendary moment in music hall history: Marie Lloyd stayed out, Lockhart's Elephants carried on.

Marie Lloyd was one of the great stars who stamped their character on music hall in its last great flowering, continuing to effect a collusive intimacy between artist and audience within the increased scale and pretension of the music hall as variety theatre. Music hall's continuing aspirations to dramatic legitimacy were registered in the increasing prevalence of the sketch or dramatic episode. The character of such pieces ranged from raucous knockabout to revue-style sophistication but its displacement of other traditional items confirms in part a conscious shift in programming to cater to a more numerous lower-middle- and middle-class element in the audience. This concern to capture a more respectable clientele was a long-held preoccupation of the big caterers; in the 1890s, with their penetration of the suburbs, they were achieving something of their aim — E. M. Forster took his mother and aunt to a music hall in 1896.[4] But the symbolic apotheosis of music hall for most commentators was the Royal Command Performance of 1912 when 'the Cinderella of the arts finally went to the ball', an awesome but deadening occasion as it proved.

There was no abrupt terminus to music hall's career but its problems were now more than those of outfacing puritans without and unionists within. By 1912 music hall was well into a crisis of overproduction and reduced profits. Overexpansion was compounded by the rival claims of new forms and new technology, most notably film, accommodated since 1896 as one more novelty item on the variety bill but increasingly exercising its own singular appeal in purpose-built movie houses from the early years of the new century (the phonograph was as yet a less potent rival). The infiltration of American song and dance forms, a process with an even longer history of accommodation, became not only an invasion but an occupation of home territory with the success of the revue *Hello Ragtime* in 1913. Music hall survived the First World War (despite an entertainment tax and the reintensification of calls for moral surveillance) and took its share of the immediate post-war boom before being confronted with another powerful rival in radio. Yet British music hall remained, until the 1950s and the advent of television, a prominent and extensive institution, no longer the dominant entertainment industry, but possessed of enough confidence and vitality to laugh off its many premature obituaries.[5]

The majority of writings on the music hall, according to its most recent bibliographers, are 'redundant, superficial [and] unreliable', yet for all its fallibilities in furnishing an accurate historical account this rank and rambling corpus does offer a historiography with some more or less distinctive interpretative preoccupations.[6]

The first readily identifiable position is that generated most insistently within the music hall industry itself, particularly from the 1890s when it was so anxious to publicise a social rationale that would both appropriate the past and secure the future. By this I mean the 'pot house to variety palace' thesis with its celebration of those helmsmen of popular taste like Charles Morton who were credited with rescuing variety from its lowly pub origins and establishing its status as a respectable form of modern entertainment. It has its mythic parallels in other shorthand formulations of the history of popular forms — from the brothels of New Orleans to Carnegie Hall in the story of jazz — and in a larger sense it is music hall's equivalent of the Whig or Liberal interpretation of history with its proprietors cast as friends of the people directing the march of progress along its evolutionary and meliorist path . . . onwards and upwards via the bigger and better. The pursuit of profit is not denied but, in the words of John Hollingshead, it was subordinate to 'the rules of good citizenship'. Typically embodied in the life-careers of the great caterers, it was a perspective that could move even the most austere of these to flights of romanticism. Thus Oswald Stoll, recalling his beginnings in the tiny and shabby Parthenon in Liverpool in the 1870s, saw 'that little Stage coming down that avenue of trees of time — coming forward and growing larger, recording triumph after triumph in the travels through life'.[7]

Less grandiose but more insidious in its romanticism is a second position, more complex and more widely diffused, which might be called the folk or idealist interpretation of music hall history. In its vulgarised form it is most obviously celebrated in innumerable compilations of the Good Old Days, Winkles and Champagne, Twenty Shillings in the Pound genre, and flourishes still in present-day television and theatre reconstructions. Here the people not the caterers are the heroes. This representation nurses the legend of an industrial or at least urban Volksgeist, of a sturdy and self-reliant people laughing and crying at life but above all enjoying it, and sharing that enjoyment with those of its class superiors who sought its rough but oh-so-congenial embrace: 'Ambrosian were the nights . . .', as Sir Lewis Fergusson wrote.[8] Unlike the Whig interpretation, it has no central point of provenance or historical perspective, or rather, it foreshortens history in that it remains fixated on the whiskers and waistcoats of the Edwardian wonderland. In more sophisticated form, the idealist interpretation seeks to identify the essence or core of music hall and finds expression in the musings of a number of more intellectual commentators. There is a common note here of the directness of music hall as an unselfconscious expression of the popular voice, 'a capacity', as T. S. Eliot put it in writing of Marie Lloyd, 'for expressing the soul of the people'. Virginia Woolf, though she tried to resist the intellectual simplicity of such a conclusion, was forced to acknowledge 'you can't help feeling it's the real thing, as in Athens one might have felt that poetry was'. Woolf also noted that music hall humour was 'something natural to the race' and the sense of its definitive Englishness was also commonly identified as a prime source of its appeal. Historically this intellectual and bourgeois embrace for the demotic genius of music hall came late and, one suspects, often at second hand. An institution which for much of its history had been represented as an agent of moral and cultural degeneration became part of the World We Have Lost, by a kind of reverse Whiggery in which the past becomes authentic and the present embattled with the hybrid, the artificial, and the alien — in this case, as Kipling bemoaned in the 1930s, with 'the imported heathendom' of 'Americanised stuff'.[9] This interpretation is just as selective as the more 'official' one (for example, it begs the question '*whose* England?'), but we should not feel too superior to it, for there is still a tendency to accept unquestioned that music hall was the great success story of nineteenth-century popular culture and a prime locus of an authentic working-class sensibility. The idealist lens has coloured the vision of some tough-minded commentators. Hoggart notes that 'Even a writer as stringent and seemingly unromantic as Orwell never quite lost the habit of seeing the working classes through the cosy fug of an Edwardian music hall'.[10]

There are further strictures to be made on these two older positions but they can be dealt with more conveniently in a discussion of interpretations offered in recent scholarly work; though there is no precise coherence to this still modest corpus, the general thrust is one of cultural materialism or sub-Marxism, written mostly within the expanding discipline of social history.[11]

Social historians have become interested in the halls as part of their concern to recover the wider experience of everyday life, in leisure as well as work, but to integrate this with an understanding of structure and process in the formation of class cultures in a capitalist society. By this interpretation the general line of development from pot-house to palace is represented as a product of conflict rather than consensus, of choices imposed from without rather than volunteered from within working-class culture. 'The evolution of the music hall', writes Penny Summerfield, 'was a process of deliberate selection, later made to look natural and inevitable.' There is an obvious analogy here with the capitalist transformation of industrial manufacture: the caterer's conversion of the pub sing-song into modern show business can be likened to the shift from domestic to factory production, with the same organisational imperatives to economies of scale, division of labour and the specialisation of plant. Within such a model the performers can be represented as alienated labour in rebellion against a new work discipline and the rationalisation and speed-up of programming that came towards the end of the century. In its later victories capital extends its disciplines to the audience who are reduced to passive consumers of an increasingly commoditised form of entertainment which is both wholesome and 'bright'. The convergence of profit, morality and good order is assisted by an interventionist state via the localised input of the licensing system. In this schema music hall not only manufactures entertainment but a particular ideology which further assimilates its public to capitalism. In his influential account of the remaking of working-class culture in late nineteenth-century London, Gareth Stedman Jones sees the process as rooted in deeper material changes in work and the urban ecology which sap the strength of an older more independent artisanal culture. Music hall fulfils a crucial role in this transformation by enfolding London workers in 'a culture of consolation' which, while far from soporific, is none the less socially conservative, aggressively patriotic and politically disabling.[12] This is, then, hardly a success story for popular culture; it is culture for the people not of the people. One recent study of music hall songs represents them as an almost wholly artificial product with little or no demotic authenticity, while a piece of regional research questions the class specificity of the halls after a certain point, identifying them as a more typically petty-bourgeois than working-class form.[13]

This perspective plainly challenges the rhetoric of the official version and the more sentimental fictions of the idealists, but it has its own shortcomings. The idea of a single trajectory of development, while now more realistically seen as capitalist and manipulative rather than benevolent and progressive, pays little attention to contradictions and exceptions to the model. Some of these, such as the persistence of traditional practices and the co-existence of the extensive world of the free halls alongside the syndicate juggernauts, may be accommodated within the valuable modification of the 'combined and uneven development' of capitalism, but they need also to be understood on their own terms, not just as hold-outs. There is no acknowledgement of the particular properties of artistic labour on the halls which give it a distinction not only from a proletariat but from other cultural workers. Above all, and this

is unusual given the culturalist strand in social history, the people who constitute the music hall public are represented as largely ineffective figures, boisterous, demonstrative and claiming the halls as their own, yes, but otherwise
entrapped and neutered by the music hall bosses and the ideological
apparatus. One writer bridles at the use of a social control model which
denies any agency of the subject, but given the more dialectical concepts of
cultural hegemony and relative autonomy favoured by neo-Marxism there
has been little application of their sense of culture as a site for exchange and
negotiation in music hall studies.[14] Indeed in its tone of cultural pessimism,
modern scholarship on the halls seems to have substituted a revised idealism
with distinctions between an authentic and a bogus popular voice, an echo of
the mass culture critique which disallows that the production of culture is a
dynamic process in which the consumer continues to play a constitutive role,
and the 'authentic' is a property of ever imperfect and contested definition.
At the empirical level, recent studies still concentrate too exclusively on London (a point everywhere acknowledged), and rely too heavily in their treatment of music hall entertainment upon a very narrow set of examples — the
cultural journey from G. W. Ross's 'Sam Hall' to Albert Chevalier's 'My Old
Dutch' has become as predictable as that from pot house to palace.

We may now agree that music hall is not a radical mode, that in many of
its features it is deeply conservative, but that is no reason to intone the valuable but partial truths of the 'culture of consolation' tag as some kind of critical epitaph. Like all compensatory models it is too dismissive and shifts the
burden of significance too far onto extrinsic phenomena while often
exaggerating the fit of text and context. As a hegemonic order on a mass
scale over several generations we should expect the ideological apparatus of
music hall to be both more sophisticated and extensive but also more obviously subject to the strains and lesions of reproduction, particularly in the
field of leisure and popular culture where there was as much disagreement
as consensus among dominant groups.

If recent scholarly work has nevertheless established the importance of
music hall as a prime site for the interaction and contest of market forces,
cultural hegemony and popular or class consciousness in a period of deep
structural change, it has done little to advance our understanding of music
hall as a cultural form in terms of its specific content — its own internal codes
and processes. In this sense, music hall continues to be taken for granted,
rather than as an interpretative challenge. Fundamental to music hall is its
entertainment, of which each form constitutes a particular cultural text or
signification with its own history and meaning, to be worked through in
terms of content, performance and reception. Is the mix of such often
diverse forms arbitrary and accidental or organic and patterned? Are there
larger typologies or latent structures which give unity and meaning to Champagne Charlie, Blondin cooking omelettes on the high wire, Pongo Redivius
the man-monkey, Madame Leonore and her *poses plastiques*, and George
White, 'the Man With No Legs' ('See Him Jump' as the ads beckoned)? This
is a question that ought to stimulate rather than dismiss serious enquiry.

Working outwards from the entertainment, we need a more searching examination of music hall as experience, dispelling the tableau effect of so many representations; the truism that it was a participatory form needs re-animating. At its optimum music hall was a highly charged social space, a consequence of its genius of place and the particular dynamics of its performance. In its social logistics, the music hall combined something of the features of both pub and theatre. Like the pub it was both a public and private place, where the multiple intimacies of its crowd — a more helpful designation than audience — paradoxically afforded a kind of privacy. Like the theatre it reduced the promiscuous social mix of city streets to some kind of territorial order while keeping open mutual contact of sight and sound among its different social elements. In this setting, the crowd were as much producers as consumers of a form of social drama, in which styles and identities were tried out and exchanged, inducing what T. J. Clark, in his study of the Parisian café-concert, called 'a kind of social vertigo'.[15] Participation also included ritualised forms of popular jurisdiction in which sections of the audience claimed customary rights to the control of territory and performance in the halls, and exacted a *taxe populaire* from management, performers and visitors.[16] The reordered proportions of open, closed and negotiable space and the more rigorous policing of 'nuisances' in the later halls or theatres of variety probably reduced but by no means extinguished the situational autonomy of the audience-crowd — promenades, for example, despite the campaign against the Empire, remained a significant feature of new suburban and provincial halls after the turn of the century and we should be alert to the persistence or displacement of other expressive dimensions to music hall experience.

In their relationship to the performance on stage the music hall audience has too often been represented as an undifferentiated lump with a simple reflex role in chorus-singing and banter, whereas the interaction was more complex. Notable here, I would argue, was a running drama of inclusion and exclusion as songs and acts celebrated or satirised particular types or groups, sometimes doing both at the same time, drawing their targets from inside as much as outside the audience, inviting identification or discrimination simultaneously. The bulk of the music hall crowd were working-class, but as an audience they constituted a different and more volatile collectivity, dissolving and recomposing as members of other groups by nationality, age, gender and stratum as invoked in performance. Neither a particularly cruel nor fractious exercise, its general effect was no doubt to reassert an overall community of feeling, but arguably this agreeable closure had to be negotiated anew each night. A recent reassessment of working-class life in the pre-1914 period notes that together with its 'extraordinary mutuality' went 'real social distances and much hostility between members'.[17] If music hall signified community it was a meaning that came not simply as a reflection of a self-evident given but as a resolution of contradictions in real life. It was the particular concentration of such ambiguities within the marginal culture of the lower middle class that gave music hall's comic realism some of its richest material and most plausibly qualifies it as more petty bourgeois than proletarian in its sensibilities.

Music hall also deployed an extravagant and insidious style that exercised its own determinations both within and beyond the sub-culture. If it is necessary to get behind the gush and glitter of music hall hyperbole to reveal the politics of profit and control, it is further necessary to understand how style and surface mediated and inflected the relationships of power and production. It is worth considering too how, in a more general sense, music hall's particular mode of conceit, parody and innuendo constituted a second language *for all classes*, whose penetrations had a powerful integrative force in English society. It was perhaps in this sense that Orwell could pronounce the comedy of Max Miller 'intensely national', a suggestion that may be more fruitful than locating the Englishness of music hall in the soul of the people or its patriotic excesses.[18]

What we have yet to treat with adequately is music hall as a specific discourse of pleasure and sociability, or, put more simply, a way of having a good time — its definition, production and regulation. A classic historic locus for the good time is the carnival or feast. The richest studies of the carnivalesque are located in 'pre-industrial' popular culture where its ritual process and symbolic order are compact and articulate. Modern popular culture does have a significant ritual and symbolic content, but its expressions have become fragmented, displaced and optional, and the student must recompose the larger coherence. Thus, in its overall homology, music hall might be understood as a feast.[19] The working-class naturalism of many music hall songs does suggest the consolation of small pleasures — 'A little bit of what you fancy does you good' — but these were purveyed within a larger field of signification in which pleasure is represented as an abundance. In the grand style of its architecture and amenities, the hyperbole of its address, and the scale and variety of the programme, music hall was a site and occasion for liberality, profusion and plenitude, however bogus. What then becomes interesting is how the industry contrives to maintain the relish of the feast day that comes every week and reconcile an invitation to indulgence with the newer norms of orderly consumption. Contrasted with the dispensations of employers, philanthropists and municipalities, music hall projected a relatively unconditional generosity of intention, but in its reduction of the good time to a measured and commoditised abundance it did indeed contribute to the making of the modern consumer, though in ways that have yet to be fully examined. This is not to argue that the feast and by extension the carnivalesque offer an exhaustive or universalist paradigm for deconstructing the music hall — in some hands carnival is becoming more cliché than tool — but it does suggest further ways of reading a specific institution in terms of other social and associational forms in the history of the good time.

To talk of reading cultural phenomena as complex and contradictory texts is to make an uneasy excursion into the territory of what has come to carry the generic label 'cultural studies' — an extensive, confusing and sometimes meretricious field where it can be difficult to find a secure footing. There are many who have no taste for its full frontal theoreticism, its often laboured conflation of the abstruse and the banal, and its tendency to overcomplicate. Historians with a traditional grounding in liberal empiricism may in particular distrust propositions which can neither be proved nor disproved, and find it difficult to discern any useful coherence in an academic variety show that sometimes presents more of a mash than mesh of several specialist disciplines or schools — linguistics, semiotics, anthropology, sociology, structuralism and other critical practices. This is not to ignore work which has successfully combined different practices, but to argue for their more sustained and enterprising employment in disclosing the fuller meaning of music hall and its compelling engagement with its public. We can then more effectively recontextualise music hall socially and historically, relating it to other major forces (intertextuality) in the formation of popular and class cultures — the press, sport, the rise of the mass market — and the determinations of the work-place, politics and the state. Ideally, of course, the study of text and context should proceed in conjunction, and we need a precise chronology as well as an anatomy, but ultimately it is only as a more imaginative as well as more thoroughgoing exercise that the history of the music hall can be made to make its significant contribution to the bigger questions of culture and ideology, agency and structure in a modern capitalist society.[20]

One retort to this rather windy critique-cum-manifesto may be that the language in which I would re-animate music hall is more likely to strangle it, or simply offer new clichés for old — thus carnival is rendered as 'a surplus of signifiers', and the 'life and colour' of conventional account becomes the 'highly charged social space' of critical newspeak. Certainly there is a need to blend effective analysis with a style of appropriate wit and humanity; I can only offer that this is a running challenge that must be acknowledged and met by anyone who seeks to capture as well as demystify the expressive vigour of popular cultural forms, but particularly so for those who would make sense of the fat, rich pudding of music hall.

In keeping with our subject this is no doubt the point at which to produce the Barthian showstopper, revealing the latent structures that pattern the surfaces of music hall style as signifying practice, relating Lockhart's Elephants and George Formby's 'Little Stick of Blackpool Rock' to the ideology of the capitalist system and the struggle for the sign. But this is not only facetious and defensive, it is presumptuous, for such interpretations are of little value without some rooting in an understanding of the conditions of practice in music hall as a social and economic institution. If we want to know what music hall means, we must know how it works, for meaning is constructed in action and through relationships. Music hall was primarily about pleasure and entertainment, but the development of its particular aesthetic took place within and was determined by the structures of music hall as a business, and this is the principal concern of this volume.

We start, quite literally, with structures, as John Earl charts the obscure and haphazard evolution of building form, demonstrating the architectural variety of the emergent variety theatre and its determination of the social logistics of the music hall experience. My own piece on London music hall management before syndication is an attempt to give some historical specificity to the legendary glow of music hall *bonhomie* by examining the assumptions and practice of friendship as a stylistic and operational code within a socially intensive business. In a necessary excursion outside London, Jeremy Crump provides a provincial case history in his study of music hall in Leicester, looking at the specific determinants of the local social and economic environment and comparing this with the standard representation of national development. Also drawing primarily on provincial evidence, Dagmar Höher is concerned to provide a more specific and testing analysis of audience composition, its patterns of membership and degree of community. In her study of the collective action of the performers, Lois Rutherford constructs a social and ideological profile of the profession and charts its uneasy relationship with the entrepreneur in the shift to more formalised business practices. Music hall's embattlement with licensing agencies and reform lobbies is the theme of Susan Pennybacker's enquiry into the politics of regulation under the new regime of the London County Council which mediated the struggle between profit and morality; the author finds the role of the local state to be more ambiguous than hitherto represented. In conclusion, Chris Waters takes us on another trip away from the capital, though he cannot leave its influence behind as he examines the history of Manchester's Palace of Varieties, where expansionist London interests found themselves confounded by Manchester morality in a controversy that exemplifies the shifting complexities of cultural politics at the turn of the century.

Thus the volume variously opens up neglected areas, re-examines familiar territory, and tests both received opinion and newer interpretations in the history of the halls. At the same time as engaging with the broader categories of historical analysis and debate, an important emphasis has been on the task of accurate recovery in an often obscure, underworked and overromanticised territory. While steering clear of the hidden shallows of music hall antiquarianism there is a great need here for meticulous and informed exercises of descriptive or 'narrative' history proceeding hand in hand with more speculative enquiry.

In addition to more extended work on the topics in this volume, there are many other areas for related research: the rise of the agent; the business of commercial song production; the relationship of music hall and theatre — in repertoire, at law, and in the market; cross-cultural studies of music hall and its equivalents in France and the United States. The study of music hall as a prototype modern entertainment industry and dominant popular medium needs integrating with and comparing to that of the rising forms of cinema and radio. Generally there is a need for more counting, locating and classifying and, to repeat, scholarship has yet to move up beyond 1914 (an opportunity in oral history[21]) and outside England.

The sources exist to support such work, though there are many frustrations to their use. Overall, as mentioned before, they are voluminous; but the student in pursuit of certain themes will find them diffuse, fragmented and elliptical. In few fields is one obliged to read so much that seems of stunning inconsequence. Some materials, such as accounts or business figures for the earlier period, seem virtually non-existent; others are plentiful yet unexploited, as in the later business records in the Public Record Office, visual evidence of several kinds, and most notably, the music. Generally the tendency has been to treat all sources as unproblematic except in a mechanical sense. A most useful service here would be a study of the music hall press, not only as source but as agent and discourse in constructing style and ideology. In particular, the revered tablets of the *Era* (Bible and Wisden to theatre as well as music hall students) cry out for more critical reading.

It is ironic that, in all this considerable agenda, one of the greatest gaps is that emphasised in the division of territory between this volume and its companion, between music hall as business and music hall as performance. Those who read Bratton as well as Bailey will find some connections made or waiting to be made, but the relationship between the two areas is one where some of the most necessary work has to be done. Only then can music hall pass from being cliché and myth to an intelligible form within a satisfactory history and theory of modern British popular culture.

Notes

(Place of publication is London unless otherwise stated.)

1. For fuller recent accounts, see P. Bailey, 'Custom, Capital and Culture in the Victorian Music Hall' in R. Storch (ed.), *Popular Culture and Custom in Nineteenth Century England*, 1982, pp. 180–208; P. Bailey, *Leisure and Class in Victorian England*, 1978, pp. 27–34, 147–68; P. Summerfield, 'The Effingham Arms and the Empire: Deliberate Selection in the Evolution of Music Hall in London', in E. Yeo and S. Yeo (eds), *Popular Culture and Class Conflict*, Hassocks, 1981, pp. 209–40; B. Waites, 'The Music Hall', in the Open University's Popular Culture course booklet, *The Historical Development of Popular Culture in Britain, I*, Milton Keynes, 1981, pp. 43–76; M. Vicinus, *The Industrial Muse*, 1974, Chapter 6; L. Senelick, 'A Brief Life and Times of the Victorian Music Hall', *Harvard Library Bulletin*, vol. 19, 1971, pp. 375–98. D. F. Cheshire, *Music Hall in Britain*, 1974, is a valuable source book. Among older general histories, the following are still useful: C. D. Stuart and A. J. Park, *The Variety Stage*, 1895; H. Scott, *The Early Doors: Origins of the English Music Hall*, 2nd edn., 1977; R. Mander and J. Mitchenson, *The British Music Hall*, 2nd edn., 1974.
2. Quantification is generally problematical because of vagaries of definition and record. These figures, from the *Era Almanack*, take no account of the smaller pub or 'free halls'. Sampling in the same source reveals a considerable dip in numbers by 1900, though we may assume that the overall audience for music hall continued to grow, housed in fewer but much larger halls. The figures pick up again by 1910, with a count of 63 halls in London and 254 for the rest of the country.
3. The history of the free halls can be studied in the *Magnet*, published weekly in Leeds from 1866 until 1926.
4. He wrote an account for his old school magazine, in Latin. See P. N. Furbank, *E. M. Forster: A Life*, vol. 1, 1977, p. 51.

5. For the latter period, see R. Wilmut, *Kindly Leave the Stage! The Story of Variety, 1919–1960*, 1985.
6. L. Senelick, D. F. Cheshire and U. Schneider, *British Music Hall 1840–1923: A Bibliography and Guide to Sources*, Hamden, CT 1981. For London, see D. Howard, *London Theatres and Music Halls, 1850–1950*, 1970. For continuing interest and research into the halls, see *Music Hall*; *The Call Boy* (official journal of the British Music Hall Society); and a valuable newcomer, *Theatrephile*.
7. *Entr'acte Annual*, 1900, p. 13; O. Stoll, 'Foreword' to V. Tilley, *Recollections*, 1934, p. 7.
8. Fergusson, *Old Time Music Hall Comedians*, Leicester, 1949, Prologue.
9. T. S. Eliot, *Selected Essays*, 1951, pp. 456–9; Woolf, *Diaries, 1915–1918*, 1977, quoted in Senelick, Cheshire and Schneider, *British Music Hall*, p. 145; Kipling quoted in J. B. Booth, *The Days We Knew*, 1943, p. 30. For the ambivalent attitudes of the Fabians to music hall, see I. Britain, *Fabianism and Culture: A Study in British Socialism and the Arts, 1884–1918*, Cambridge, 1982, pp. 228–9, 235–40.
10. R. Hoggart, *Uses of Literacy*, Harmondsworth, 1958, p. 15. See also, C. MacInnes, *Sweet Saturday Night*, 1969, p. 25.
11. See most of the recent titles in fn. 1, above, to which add G. Stedman Jones, 'Working-Class Culture and Working-Class Politics in London, 1870–1900', *Journal of Social History*, 1974, reprinted in his *Languages of Class*, Cambridge, 1983, pp. 179–238; S. Yeo, *Religion and Voluntary Organisations in Crisis*, 1976, Chapter 7, and the Yeos' interpretative essays in their *Popular Culture and Class Conflict*; H. Cunningham, *Leisure in the Industrial Revolution*, 1980, pp. 164–76. See also M. Chanan, *The Dream that Kicks: The Prehistory and Early Years of Cinema in Britain*, 1980.
12. For the most recent emphasis on music hall as disabling ideology see I. Watson, *Song and Democratic Culture in Britain: An Approach to Popular Culture in Social Movements*, 1983, pp. 49–52. For a more considered view of the patriotism question, see Summerfield, 'Patriotism and Empire in Music Hall Entertainment, 1870–1914' in J. Mackenzie (ed.), *Imperialism and Popular Culture*, Manchester, pp. 17–48.
13. L. Senelick, 'Politics as Entertainment: Victorian Music Hall Songs', *Victorian Studies*, vol. 19, 1975, pp. 149–80; D. Harker, 'The Making of the Tyneside Concert Hall', *Popular Music*, vol. 1, 1981, pp. 27–56. See also R. Poole, *Popular Leisure and Music Hall in Nineteenth Century Bolton*, Lancaster, 1982.
14. Waites, 'The Music Hall', p. 75. For cultural hegemony, see the readings in T. Bennett, G. Martin, C. Mercer and J. Woollacott, *Culture, Ideology and Social Process*, 1981. For a less doctrinaire equivalent of the idea of exchange, etc., see the recent emphasis on appropriation, in the contributions of R. Chartier and D. Hall to S. Kaplan (ed.), *Understanding Popular Culture: Europe from the Middle Ages to the Nineteenth Century*, Berlin, 1984.
15. T. J. Clark, 'The Bar at the Folies-Bergeres' in J. Beauroy, M. Bertrand and E. T. Gargan (eds), *Popular Culture in France from the Old Regime to the Twentieth Century*, Saratoga, CA, 1977, pp. 233–52. Walter Benjamin, *Charles Baudelaire*, 1973, is also suggestive on the big city crowd; they knew each other, he said, as debtors and creditors, salesmen and customers, employers and employees, above all as competitors. See also B. Sharratt, 'The Politics of the Popular' in D. Bradby, L. James and B. Sharratt (eds), *Performance and Politics in Popular Drama*, Cambridge, 1980, p. 276.
16. Bailey, 'Custom, Capital and Culture', pp. 193–4.

17. R. McKibbin, 'Why Was There No Marxism in Great Britain', *English Historical Review*, vol. 99, April 1984, p. 305. For other recent treatments of the remaking (unmaking?) of working-class culture, see E. Hobsbawm, *Worlds of Labour*, 1984, Chapters 10 and 11; and H. Cunningham, 'Leisure' in J. Benson (ed.), *The Working Class in England, 1875–1914*, 1985, pp. 133–64.
18. G. Orwell, 'The Art of Donald McGill' in *Collected Essays*, vol. 2, 1968, pp. 161–2.
19. For modern projections, see G. Thompson, 'Carnival and the Calculable' and T. Bennett, 'A Thousand and One Troubles: Blackpool Pleasure Beach', *Formations of Pleasure*, 1983, pp. 124–37; 138–54. For a historian's investigation of the good time, see P. Bailey, '*Ally Sloper's Half-Holiday*: Comic Art in the 1880's', *History Workshop*, Autumn 1983, pp. 4–31.
20. For sophisticated primers in cultural studies, see the booklets and readers for the Open University's Popular Culture course, including Bennett et al., *Culture, Ideology and Social Processes*. See also the various publications of the Centre for Contemporary Cultural Studies, particularly J. Clarke, C. Critcher and R. Johnson (eds), *Working-Class Culture: Studies in History and Theory*, 1979, for the work of historians. S. Hall, 'Notes on Deconstructing the Popular' in R. Samuel (ed.), *People's History and Socialist Theory*, 1981, pp. 227–40, says a lot in a short space. D. Hebdige, *Subculture: The Meaning of Style*, 1979, is already a minor classic, and S. Frith, *Sound Effects: Youth, Leisure and the Politics of Rock 'n' Roll*, 1983, offers a suggestive model for comparative analysis.
21. See M. Vicinus, '"Happy Times . . . If You Can Stand It": Women Entertainers During the Interwar Years in England', *Theatre Journal*, vol. 31, October 1979, pp. 357–69; B. Dickinson, 'In the Audience', *Oral History Journal*, vol. 11, 1983, p. 52–61.

1 *Building the Halls*

JOHN EARL

Buildings and people

On Tuesday evening at this house
Is held what's termed a free and easy;
The Chairman's like the fatted boy
But much more dirty — far more greasy.

In filthy songs and beastly toasts
The snobby crew dispel their cares;
And modest females creep by stealth
To listen on the first floor stairs.
> *The Town* writing of Hemmingway's Mile End Saloon, 1840

The magnificent and brilliantly lighted hall in which the
Concert is held, exercises no little influence upon the minds of
the audience. There is a harmony between it and the
entertainment which produces a beauty of *ensemble* more easily
felt than described.
> Charles Morton describing his Canterbury Hall, 1857

There is seating accommodation for 5000 and the fare promises
to be excellent . . . Slowly but surely 'the halls' have changed
their character. They are more like theatres than ever and the
quantity and quality of their programmes contrast more and
more forcibly with the mostly meagre bills of the 'legitimate'
houses.
> *Building News* reporting the opening of the Palladium, 1910

Specialised building types come into existence to meet specific needs, but once a building exists it begins to mould and modify, sometimes in quite subtle ways, the activities which take place within it. In any entertainment building the performer learns to exploit its shape and acoustic and other properties. Similarly, the behaviour of the audience is directly influenced by its physical surroundings and indirectly by the psychological effect of

the intimate or formal relationship set up between entertainer and entertained.

A study of the architecture of the music halls must concern itself with
issues of this kind. The silent auditoria and sparse ornament of a Wilton's or
a Glasgow Britannia tell us very little if we do not ask the right questions.
Who built this hall? Why here? What were its forebears? How was it used?
Did the people sit at tables, talking and drinking, or in fixed rows of seats, all
facing one way? Did they feel free to move about during the performance?
Were the singers seated at a table? Or did they move to a low platform at the
corner of the room? Or were they separated from the audience by a row of
guarded footlights on a high stage? How well could they be seen and how
attentively were they heard?

The exceedingly varied buildings we have to lump together under the
single term 'music hall' demonstrate that the answers to these questions must
have been quite different at different times. As the entertainment evolved,
the buildings suffered a continuous process of adaptation and replacement.
At every stage, proprietors and their architects found new ways of attracting
patrons, increasing takings and reducing outgoings and these in turn
triggered off further changes in performance conditions and audience
experience.

The processes of interaction were complex and subject to continual external interference. At different times the impact of safety regulations and the
views of the governing class on temperance, propriety, sexual morality and
social order all influenced the physical shape as well as the life of the halls.

It would be pleasing to be able to explain the development of this special
building type with a sequence of pictures like time-lapse photographs of a
caterpillar-chrysalis-moth metamorphosis. The record is, unfortunately,
gapped and it is at present particularly deficient in the chrysalis stage.
Nevertheless, fairly extensive records do exist of some of the later stages of
development and sometimes they contain clues to the missing 'frames'.

This chapter attempts to construct an account of the evolution of purpose-
built music halls, with special emphasis on the critical period from about
1840 to 1875. It also aims to shed some light on the circumstances in which
the first music halls came to be built.

There is still a great deal for the historian to investigate and interpret. All
that is claimed for this London-orientated essay is that its surmises and conclusions are not unreasonable in the light of the evidence so far seen.

The seven ages of music hall provision

A crude framework of reference may be constructed by retelling the familiar
strip-cartoon story of the emergence of music hall entertainment 'from pot-
house to palace', and identifying typical building forms for each stage.

Phase 1 is the prehistoric 'convivial meeting' stage (Figure 1.1). Mr
Wilkins, licensee of the Swan, has a parlour which is used twice weekly by a

dozen hearty drinking companions calling themselves (to themselves) the Harmonious Stevedores, the Nightingales or the Warblers. It matters very little whether the cronies are comfortable tradesmen, priding themselves on their alto, tenor, baritone and bass voices and working their way through a favourite glee book, or workmen with a part-oral tradition, enjoying a 'free and easy' and taking turns with a verse and a chorus. Their needs are simple. Almost any room will do provided it is not too large and is adequately furnished with a table and chairs. An overriding necessity is, of course, access to refreshment. The time could be any time up to the present day, but let us say that it is about 1820 to 1830.

Figure 1.1. The Nightingale Club, a convivial meeting of tradesmen in a room at the 'Cabbage and Shears' in 1826. The club rules are pinned up behind the chairman. Non-singers are penalized by being forced to drink a pint of salt water.

The geography of such a self-made entertainment is almost entirely dependent on the shape of the room, the position of such features as the door and the fireplace and the character of the landlord's furnishings. A round table at the centre of the room would not be uncommon. Otherwise, and particularly if there are fixed settles, a long table may be drawn up to one side. Once a chairman has taken his place and the glasses are full the entertainment may commence.

Phase 2 is what we may call the 'open harmonic meeting'. Wilkins, observing that a song has a capital effect on drink sales, knocks two rooms into one to provide accommodation for as many as may be attracted to attend. He occasionally takes the chair himself but he has a regular arrangement with the chairman of the Warblers, a competent baritone and something of a rough wit, whose presence is a guarantee that the best local talent will attend and contribute to the entertainment. 'The best' include one or two soloists of semi-professional standard. They occasionally sing comic songs 'in character' and a piano is provided to accompany them.

Phase 3 is the beginning of an evolution towards professionalism. The movement from phase 2 may at first be barely perceptible. In effect, it is a movement from an informal meeting to a 'regular concert'.

The meetings in the singing room have been popular beyond Wilkins's expectations. The entertainment remains in the same room but it becomes steadily more ambitious. Professional 'room singers'[1] are engaged who work a number of such establishments. Most of them are all-purpose entertainers who are as likely to be seen in the minor theatres as at the concerts. The outward appearance of the harmonic meeting may be maintained for some time — there are still accomplished amateurs at the chairman's table (which is no longer the only table), glees are still sung and the audience joins in familiar choruses, but the pretence of a private entertainment in which all who attend must make a personal contribution is fading rapidly.

The professional singers have actor's skills and their character impersonations need to be seen as well as heard. Wilkins provides a low dais for the purpose, alongside the singers' table. The Swan still has no purpose-built room, but it is a proto-music hall, a licensed entertainment house.

By 1845 a new movement is afoot. The Theatres Act 1843 has made the world safe for the minor theatres.[2] This has produced no immediate or particularly visible change in the theatre heartland, but it is having interesting side effects in the field of miscellaneous entertainment. One effect is to force a choice on the proprietors of small saloon theatres — in fact, on any tavern room or garden presenting quasi-theatrical confections. Either they must apply for a Lord Chamberlain's licence, which permits them to present drama but forbids drinking in the auditorium, or they must give up all theatrical ambition and operate with a magistrate's music and dancing licence. Some proprietors, like Matthew Eltham[3] (his pub is later to achieve fame as Wilton's) wobble before deciding which way to go, but the advantage enjoyed by the proto-music halls in having drinking during the performance is now thrown into sharp relief. A little building boom is imminent.

Wilkins sees profit in going farther along this road and, following the example of others, he knocks down his skittle shed and back yard urinal and puts up a purpose-built hall covering the whole of what was once the pub garden. In *Phase 4* what we see is still likely to be called a concert room but it is in truth a music hall. The entertainment is now, beyond doubt, a professional concert. Wilkins employs the best singers and comedians he can afford, with occasional acrobats and speciality acts appearing in formal succession.

The new hall is a plain, oblong room with a fireplace on either side, an open platform across one end and a little balcony at the other end. No architect has been involved. The chapel-like structure, on a totally enclosed site with no street elevations, has been run up by a builder with not much more than a rough sketch to guide him. The plaster ornament is sparse and the iron balcony fronts have been chosen from a manufacturer's catalogue.

As such rooms become more common, differences of arrangement and furnishing may be observed, but a pattern soon begins to emerge. A chairman sits with his back to the stage, viewing the performance in a dressing mirror.[4] The bar under the balcony is crowded with standing patrons. Women — sweethearts and wives — are more in evidence than they were in the old room. The atmosphere is one of conversational ease, but there is now a conscious attempt to instil a feeling of luxury and 'occasion'. The admission tickets and the rudimentary song books (modelled on Evans's) are straws in the wind. The glittering chandelier, highlighting the polished marble tops of the supper tables, is the chief advertisement of the proprietor's new ambitions.

Before the concert room is a year old, Wilkins is engaged in buying two or three houses adjoining the Swan in order to obtain additional backland. Within two years he has established the superiority of his 'entirely new' entertainment over all other local pub concerts by upgrading his programme with performers of metropolitan quality. The Swan Music Hall (so styled in its occasional advertisements, but universally called 'Wilkins's') is a money-spinner. A bigger hall would make even bigger profits, but the proprietor has insufficient funds to undertake the next step alone.

Several providers of entertainment arrive at this point at about the same time in the mid-1850s. Wilkins follows in Charles Morton's footsteps[5] by mortgaging his property with a major brewery company, becoming 'indebted in trade' (in practical terms tied to the sale of that brewer's beer) for the amount needed to prime his next project.

Phase 5 is a historical watershed. The 'grand music hall' has arrived. Wilkins, running with the leaders of the race, employs an architect to design an enormous new room, several times bigger than (but entirely concealed behind) his pub. The architectural precedents for a performance room of this kind are not difficult to find. A galleried church has similar requirements of audibility and visibility — but the mid-century music hall also has much in common with grand ballrooms and polite concert rooms, like Almack's, the Novosielski concert room at Her Majesty's Theatre, the Hanover Square Rooms and the Freemason's Hall. Wilkins's is modest compared to these, but its walls are ornamented with coupled Corinthian pilasters, the ceiling is gently curved and the stage has an architectural backdrop in the form of a triumphal arch relief.

Stylistic considerations do not, in fact, worry Wilkins too much. His firmest injunction to the architect is that the works must not require closure for more than three or four days.[6] The old concert room remains open until it is practically enclosed by the rising walls and half-completed roof of the new music hall, which is poured into the back garden site, blocking the rear windows of the pub and bringing promise of unrelieved misery to adjoining residents.

A house adjoining the pub is demolished to make a separate entrance with a pay-box and bar. The narrow façade so formed, penetrated by an arched doorway with a big bracket gas lamp, bearing the name of the hall, provides the only opportunity for external architectural display. It gives no hint of what the visitor will discover on paying a few pence and passing through a curtained door or climbing the stone stair at the end of the corridor.

The first sight of this 80-foot room, brilliantly lighted with crystal chandeliers and hundreds (the advertisements say tens of thousands) of gas burners, is breathtaking. Spindly iron columns on three sides support a heavily gilt balcony front. There are splendid mahogany bars and serveries, and waiters in clean aprons wind in and out of the lines of supper tables. The hall links directly with the pub at both levels. There is still only one direct way in and this doubles as the only exit. No provision has been made for rapid escape in case of fire or panic.

We should pause for a moment over the new hall because we have now arrived at a new building type. Disused and stripped of its furnishings (as we see the only surviving grand music hall today, Figure 1.2) it could, as we have already observed, be taken for a ballroom or 'respectable' concert hall. But this is a true music hall, a huge supper room in which the principal source of income is the sale of liquor. The audience is presided over by a chairman, but he now introduces a programme as formally organised and advertised as any theatre bill. A large number of people come and go in the promenade spaces at the rear and sides of the hall, meeting friends, chatting and drinking and occasionally standing in silence to hear a particularly good song. They are becoming an informed and critical audience. Their tastes and expectations will give employment to a whole new generation of entertainers whose life's work will be dedicated exclusively to 'the halls'.

The doorkeeper refuses entry to some unaccompanied women and drunken men to uphold the hall's claim that it is a high-class establishment raising the cultural tone of the neighbourhood. As additional reinforcement the popular engravings which hung round the walls of the old room are assembled with one or two specially purchased paintings to create an art gallery — in the entrance hall. The walls of the music hall under the balcony are lined with rococo-framed, cut and acid-etched mirrors. Above the balcony the walls are painted with stencilled ornaments.

There is no proscenium and therefore no act drop. The performers enter in full view through the curtained archway. The stage has a row of footlights, like a theatre, but it is furnished with a Broadwood piano, a harmonium and two multi-branched gas standard lamps. There is no scenery. The choir, the resident soloists (no longer mere local talent) and the chairman are all in evening dress. The comedians are dressed in character. On arriving from their last venue they repair their make-up in minimal dressing rooms under the stage.

An important fact about this kind of big pub music hall — the grand music

Figure 1.2. Wilton's Music Hall, Stepney. Sole survivor of the giant grand music halls of mid-nineteenth-century London. The proscenium replaced an original apsidal stage by the 1870s. After a fire in 1878 the auditorium was reinstated with a raked floor instead of the old, flat supper-room floor.

halls of the mid-Victorian building boom — is that they were never particularly numerous and they did not last long. As the music hall industry took
off, success led to alterations in practically every hall. By the 1870s music
halls were beginning to look quite different, while by the late 1890s the classic grand music hall was a fading memory, totally eclipsed by a new building
type and a new style of presentation.

The first stage in the transition may be labelled *Phase 6*, the 'grand music
hall modified'. To return to our comic strip: Wilkins Jr (who has taken over
from his father) finds that a room full of supper tables limits capacity without
guaranteeing that every seated member of the audience will drink heartily.
He reduces the number of tables and corrals them into half (and later an
even smaller portion) of the flat-floored auditorium. An 'area' like a theatre
pit, with rows of bench-seats, fills the rest of the space. This not only increases
the notional capacity but also has a beneficial effect on total evening atten-
dances, since the benches, like the promenade, accommodate stays of varying durations. Many people 'drop in' to the music hall during the course of
the evening. There is good value to be had in any sampling of the programme, however brief.

Wilkins Jr is, in any case, an experimenter who sees the open stage hall and
supper-room-style entertainment as hopelessly outdated. He has no resident
corps. Glees and operatic selections in evening dress are abandoned under his
management. Comic singers and serios account for most of the programme
but he begins to present elaborate *ballets d'action*. A proscenium is installed
and scenery is used for the ballets and, although the stage remains shallow
and inflexible, a movement toward theatrical conditions is now under way
for both audience and performer.

In the late 1880s, Wilkins Jr, who has taken a partner and acquired an
interest in another large hall a couple of miles from the Swan, falls foul of the
licensing authorities. Armed with new and stringent powers, their officials
serve a schedule of safety requirements which must be satisfied before the
hall will be certified as suitable to receive an audience.

The alterations needed are extensive and Wilkins, whose enterprise is
coining money, takes the opportunity to make further reforms, doing away
with the chairman and the last relics of his reign. The supper tables disap-
pear, to be replaced by comfortable stalls seats. Mahogany bar counters with
beer pumps and rows of bottles remain in the auditorium for the time being,
but pressure from the licensing authority will eventually force drinking out
of the auditorium and into separate bars. There is still a promenade, but the
greater part of the audience will probably remain seated, as at a theatre, for
the whole of the advertised programme.

The change seems logical, but it is mistaken. The 'improved' hall (call it
Phase 6a) is an uncomfortable hybrid. A rectangular flat-floored room with
long side balconies is far from ideal for the ever more ambitious stage scenes
now being attempted. The audience begins to dwindle.

Wilkins and his partner call in the architect who supervised the last alterations, a specialist who knows his way forward and back through the web of

building regulations and safety requirements. He demonstrates that the sightlines cannot be improved without going to the unreasonable expense of raking the auditorium floor, reconstructing the balconies, raising the roof and rebuilding the proscenium. He presents an alternative scheme for a completely new variety theatre in the latest style, but his proposal is never adopted.

The proprietors of Wilkins's can see the writing on the wall. They lack both the financial resources and the spirit to enter into serious competition with the rising syndicates which are employing Frank Matcham and the new breed of theatre architects he represents[7] to build gorgeous variety palaces in every suburb. The old hall lingers on for a few years but it has the marks of death. Its final closure and sale as a furniture repository attracts no comment in the local newspaper.

The local Empire Palace, which has already given its name to a tram stop, belongs to a different world. Magnificently enriched, with comfortable tip-up seats and padded gallery benches, it offers an excellent view from any part of the house. With this development (*Phase 7*) we have reached the end of the road. No further evolution is to be looked for, since the building types appropriate to the rival entertainments, theatre and music hall, have converged. This is in fact a theatre in all but name and programme. The stage is equipped like a theatre stage for any kind of performance. The audience for the twice-nightly entertainment is as static as a theatre audience. Standing is permitted but promenading in the old sense is not encouraged. The bars are separated from the auditorium and there is neither viewing from the one nor drinking in the other. The practice of lowering the house lights is becoming universal.[3] And this is, perhaps, the most telling evidence of what has happened to the music halls. They have turned their backs on their own most durable tradition. They are no longer brilliantly lighted rooms where friends meet to drink and listen to a song. They are theatres where audiences assemble to be entertained.

At this point it will be appropriate to drop the historical present tense, since the narrative is at an end. The variety palace boom went on into the early years of the twentieth century but well before the First World War a new specialised type of entertainment building was beginning to appear. The electric palaces and hybrid cine-variety theatres of this era belong to a new line of development which does not concern us here.

Looking at buildings

Like all strip cartoons, this introductory account has been over-simply drawn. No account has been taken of the many byways and dead ends of music hall development. The line of evolution was neither uniformly direct nor neatly consecutive and several different kinds of music hall existed simultaneously, drawing from the same pool of talent but serving different audiences and offering widely differing ambiences. The crude scaffolding we have constructed may, nevertheless, serve as a platform from which to view specific architectural events. Let us, however, note from the outset that 'architecture' in this context carries no necessary implication of refined architectural ambition.

Here is the first of the traps we have to avoid in looking at music hall buildings. They cannot be made to fit tidily into any mainstream art-historical sequence. Their architects — when they can be named at all — tend to be either unremarkable local men, glad of whatever commissions might come their way, or (especially in phase 7) theatre specialists who dressed their functionally efficient shells with eclectic extravagance, in fine disregard of what was happening elsewhere.

Second, we must not suppose that surviving music hall buildings, however exciting they may be, can convey to the uncritical observer a complete impression of what they were like in their prime. To understand them fully our imagination must furnish, drape, decorate and fill them with the sound, colours and odours of their time,

This kind of recreation is essential to an understanding of the music hall experience, but the student must be warned that no single source of information provides all that is needed and some sources must be treated with caution. Contemporary illustrations and descriptions, plans submitted to licensing and safety authorities and the related correspondence, together with deed plans, schedules of contents, business correspondence (where any of these things exist), examination of the standing fabric (again, where any exists) — all such sources must be used and compared to piece together what may still be an incomplete account.[9]

The examples following are intended to do no more than show what is discoverable over the range of music hall types and to encourage the reader to develop a critical eye in looking the often reprinted pictures of music halls.

Case studies

Deacon's — from Crib to music hall

An old drawing of Deacon's Music Hall (redrawn here as Figures 1.3 and 1.4) offers remarkable evidence of four distinct stages of development — roughly speaking phases 1, 3, 5 and 6 — in one building. The drawing itself is dated 1886, but it speaks first of the 1830s and the Sir Hugh Myddelton Tavern.

The pub, which was rebuilt in 1831, had a popular tea garden attached to it and a convivial meeting tradition established in the eighteenth century. Renton Nicholson, writing in 1837, describes two rooms which can be identified on the plan. The 'Old Crib' or club room was the scene of discussions and other meetings under the chairmanship of the licensee. A charge was made for admission, but it seems to have been a room for cronies, rather than a truly public room. Next to it, at the back of the house, was the Long Room, successor to an earlier public concert room.

By the mid-century, the Long Room had become a proto-music hall. In 1861 the remnant of the old tea garden was built over with a new music hall, 80 feet long, seating 600 and with a total capacity (including promenades) of 800. In 1884 it was increased in width to the irregular shape seen here, with a total capacity of 1,030. The extension 'outboard' of the columns to the left of the stage represents the 1884 works. The Crib and the Long Room survived (with their old names) as bars, open to the promenade.

Deacon's was a ramshackle affair, stitched together rather than architected, but it must rate as a grand music hall. The hall and its roof completely blinded the back windows of the pub and there can be little doubt that it had become much more important and profitable than the building it was attached to. At the date of this drawing, however, it must be rated as old-fashioned, retaining the full complement of supper tables and the open stage typical of the classic grand music halls of 20 and 30 years earlier.

The long section shows clearly how it worked. The hall had its own entrance from the street, past a little pay-box, but once within the visitor could pass freely from the seated areas to the promenades and bars. The chairman was perched on a little dais in front of the orchestra within an enclosed, higher price stalls.

In cross-section can be seen the dizzy stacking of some of the seats in the balcony extension, which would otherwise have had no view of the stage. Sightlines in the strict theatrical sense were not, however, of great importance. The performers made a profession of audibility and they created characters with an accuracy and intensity to triumph over all limitations. None the less, we see here a tentative move toward theatrical conditions in the presence of a curtained proscenium arch — but note that the singer and the footlights are a good ten feet *in front* of the arch. The intimate contact between performer and audience is not unlike that existing in Georgian playhouses (the Marylebone music hall, as late as the 1880s, exhibited a stranger throwback with proscenium doors topped by little boxes).

Unlike a theatre, the classic grand music hall had windows and rooflights, but additional ventilation was needed to cope with the fruity atmosphere generated by a thousand drinking, smoking and sweating patrons. The louvred outlets above the roof would have improved matters a little, but the principal benefit was provided by the 'sunlight', the multi-burner gas chandelier in the centre of the roof, whose flue heated the air in an outer concentric shaft, producing a forced updraught.[10] Even so, the long narrow urinal near the entrance must have declared its presence on hot summer evenings.

Early doors — the Cyder Cellars and the Grapes

Deacon's has taken us too far and too fast. If we return now to two of the most important precursors of the classic music hall we shall find that they differ noticeably in physical form not only from the later Deacon's but also from one another. In other respects, however, they were probably not so different as contemporary illustrations might suggest.

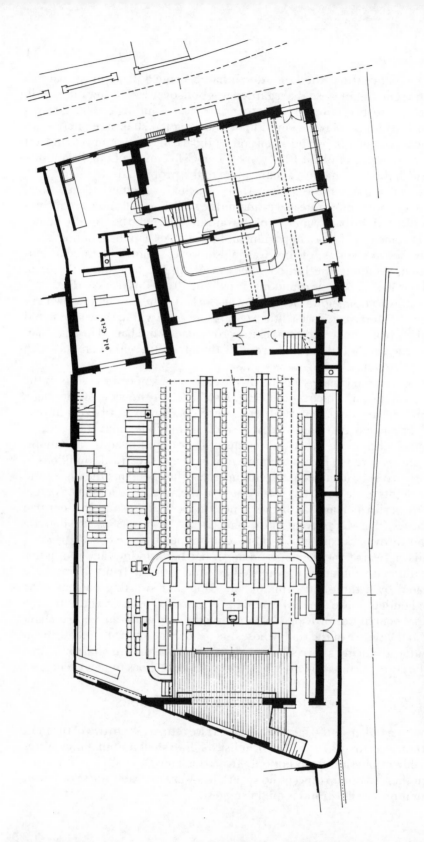

'Old Crib'

Figure 1.3. Deacon's Music Hall: plan as completed in 1884. Redrawn by the author from an original drawing in the Greater London Record Office.

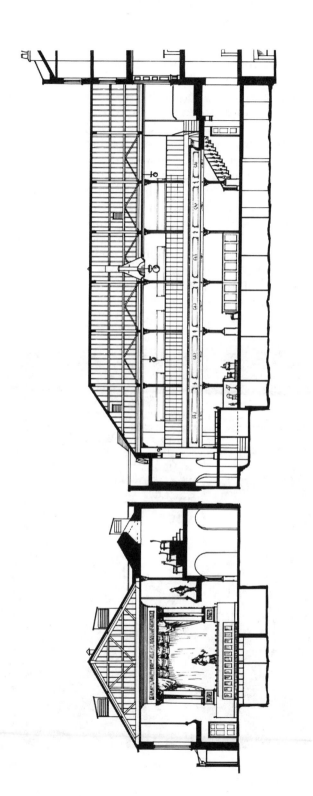

Figure 1.4. Deacon's Music Hall: sections.

The formal banquet room appearance conveyed by plans and conventional view of such historically crucial halls as the Grapes Grand Harmonic Hall of 1846 (seen here, Figure 1.7, as the Surrey) or the Canterbury Hall of 1854 (Figure 1.9), needs to be corrected by referring to Figure 1.6, Dicky Doyle's cartoon of the Cyder Cellars and Figure 1.11, an unnamed music hall (the Middlesex has been suggested) illustrated in the *Graphic* in 1873.

The apparent contrast between the views of the Cellars and the Grapes needs to be looked at with particular care. The Cellars, seen here in 1849, had recently become what it was to remain almost to the end, a 'phase 3' proto-music hall. It was a rectangular room which, ten years earlier (Figure 1.5) had been tidily laid out with three long refectory tables, the chairman being seated at the head of the centre table, where glees and solo songs were performed. The *Punch* cartoonist has caught the room almost at the moment of change. By the late 1840s the success of character singers like W. G. Ross and songs like 'Sam Hall' had led to the introduction of a little corner platform and the crowding in of as many tables and chairs as the place would hold.

Figure 1.5. Cyder Cellars, Maiden Lane, Covent Garden – the new room built about 1840. Engraving from a handbill.

Figure 1.6. The Cyder Cellars: the purpose-built supper room of c. 1840 transformed to a proto-music hall, with W. G. Ross singing 'Sam Hall' from the corner platform, installed c. 1847–9. From an illustration by Richard Doyle to Mr Pips Hys Diarye, *1849.*

Doyle has probably not greatly exaggerated the visual confusion of the Cellars. Note the folding screen (presumably a quick change slot) behind Ross and the piano squeezed into a bit of dead space on the end wall.

The slightly earlier Grapes looks orderly by comparison, but this kind of view understates the casual behaviour of an early music hall audience, treating the figures as necessary furnishings to an architectural perspective and ignoring the competing foci of bars and refreshment counters. The movement towards completely stage-focused theatrical conditions was certainly farther off in the 1840s than this engraving makes it appear. The Grapes hall had been thrown up in great haste by an architect named Hiscock for Richard Preece the Elder. It had a proscenium stage with provision for simple scenery, but it was an oddity — a survivor as well as a precursor, combining characteristics of the dying race of small saloon theatres and the rising generation of music halls.

Ten years after Preece's transitional hall, the phase 5 grand music halls had nearly all adopted the open stage form and presented a scene of busy informality more like the Cellars than any regular theatre.

Figure 1.7. The Grand Harmonic Hall at the Grapes Tavern (Surrey Music Hall or Winchester Music Hall), Southwark. From a handbill.

The grand music halls: the Canterbury

The classic 'phase 5' music hall is superbly illustrated in the *Graphic* picture, which may stand for Deacon's or the Canterbury or any other product of the mid-Victorian boom. It should be read with the conventional 1854 view and the plan of the Canterbury complex as completed by Charles Morton in 1858 (Figures 1.8, 1.9 and 1.10).

The plan shows how even the most magnificent of the pub halls had to be pummelled and punched into whatever space was available with little thought for sophisticated architectural effect. Most such halls were practically invisible from any public place. Management of the internal volumes within the confines of an enclosed site and the commercial imperatives laid down by the proprietor called for ingenuity rather than innovation. At this stage, architectural splendour was measured almost entirely in terms of more or less ornament, richer or plainer furnishing. The conditions which produced the boom music halls often made for an extremely seductive visual complexity, but it would be a mistake to read into this the existence of conscious design ambitions.

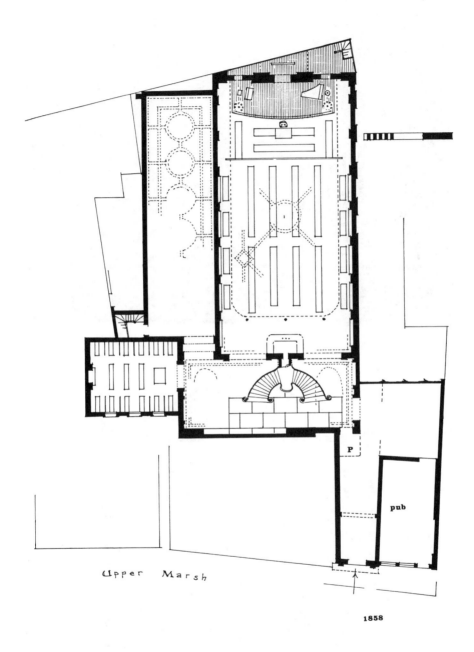

Figure 1.8. Canterbury Hall, Upper Marsh, Lambeth: the complex as completed by Charles Morton in 1858. Plan reconstructed by the author from plans and sketches in Greater London Record Office and from contemporary illustrations.

Figure 1.9. Canterbury Hall: Morton's second hall of 1854 as depicted in the Illustrated London News of 1856.

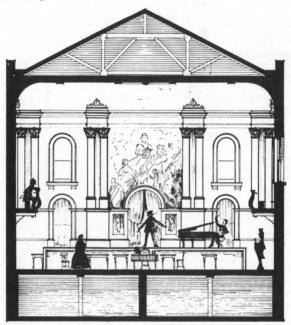

Figure 1.10. Canterbury Hall: cross-section with figures drawn to scale (contrast with Figure 1.9). Author's reconstruction.

Figure 1.11. Unidentified music hall illustrated in the Graphic 1873.

In the Canterbury we see the 'paste-on' design process at work, with a 'fine art gallery', supper room, vestibule, grand staircase and billiards room added to an already existing music hall and filling every corner of an irregular site assembled by a complex series of purchases. The staircase seems almost too big for the space it occupies and the approach from the street is far from grand — almost as casual, in fact, as the winding corridor which, six years earlier, had linked the back of the pub to its little concert room.

It is a pity that Sickert (unborn in 1858) could not have brought this immensely important hall to life for us, but the *Graphic* artist probably takes us as close as we will now get to the reality of this kind of hall.

It is not immediately apparent where the observer is placed in relation to the main axis of the room and uncertainty is doubled by the fact that none of the figures in the foreground seems to be taking the slightest notice of the performer. The view is, in fact, taken from the promenade. We have already observed that a music hall audience was not static. It did not arrive for curtain-up and sit obediently in a fixed seat for hours at a stretch. The artist has emphasised but not overstated the function of a music hall as a meeting place, a social club and a monkey-walk. If we could push through the promenade and the throng of men and women in hats and outdoor clothes, we

should find an organised architecture and orderly furnishing, but everything seen, from the basic planning of the spaces, down to the details of the
decorations (hard-wearing up to shoulder level, dazzling above) would have
been geared to the character and behaviour of a casual, determinedly mobile
audience to whom liquor must be sold in quantity if the hall was to prosper.

Seen against the set piece *Illustrated London News* view, the *Graphic* provides
a convincing smell of real life. It is also a corrective in terms of scale. The
artist has drawn real people, not the conventional 4ft. 6in. midgets who make
the *ILN* Canterbury look so enormous and boringly polite. The Canterbury
was, nevertheless, big enough. The dry official who inspected the building in
progress in 1854 was moved to remark: 'Although this room comes before
[us] under the unpretending form of a room attached to a public house, it is
of much importance as a concert room capable of holding some 1500
people'[11] — but his surprise stemmed from the where rather than the what.

Before proceeding to the next example we should, perhaps, consider what
has been learned so far as to the value of different kinds of evidence about
music hall buildings. Official building and licensing records can provide
some bare facts. Scale plans, where they exist, are the most reliable guide to
the physical character of buildings, especially when they can be checked
against other records, but they say little about the interaction between
architecture, artiste and audience. If we fill gaps from the impressions of
contemporary artists and writers we must beware of deliberate and 'recognised' distortions as well as misrepresentations arising from the background
and conditioning of the reporters, a minority of whom 'belonged' in a music
hall.

The smaller halls — Rodney's Head

The plan and section of the Rodney's Head (Figure 1.12) takes us to the
other end of the market. It is exactly contemporary with the second Canterbury, an East End long room of 1854 (seen here with seating arrangements
of the 1880s) of one building plot's width, covering all the land at the rear of
a narrow-fronted pub. Entry and exit are by way of the ground-floor bars,
passing a pay-box. A fire in the pub would have trapped the entire audience.

The room itself is about as simple as a balconied hall can be. A wood and
canvas proscenium frames a stage which can only be entered through the
body of the hall (not even, as it was at the second Canterbury, through the
cellars). The chairman is a lone figure with a gavel. There is no pretence of
a top table and most of the audience sits on ranks of benches, each with a
shelf for glasses on its back rail. If there were more tables when the hall was
first built the capacity must have been unprofitably low.

The persistence throughout the nineteenth century of large singing
rooms in pubs and a number of unambitious 'phase 4' concert rooms of the
Rodney's Head kind accounts for the confusing statistics we see quoted for
music halls in London at different times. A crude count of magistrate's music

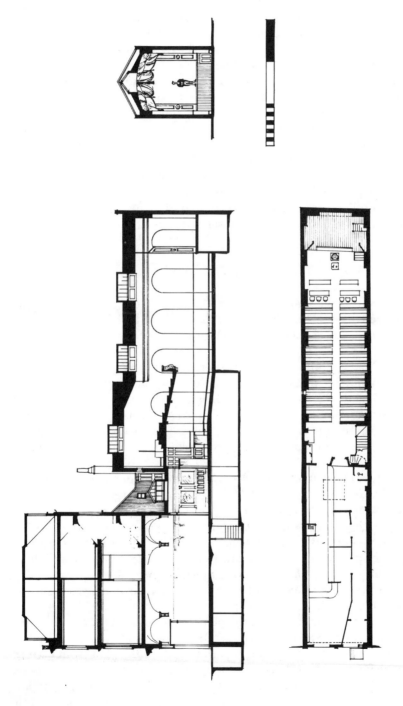

Figure 1.12. Rodney's Head, Whitechapel, a small East End pub 'music room' run up by a local quasi-architect in 1854. Plan and section redrawn by the author from original drawings of 1884 in Greater London Record Office.

and dancing licences reveals nothing of the scale of provision, the tone of the entertainment or the architectural and social chasm which existed between, say, the Alma singing room or the Rodney's Head and the Oxford. The two last may quite reasonably be described as music halls, but only as No. 8 Paradise Row and Chatsworth may be described as houses.

Even where size and plan form appear to match closely there may have been extreme variations in character. The room recorded in Alfred Concanen's excellent lithograph (Figure 1.13) is very like the Rodney's Head (a little simpler, since it has no balcony) but apart from a few tables set round the walls, the floor is kept clear for dancing. It is all promenade. Music (one suspects it came from a mixture of traditions, oral and 'polite') and some kind of rough variety entertainment is provided, but the audience is active and rowdily self-entertaining in a way that the patrons of the Rodney's Head, just over a mile away, could not be. The Concanen view is of a Ratcliff hall — the Gunboat — itself a scene of splendour compared to the neighbouring Globe and Pigeons, which had whitewashed walls and no stage.

Climax of the grand music hall: The Oxford

Returning now to the mainstream, the Oxford of 1861 (Figures 1.14 and 1.15) marked Charles Morton's move from Lambeth to the West End with a display of architectural magnificence. Here is the first cathedral of the music halls.

Four halls had already opened up the territory: Evans's in 1855, the short-head loser to Morton in the race to build the first grand music hall; Weston's in 1857, designed, like Evans's and the Britannia Theatre, by William Finch Hill; the first London Pavilion in 1859, a less than permanent affair, formed by roofing over an inn yard, and (not far ahead of the Oxford) the Alhambra in 1861, an architectural oddity, converted from the old Panopticon building.

Morton's Oxford put all its predecessors in the shade. The old galleried Boar and Castle Inn was completely demolished to be replaced by the first complex in which tavern and music hall were conceived as one.

Sam Field, the architect of the Canterbury, had no hand in the Oxford. The design was entrusted to William Finch Hill and his partner Edward Paraire. They combined the best features of all earlier grand music halls to produce a prodigious balconied room, flowing into spacious promenades, bars and buffets, approached through its own portico and vestibule, yet tightly integrated with the frontage pub.

It is interesting to observe from the plan that, even with the freedom of a cleared site, a magnificent hall like the Oxford was still, in many respects, designed as if it were an addition. A path traced on the plan from Oxford Street to the farthermost corner of the long promenade reveals a route beset by as many choices of direction, as much visual incident and as many opportunities for personal encounters as any casually created backland warren.

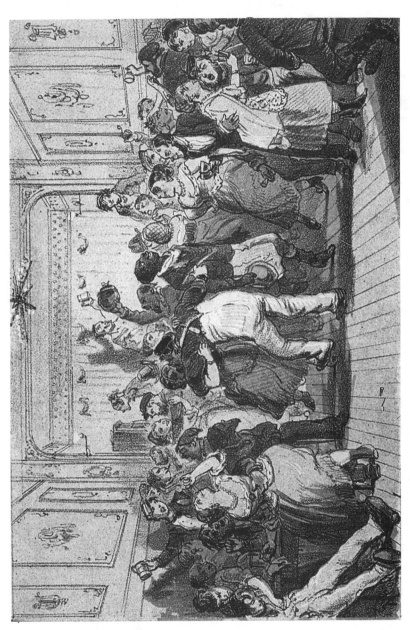

Figure 1.13. A small dockland music and dancing hall in Shadwell High Street, built 1860 or earlier. Lithograph of 1876 by Alfred Concanen.

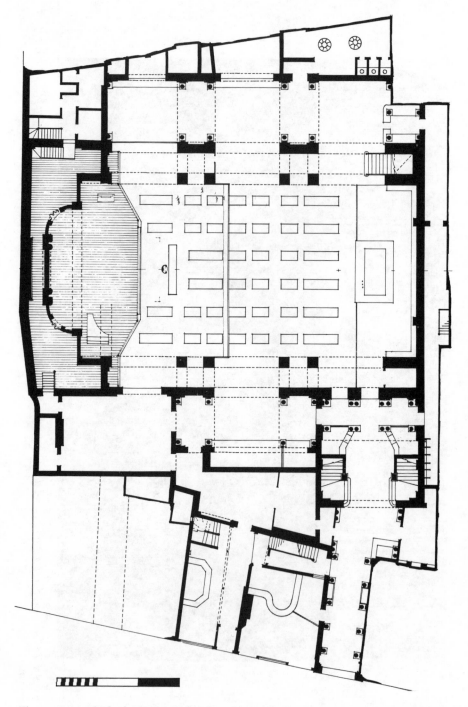

Figure 1.14. Oxford Music Hall: plan of first hall of 1861–9. Reconstructed by author from later plans and contemporary views and descriptions.

Figure 1.15. Oxford Music Hall: view of auditorium as built in 1861, from a lithograph by Thomas Packer.

How far Finch Hill and Paraire may, in this case, have exploited the architectural potential of its labyrinthine character could now only be tested fully by making a model.

Although, as we have seen, 'phase 5' halls persisted, with varying degrees of modification, to the last years of the century, the Oxford represents the climax of the type. After only seven years of existence (from the building of the second Canterbury) the grand music hall could develop no farther.

The original 1861 Oxford design survived recognisably through two rebuilds, but by 1873 rows of fixed seating had replaced the supper tables (Figure 1.16) and the stage had acquired a proscenium. Progress toward a new type of music hall had, in fact, begun at least four or five years earlier with Holland's improvements to the Canterbury and Villiers' rebuilding of the South London Palace (Figure 1.17).

Transition: early evolution of the variety theatre

The South London of 1869 took a significant step in the movement toward theatrical conditions. With its curving balconies it was in a different class

Figure 1.16. Oxford Music Hall: as altered after the fire of 1872 (from a souvenir programme).

Figure 1.17. South London Palace, London Road, Elephant and Castle, a transitional hall by W. Paice for R. E. Villiers, 1869.

from the old hybrid at the Grapes or any of the later rectangular halls which had suffered modifications typical of phase 6/6a. It could easily be taken for a contemporary theatre in this illustration (Figure 1.17), were it not for the visible attributes of a music hall, the bars and tables.

Perhaps the first, almost accidental move in this direction occurred when the Panopticon rotunda opened in 1861 as the Alhambra Music Hall,[12] with a big proscenium arch cut into its circumference to give it the combination of tent-like auditorium, encircling promenade and spectacular dance stage adopted in Paris (also in the 1860s) at the Ba-ta-clan[13] and the Folies Bergère — and also much later at Verity's Empire, just across Leicester Square from the Alhambra. It was, however, Villiers' rebuilding of the Canterbury in 1876 and the London Pavilion in 1885 which made the most positive advances towards variety theatre form (that is, towards phase 7). At the Pavilion in 1886 all the tables at last disappeared to be replaced with reservable tip-up seats with neat little shelves for glasses screwed to their back rails.

The final stage was reached in the last decade of the century with the tightening of safety controls and the dominance of the syndicates, leading to the perfection of a fully theatrical form of variety house whose architecture was geared to safety, order and profitability.

The new boom carried all before it. Curious old survivors like Edward Clark's Metropolitan, Edgware Road (a sort of poor man's Alhambra in architectural form) were rebuilt by Frank Matcham and his contemporaries. The old hexagonal Metropolitan of 1862 with spindly iron columns supporting a single balcony is shown here (Figure 1.18) just before its final metamorphosis.

The chairman's table had, by this time, disappeared. Entering by the vestibule (V) and passing the pay-desk (P), one turned left for the tables or comfortable settles of the stalls (S) and the upholstered seats of the orchestra stalls (O), or right for the benched area (A). In the unbenched promenade to the left of the triangular stage there were narrow shelved rails for elbows and glasses. The changing character of the halls is shown in this plan by the presence of a scene painting room (sp) and the comparatively generous lavatory provision (m and l) as well as the growing subdivision of the audience, but the bars in the auditorium (B) still tell of a pub concert room ancestry.

The second plan (Figure 1.19) shows how Matcham's 1897 transformation followed the usual time-saving practice of using as much of the existing structural envelope as possible, but without preserving the faintest memory of the old flat-floored room. The pub remained embedded in the frontage, but the theatre was otherwise independent. The glazed screen to the stalls bar marks the first step toward the complete removal of drinking from the auditorium in those palaces which were rising on virgin sites in the suburbs.

The variety theatres

The exotic splendour of the Hackney Empire (Figures 1.20 and 1.21) may stand for an entire generation. It is a building which outshines nearly every

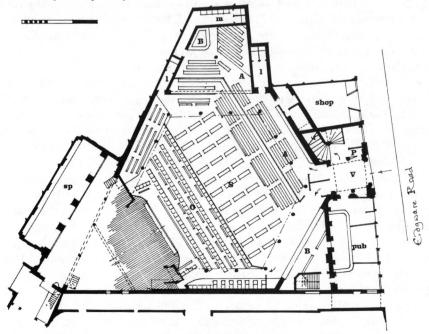

Fig. 1.18. The Metropolitan, Edgware Road, by Edward Clark, 1862. Redrawn by the author from a plan of 1884.

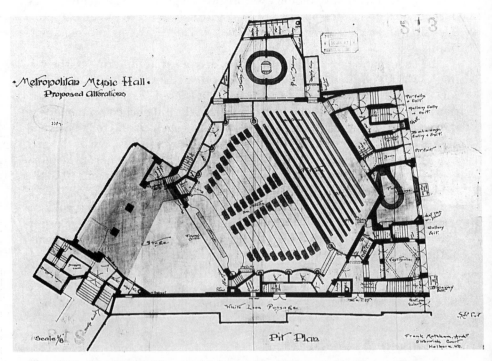

Fig. 1.19. The Metropolitan: Matcham's Plan for reconstruction 1897 (Greater London Record Office).

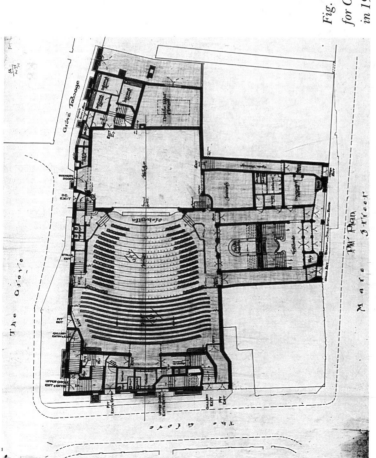

Fig. 1.20. Hackney Empire: plan dated 1900 by Frank Matcham for Oswald Stoll's fourth London suburban variety palace, opened in 1901.

Figure 1.21. Hackney Empire: the exotic Indian decoration of the auditorium. The name 'music hall' continued to be applied to sumptuous variety palaces of this kind, long after the flat-floored drinking halls had been killed off by the safety regulations and the anti-music hall campaigners in the licensing authorities.

regular theatre existing in London when it was built in 1901. From the point of view of safety it approaches the ideal, with exits on three sides and separate escape staircases from each level — a separation which has the effect of reinforcing social divisions.[14] In this respect it is quite unlike the earlier music halls where the visible divisions were slight. Here each section of the audience is directed to its proper place by the pricing structure and the careful separation of the entrances, each mingling only with its own kind and all confined to seats of varying degrees of comfort — but all, it must be said, enjoying better conditions than they would have found in most theatres.

The architecture, internal and external, of the Hackney Empire, was and is opulent, almost erotic in its appeal. By the turn of the century the great rectangular rooms, blazing with light and alive with movement, were all gone, to be replaced by wonderful caverns of gold.

The professional entertainers adapted readily to their new conditions without material change to the style created 40 and 50 years earlier by Sharp, Cowell, Collins, Mackney, Mrs Caulfield, Jenny Hill and other pioneers. Historical continuity in the performance can be traced much farther back. The Empire certainly heard songs and patter with recognisable antecedents in the songbooks of the Regency concert rooms. But the architectural setting, the experience of 'going to hear a song', the pretences of the entertainment magnates and the behaviour of the audience had changed out of recognition in less than 20 years.

Notes

(Place of publication is London except where stated otherwise.)

1. The useful term 'room singer' seems to have been current by the 1830s (it is used by Renton Nicholson in *Town*). The room singer was paid, unlike the modern folkclub 'floor singer' who is generally unrewarded.
2. It was a regulatory rather than a revolutionary measure, giving legal recognition to a state of affairs which already existed.
3. Eltham's back additon to the Mahogany Bar was licensed by the magistrates as a concert room for four years up to 1843. In that year it was modified (as the Albion Saloon) to make it suitable for a Lord Chamberlain's stage plays 'saloon theatre' licence under the new Act. By 1853, when John Wilton built his first small hall over the same site, it had reverted to concert room use (Public Record Office, Lord Chamberlain's records (PRO LC) 7.5; 7.6 and 7.13; Metropolitan Buildings Office (MBO) Cases of Special Supervision V. 16 p. 223).
4. This was the standard but not quite invariable arrangement. At the Borough Music Hall, for example, the chairman sat at the side of the stage in the modern Players' 'Late Joys' fashion (woodcut in *Peeping Tom c.* 1858–9).
5. Morton's progress is detailed in J. Earl and J. Stanton, *Canterbury Hall and Theatre of Varieties*, 1982, pp. 15–16.
6. Ibid., pp. 24–6.
7. For more detailed background to the emergence of the new generation of architects, see Victor Glasstone, *Victorian and Edwardian Theatres*, 1975, p. 59ff; and B. Walker (ed.), *Frank Matcham: Theatre Architect*, Belfast, 1980, *passim*.

8. As late as 1896, Clement Scott could still contrast the bright interiors of the Empire, the Alhambra and the Palace with the 'catacomb' effect of those theatres which had adopted lowered house lighting (*Illustrated London News*, 2 March 1896).

9. In this chapter the principal sources used have been Greater London Record Office (GLRO) theatre drawings; GLRO MBO records; GLRO Metropolitan Board of Works records; GLRO reports and *Presented Papers* of the various London County Council committees concerned with the licensing and safety of theatres and music halls; PRO LC records; and prints, drawings and periodicals in various public and private collections.

10. See Terence Rees, *Theatre Lighting in the Age of Gas*, 1978. Complete examples of sunlights, sunburners or starburners are now extremely rare. A flue still exists inside the roof of Wilton's Music Hall, whose timbers were charred in places by the intense heat. Sunburners can be seen in the private theatre at Normansfield, Teddington and Buxton Opera House. Sun and starburners exist in St Botolph's church, Aldersgate. The Buxton example is, uniquely, in working order.

11. GLRO MBO Cases of Special Supervision V. 18, report by Ambrose Poynter, 14 August 1854.

12. F. H. W. Sheppard (ed.), *Survey of London*, vol. 34, 1966; R. Mander and R. Mitchenson, *Lost Theatres of London*, 1968.

13. For the Ba-ta-clan and other Parisian parallels, see F. Cardec and A. Weill, *Le Café-Concert*, Paris, 1980.

14. Even in mid-century there was no such thing as a 'standard', homogeneous music hall audience, working-class or otherwise. The Oxford and the Alhambra attracted a different mix from, say, Paddy's Goose in Dockland, but in all of them the various sections of working- and middle-class society could mingle as in a public place. The relaxed, unsegregated freedom of the halls was an attraction to the well-heeled men about town who completed the spectrum in the West End and its fringes. For the social composition of audiences, see the contributions of J. Crump (Chapter 3) and D. Höher (Chapter 4) in this volume. For a recent consideration of a related question, see G. Harris, 'Audience and Class in the Café Concert', *Theatrephile*, no. 6, 1985.

2 A Community of Friends: Business and Good Fellowship in London Music Hall Management c. 1860–1885

PETER BAILEY

In his address to the audience at his grand benefit night in 1869, William 'Billy' Holland, the proprietor of the Canterbury music hall in London, 'first begged permission to substitute the word "Friends" for Ladies and Gentlemen, and then very properly remarked that when prices are raised on benefit night, a man finds out who are really his friends'.[1] In this artful reconciliation of the ingratiating and the obligating, the affective and the instrumental, Holland animated an ideological motif central to the culture and operation of early music hall, for in this world the language of friendship was the language of business.

Though music hall is much celebrated for its legendary *bonhomie*, there has been little analysis of the specific dynamics of its sociability — how it worked and what it meant. This essay attempts to understand friendship in the music hall as a stylistic and operational code within a distinctive set of relationships in what is characterised as a socially intensive industry. It concentrates on the role of the proprietors who rode London's first music hall boom, their conduct of business and their relationships with the performers, other workers, the audience and the community. Particular attention is paid to the ritual occasion of the benefit night, which disclosed the contradictions of business and good fellowship while celebrating their mutuality, and the essay concludes with some general observations on the significance of friendship in the culture of the period.

I

Although neither they nor the record were reticent on their behalf, the proprietors have received little attention in music hall history compared with that lavished on performers and the sacred sites of the halls themselves.[2] There is unfortunately no space here for an adequate group biography;

what is offered is a brief sketch of the London proprietor or 'caterer', as he was called, as an occupational and social type.

The majority of metropolitan proprietors from this period were drawn from the swarming world of small to medium-sized independent businesses in the service and retail trades. A number of them entered music hall management through the theatre or showmanship, but among some very mixed and mobile careers the commonest way-station en route to full-blown proprietorship was that of publican, and the identification with the licensed trade remained strong. Most of the halls were run conjointly with the taverns with which they still shared their sites, and the new caterers gave freely of their halls and services to the extensive social and charitable functions of the trade.

In social terms, the bigger proprietors had made it from the classic petty bourgeoisie to the more substantial commercial middle class. Capital-investing, property-controlling, servant-owning, the successful caterer celebrated the myth of the self-made man in a career open to talent. 'I, gentlemen,' declared Frederick Strange, who had started as a waiter, then made a fortune as a refreshment contractor at the Crystal Palace before running the monster Alhambra, 'have been . . . the architect of my own position'.[3] Yet though the rise of the music hall entrepreneur took him to the comforts and conceits of the 'paraphernalia of gentility' and commissions in the Volunteers, this self-aggrandisement was balanced with a continuing dedication to the small businessman's traditions of public service and mutuality in the intimate networks of the pub, the friendly society, the masonic lodge and the local vestry. Here service was a gregarious and social act undertaken with one's fellows in the ritual conviviality of dinners, toasts and testimonials.

The self-made man who retains the common touch is no very exceptional phenomenon, but in the music hall proprietor the mix was translated into a distinctive style in which personality was less the mark of the colourful individual than a common element in the *modus operandi* of a type. Central to this style was an effulgent social presence. Personal attention to the service of food and drink seems to have diminished to a token echo of the publican's traditional role as host, but the proprietor was habitually on the premises, his presence sometimes amplified in the appointments of the hall — Morton's monogram was reproduced in relief around the walls of the Oxford, and Morris Syers was represented in a life-size oil portrait. Proprietors took the chair on benefit night and readily allowed themselves to be called on stage. On their own territory they were formidable figures, as was noted of the boss of the Foresters in the East End: 'When I go I like to see Mr. Fort on the premises . . . his authoritative strut and the air of deliberate confidence in which he floats is very refreshing.'[4]

Presence and self-advertisement were further amplified by conspicuous consumption, not only in the accessories that took the proprietor away from the halls and his public — the broughams, the estate and the yacht — but in the manner of his dress, his eating and his drinking which was open to intimate public witness. Walter Besant's fictional caterer, Emmanuel Leweson, was discovered 'gorgeously attired in a brown velvet coat and white waistcoat

with a great profusion of gold chain and studs . . . in his hand was a tumbler
of iced soda and brandy'.[5] This is hardly a caricature, for many proprietors
were known for their grand style: Holland and Crowder of the Paragon
modelled themselves explicitly on Napoleon III in dress, manner and mous-
tache. Fulsome eating and drinking were further emblems of success, and
the symbolic role of gorging, guzzling and smoking was celebrated in the
items habitually chosen for presentation at proprietorial dinners: engraved
goblets, decanters, canteens of cultery, cigar cutters and silver snuff boxes.
Drink, of course, was the essential fuel of good fellowship. The chairman was
the arch imbiber whose direct function it was to generate profit by the glass-
ful, and it was said that proprietors kept their business head by taking their
drinks from the 'sober' rather than the 'drunken' tap. But the signs of
indulgence were plain enough in what one trade paper described as 'their
grog-blossomed faces'.[6]

Yet what we now register as consumption, the proprietor would have represented as provision. One of the most frequent terms of congratulation in
the sub-culture was liberality. Thus Holland and Sweasey were extolled on
one of their dinner nights as proprietors of 'great judgement and liberality'.
Judgement in music hall language could mean the ability to read the public
taste, to know when to drop ballet and promote gymnasts, to know how to
compile a programme of the widest appeal. In part, then, it meant intuition,
but in a more basic sense it stood for rationality and calculation, values that
were meant to complement or temper those of liberality with its sense of
lavish and spontaneous expenditure. But in music hall it was the latter, the
values of social rather than economic man, that were most applauded. After
extricating himself from the Canterbury at a loss, Holland was reproached
for his 'lack of judgement . . . his terrible mistake in giving 2/- worth of entertainment for a 1/-', and was urged to 'study a little economy'. Since this ver-
dict was delivered amid the agreeable debris of yet another proprietorial
blow-out, it was clearly more commendation than reproof.[7] If the proprietor
indulged and regaled himself, it was partly as a symbolic exemplification of
the good life in which *all* were invited to share. Fulsome public provision —
monster programmes, the best in food and drink, luxurious amenities and,
as we shall see, generous dispensations as friend and benefactor — these
were the marks of the proprietor as public caterer. Ballooning liberality
might at times float dangerously free from the restraints of conventional
business sense or 'judgement', yet in the political and emotional economy of
the music hall liberality *was* good business. Through style as much as practice
the proprietor contrived to represent himself as host of a great feast while
simultaneously charging for it.

Liberality of provision was an important part of playing the big man who
lived life beyond the scale of ordinary men. Music hall, declared the agent
Didcott, could never be a success if run like a tallow chandlery; it had to be
run 'on the heroic method'.[8] Caterers were as often cautious as reckless, but
they did court risk in a more cavalier style than other entrepreneurs, and in
true heroic tradition were called upon to confront the defeats as well as

triumphs of the venturer. Holland lost £7,000 in three days when his bullfights at the Agricultural Hall flopped, a singular improvidence on the part of a man who was president of the Music Hall Provident Fund.[9] But this was not a matter of lamentation in Holland's account; it was part of the ups and downs of the showman's life, a matter of luck good or bad. This is the philosophy of the gambler and the close relationship between the halls and gambling is well established. Here was a carry-over from the publican's membership of the sporting fraternity and, it may be argued, no index to his values in his metamorphosis as caterer; or gambling might be taken to evince a rational as much as a providential view of the world, a miniature reproduction of the mysteries of the market situation which might explain its appeal for the proprietor as a transference skill for the modern entrepreneur, rather than identify such enthusiasm as evidence of an important variation on the type. But the gambler in the music hall proprietor does suggest strongly a view of life as successive turns of the wheel of fortune rather than a condition that yields to long-term rational strategy. Such a perspective may well induce fatalism, but for these men it seems invariably to have generated confidence and resilience, for if they believed in luck they also believed in their abilities to seize the main chance and turn their luck to good account.[10]

As a self-invented élite, the proprietors were a yeasty, swanky lot, who in the face of a good deal of hostility in the larger world manufactured much of their own status. Though parvenu in fortune and manner, their roots in the ancient and (by its own lights) respectable trade of the publican gave them security of identity and the social skills to sustain their economic opportunism. Their image was that of the big man with the big heart doings things in a big way, representing himself as both larger than life and as humanity itself. It is not Charles Morton, the over-celebrated and, by one account, 'severe and dogmatic' father of the halls who is the typical figure here, but the extravagant Billy Holland, the 'Emperor of Lambeth', who appropriated the mantle of Gladstone as well as Napoleon by styling himself the 'People's William' and claiming a mission to improve the condition of the working classes. The independent music hall proprietor of the period was a liberal populist, believing in the natural merits of the open market and competitive self-advancement, yet claiming an unselfish dedication to his public through lavish personal service. It was an effective role, not only as a source of esteem, but as a means of control.

II

We turn now to examine the business in which the proprietors operated. Data for this period is scattered, inadequate and unreliable, but some general features seem plain.[11] Overall the history of London's halls in these years, though not without its alarms and casualties, seems to offer an almost perennial success story amid the mixed fortunes of the national economy. In the 1860s, their number increased more than threefold to over 40, and, as the mid-Victorian boom gave way to the great depression after 1873, the metropolitan halls retained their buoyancy, holding steady or declining only slightly in number, while audience capacity and the value and profitability of their property continued to rise. Amid reports of a further general down-swing in trade at the end of the 1870s, the music hall press found the halls, east and west, in flourishing condition. 'Everyone is talking about the profits made by music hall proprietors', noted the *Entr'acte*, amazed at 'where it all comes from in hard times like these', adding that Graydon of the recently enlarged Middlesex was negotiating for a small truck to deliver his takings to the bank.[12] In 1885, as the depression in London deepened, Villiers opened the luxurious new London Pavilion, and saw his confidence amply rewarded. Yet the trade press was forever warning that music hall was 'a perilous business', and the jeremiads deserve attention. As the capital's indi-genous and tourist population grew in number, purchasing power and expectations in these years, the market for entertainment of all kinds not only provided greater entrepreneurial opportunity but grew more volatile and competitive. Moreover, the fact that fluctuations in the music hall indus-try tended to be personal, localised or seasonal rather than industry-wide and dependent on the general economy, may have contributed to the convic-tion that, whatever its great prizes, this was a particularly capricious and idiosyncratic business.

Certainly the costs of entry were considerable and rising, whether by building or buying in. Extensions and refurbishment were increasingly expensive, the general rise in London property prices after 1870 drove up overheads, and rates rose sharply with the revaluation of 1870. The average capitalisation of halls listed in evidence to the Select Committee of 1866 was close to £10,000, but leading halls required much greater outlays. An aspi-rant proprietor might take a smaller or declining property for a few thousand, but the general escalation of costs was signalled dramatically in 1878 when the Board of Works paid £109,347 for the site of the London Pavilion.[13]

Significantly, despite the rising costs, there was little recourse to the formal capital market and the new device of limited liability; raising finance for the halls in this period was a mostly private, informal (and thus unfortunately obscure) business. Though there were several proposals for company for-mation in the 1860s and 1870s, only three reached incorporation, two of which soon failed. More generally, capital was raised by the individual owner himself or in partnership, with what was called 'the usual leg-up given by bre-wers and distillers', a suggestion that the latter subventions were necessary but not sufficient.[14] Family money was a customary way of expanding on per-sonal capital and beyond kin the caterer may have looked for funds from the professional men about town who figure among the notables in prospectuses and at table.[15] Another source may have been the more numerous compo-nent in the guest lists, the provisioning trades — grocers, biscuit and soft drink manufacturers, proprietors of cigar divans, wine and spirit merchants. Profits from the latter trade had been boosted by Gladstone's deregulation measures in 1860, and a number of merchants were parties in music hall promotion, including perhaps the last of London's old-style grandees,

George Adney Payne.[16] The role of the other trades seems to have been as necessary auxiliaries, part of the closely interested local business community that sustained the halls in other ways, by its custom, confidence and credit.

Whatever the costs, proprietors seemed to tap a ready supply of venture capital, without extensive resort to institutional funds or incorporation. In such a personalised and capricious business, direction seemed no doubt best committed to the capable hands of the big man, unencumbered by the counterweight (and expenses) of company management.And after all, this was show business, where the potential investor was himself probably an *habitué* and rational calculations might be secondary to the thrills of linking destinies with the charismatic figure of the caterer. There is a telling recollection of Holland riding the wheel of fortune in the 1860s and 1870s: after many financial failures, we are told, 'he invariably reappeared, sphinx-like, irreproachably groomed and waxed, with some confiding creature ready to finance him'.[17]

After the costs of setting up in a hall came the costs of keeping up the hall. The demands on circulating rather than fixed capital were also considerable. 'Whoever takes a hall', advised the *Entr'acte*, 'will need to be furnished with plenty of the ready.' Certainly, the big salaries of the stars, the doubling of the number of acts on the programme, and the increasing sophistication and scale of the staging drove production costs higher. In 1885 one estimate put the salary bill for artistes at a West-End hall at from £150 to £250 per week. To this would be added the bill for musicians and numerous other staff, backstage and front of house. There were also bills for gas, advertising and printing. The proprietor was said to cover these costs with takings at the door, and to look for his profit in the 'wet' money spent on drinks and refreshments.[18] Though there are some estimates of expenditure on these items there are no figures for the cost of their provision; given the range of drinks, tobacco, confectionery and 'other substantials', this would have been considerable. It is most likely that it was in this department that proprietors elasticated their assets by relying a good deal on credit and goodwill.

The important functions of credit, cash flow and business confidence come to light in an action in 1869 for slander and consequent commercial injury brought by Charles Sinclair, proprietor of Sinclair's Music Hall, off Edgware Road, against Bennett, pork butcher in the neighbourhood:

> The slander complained of was that the defendant said that the plaintiff has been arrested for debt and carried in a cab to Whitecross Street prison, whereby the plaintiff was injured in his credit. He could show that in consequence of the report getting into circulation, Mr. Stack, a tradesman in the neighbourhood, who used to cash the plaintiff's cheques, refused to do so. Mr. Rawlings, who supplied the plaintiff with cider and perry, to be consumed in the Music Hall; Mr. Harris, who supplied him with cigars; and other tradesmen withdrew from supplying him with goods.

Unable to cash his cheque, Sinclair 'was put to great inconvenience for money with which to pay his performers, and two of the band actually left him on account of the report'. Bennett the butcher, who was alleged to have an interest in a rival theatre close by, rang the death knell on his neighbour by announcing his tale to a crowded bar in the local pub, where Sinclair had previously been negotiating with a solicitor representing another artist and small-time impresario who owed him money. 'Professor' Sinclair won the case but received only a farthing damages, and did his best to repair his damaged reputation by holding 'A Proprietor's Tradesman's Bespeak' or benefit at which 'there were many friends and guest artists, all of whom made some allusion to the proprietor's goodness of heart, upright dealing in business matters and honourable conduct'. Sinclair went bankrupt the following year when it was reported that most of his debts were for money lent.[19] Sinclair's hall was small and obviously something of a hand-to-mouth operation, yet bigger men were as anxious to protect their credit and the reputation on which it rested. Syers wrote to the *Era* to correct their underestimate of his profits, for 'your former report might shake my credit if left unchanged', and Villiers clearly moved heaven and earth to secure the attendance of Stanley Vickers as chair at the dinner celebrating the rebuilding of the South London in 1869. Vickers was not only an MP — genuflection — but Villiers's principal supplier of 'gallons of wine and gin', and his fulsome testimony to the proprietor's 'honour and probity' was urgently adduced to counter those who were trying to 'talk him out of business'.[20]

The business relationship between proprietor and performer was also both critical and complex. In theory the performer was dependent but not subordinate, but the proprietor's tightening control of market access made the fiction of an equitable relationship hard to sustain, and the conventions of good fellowship had to be worked more feverishly to obscure incipient conflict and exploitation. The rise of the agent meant greater formalisation of business and contract, but many hiring agreements were still no more than a verbal exchange made face to face over a drink. In Didcott's telling description, proprietors and artists of this era transacted their business 'like farmers at a fair'.[21] The rapid and competitive growth of the halls in London may have given performers some leverage on the market in the 1860s, an advantage certainly enjoyed by the new stars. The turns system discouraged the establishment of permanent or seasonal companies, and the necessarily piecemeal assembly of programmes might make the proprietor more dependent upon the co-operation of key artists. Holland publicly acknowledged the magnanimity of the star Nellie Power who made him a gift of her services for a week over and above the terms of her engagement, and there were other signs of the exchange of favours and an amiable mutuality of interest.[22]

More often, however, the proprietor held the upper hand and the artist was the supplicant. 'Moans of a Manager', a piece in the trade press from 1870, derides the importunate pro soliciting for a job or 'shop' at a time when a bulge in supply coincident with a levelling off in the number of halls may well have compounded the insecurities of a generally overstocked profession. The piece goes on to tell how, after he has been hired, the pro turns from ingratiation to calumny and accuses the manager of 'taking half his "screw"'.[23] Summary depredations were indeed common as proprietors squeezed labour costs when business was thin: fines were imposed, unexpected commissions were levied, performers were kept waiting late for 'treasury' on Saturday night to keep up the drinking that could be discounted from their pay, and refreshment tickets or free passes might be substituted for cash.[24] Amid the clichés of companionable equality one voice spoke forthrightly and illuminatingly about where real authority lay. Fort of the Foresters Hall (he of the authoritative strut) brought a number of actions in the mid-1870s to vindicate the rights of proprietors over performers. In one case he complained that he had been misreported in saying a certain artist was his tool, offering in correction that 'Miss Thorne does as I tell her . . . she is my servant'.[25]

Music hall was increasingly labour-intensive and the proprietor had charge of numerous staff. In 1862 one of the largest halls was said to employ 80 staff, the majority of which would have been in service rather than production roles.[26] Here organisation was overtly hierarchical — 'Caste is everywhere, even in the music halls' — with authority passing down through a general manager or chairman to individual subcontractors. The status of staff was more obviously that of servant than was that of the performers, though musicians as artistic labour occupied a more ambiguous position. With low or no money wages, staff were often dependent on perquisites and tips from customers and performers, or on pilfering and embezzlement.[27] Proprietors sought to win honesty and loyalty by their paternal largess — fêtes and outings for employees became regular features in the music hall calendar, and in the 1860s proprietors began to extend the privileges of the benefit performance to individuals and groups among their support staff.

The final important relationship considered here was that of the proprietor and the neighbourhood community. Here, as already suggested, status, credit and custom were sensitively connected. A hall's function as ready source of employment — permanent, casual or bye — enhanced the proprietor's local status, as did his seat on the vestry or the board of guardians. Certainly the neighbourhood connection was crucial in maintaining a core of regular custom. It is plain that as in Morton's campaign to lure the fashionable supper-room set across the water to the Canterbury, proprietors set out to extend the constituency of their audience upwards and outwards, offering superior and separate amenities for a putative middle-class clientele and special deals for the new leisure traffic on the underground and suburban railways. But the courting of local custom was still essential even for the big halls. The *Entr'acte* scorned grandiose schemes for attracting 'society', maintaining that those who had succeeded in London music hall made local business their priority.[28]

The most obvious favour and symbol in the cultivation of local identification was the free list, the issue of complimentary passes or 'orders'. Already in disrepute in the theatre where it had originated, the practice flourished in the halls where it was claimed that those on the list were more profitable

customers than those who paid at the door. Membership of the free list —
and even better, the recognition that brought with it what was termed a 'face
pass', or the practice of 'going in on the nod' — this meant almost certain
election to the élite of local *habitués*. The group comprised mainly tradesmen
and their sons, plus clerks and shop-boys, the young men presumably entering initially on passes given their fathers and employers in return for exhibit-
ing bills for the hall. Dressed in flamboyant gentish style, the in-crowd
eschewed the common folk at their tables and clustered at the side bars
exchanging knowing nods with the chairman, shaking hands with the
guv'nor himself, and enjoying the privilege of buying them drinks.[29] Standing treats in such company conferred manhood, established status, and filled
the music hall tills. In this and other ways the generosity of the proprietor to
his friends redounded to his considerable advantage.

Music hall then was what we may usefully term a socially intensive industry; whatever its degree of needs for capital or labour, a necessary condition
of its establishment and effective conduct was an exceptionally and continu-
ously high input of social energy and skill in the direct mediation of its personal and structural relationships. Carrying out business on the halls was a
complex and demanding social exercise, a matter of self-advertisement and
personal contact, the exchange of favours and gestures of good feeling, the
nursing of networks and the wooing of public confidence. In this milieu,
drink and kind words were as potent a currency as cash and contract. Life in
this often bogus yet compelling social world was, more so than in the routine
metaphor, a dramatic performance, whose roles were rehearsed daily in the
bars, the street and the press as much as on the stage, but they found concentrated and ritual expression in the institution of the benefit night.

III

The benefit night was a traditional practice inherited from the theatre at
which the proceeds would be given to a particular member, associate or servant of the company. The amenities of the theatre and the services of the
others — lessee, players and staff — were in theory provided free, while
prices were raised. The benefit or bespeak functioned variously as a speculative device, a reward for distinction, a supplement or substitute for salary, or
aid in relief of distress when it was frequently extended to those outside the
profession. Whether a star or one of 'the small people', the beneficiary was
given the run of the stage. But while by the mid-century the benefit was falling into disfavour in the theatre for allegedly alienating the public and
depressing salaries, it flourished mightily in the London music halls.[30]

Though the benefit system on the halls duplicated many of its features in
the theatre, it was here more obviously the instrument of the proprietor.
Proprietorial benefits were the great events in the calendar, held annually as
a matter of course and on other notable occasions — farewells, inaugura-
tions, seasonal reopenings. The free list was suspended and prices were
raised, frequently threefold and sometimes more; boxes and best seats might
be put up for auction. Most of these 'bens' were sell-outs and some were

extended to two nights to accommodate the crowds. Halls were specially decorated and bills greatly extended. At the Middlesex, in October 1883, Graydon presented 56 artists in 36 turns over five-and-a-half hours.[31] The programme was supervised by a fellow proprietor or one of the big agents, and other visiting managers — the *Era* counted 16 in attendance for another of Graydon's benefits — would in turn preside as chairman, leaving the beneficiary free to receive various gifts and testimonials, to make his address and generally to disport himself among his public. At the conclusion of the entertainment (which might run till 3 a.m. by special license), the artists and special guests would be given supper and more toasts and speeches.

The functions and significance of the proprietorial benefit were various. The most obvious economic function was to raise extra money and this was clearly acknowledged where benefits were held to give direct relief to proprietors in need, as in consequences of some particular calamity or a more general reversal of fortune. Thus Villiers took a benefit after a fire at the South London; Weston and Holland announced benefits to remedy their heroic indebtedness. More covertly, the benefit could be used to rescue the marginal operation. Creditors might be prevailed upon to take the high-priced tickets in part-payment, and the prices of liquor and refreshments could be raised, though there was less precedent for this and more popular resistance. More generally, the benefit was regarded as necessary and justified to make good the season's out-of-pocket expenditures. 'Benefits here, benefits there, benefits everwhere', declared the *Entr'acte*, 'and of great benefit they are to those hard drinking managers and artists who rely upon the one special entertainment to recoup themselves the many incidental expenses attending the proper following of their employment.'[32] Whether for charitable need, overhead expenses or simple profit, the occasional report of the 'take' at proprietorial benefits suggests that London's caterers did well: Fort cleared £400 over two nights in 1874 (at a previous benefit he also received a diamond ring and breastpin worth 175 guineas); Mrs Poole at the South London took £561.12*s*.9*d*. in 1887.[33]

Yet benefits were not represented as simply money-making. Any gain was implicitly justified as a proper return on previous favours and good service. This function as an annual night of reckoning was made plain by John Wilton of Wilton's in 1862, when he explained: 'There are a great number of tradesmen and others who derive great benefit from my establishment, and others upon whom I confer favours. It is to enable these persons to acknowledge those favours that I take a Benefit.'[34] There are suggestions that this return of favours might be pursued somewhat aggressively, but though patrons were no doubt variously obliged and solicited to take tickets, the protocols of friendship put some limit on the proprietor's presumption. Tribute volunteered clearly signified more than tribute exacted, and the response from artists as well as customers was a public test of popular favour, as Holland recognised in his pride at the turn-out for a benefit of his in 1872 at the North Woolwich:

He had not issued a single ticket but depended entirely on the public; he had not asked a single artiste to come and assist him, but many had volunteered their services, and it was a pleasure to know he was as well thought of by the profession as by the public . . . he had tested the esteem with which they regarded him and the value they placed on his services as their caterer.[35]

Though its production might involve much haggling, importuning and moral blackmail, the benefit night was a great celebration of fraternal good feeling at which all were enfolded in the language and sentiments of friendship. Charles Merion, manager at the Met, said on his benefit: 'It seemed like a great meeting of friends, for wherever he turned he saw faces that he knew and people with whom he would like to shake hands.' It was also typical of such occasions that managers spoke not only of renewing friendships but of reconciling differences among their kind. Frederick Strange, for example, as a guest of Holland and Sweazey at the Royal in 1866, declared himself delighted 'to preside over so many friends . . . and to have the opportunity of setting an example to others of doing away with some of the great many jealousies that exist among our music hall proprietors.' 'Although', continued Strange, 'every man of business does the best he can for himself, it always can be done without undermining his neighbours.' Sanders at the opening of the Islington Philharmonic in 1860 professed himself 'glad to see his friend Weston and other friends who had come to give support; and if they were rivals, he knew they all felt they were rivals in a good cause (Cheers).'[36]

There was none the less a continuing note of competition at proprietorial benefits, though far from confounding the good intentions we may allow that it added to the piquancy of such encounters. Proprietors would rehearse their common interests at such occasions and declare the liberal and progressive ideals of their calling; the host and beneficiary would be lauded as an exemplar of such values, and in turn would complement his peers for their generosity in releasing their artists to appear on his bill. But within the *bonhomie* the host strove none the less to outfeast the others and score heavily in the relentless trade war between establishments. Thus the length and quality of the programme, the number and names of those in attendance and the level of prices all reflected upon the reputation of the proprietor and his effective command of the services and respect of others. As in the exchange systems observed in traditional societies, the proprietorial benefit registered the separateness, even the hostility of its chief participants even as it served to integrate them. It was like an inverted potlatch or kula, a competitive as well as fraternal display, but overall it served to renew and reinforce power at the top.[37]

Next in line as frequent beneficiaries were the performers. For them, too, the benefit was an occasion for raising extra money, the friendly exploitation of mutuality, and recognition and advancement of standing in the profession and at large. Perhaps most of all an artist's benefit night was a prime vehicle for self-advertisement. Bills and posters proclaimed the name of the favoured one. Beneficiaries met their public at the door, arrayed in their best finery, 'giving away smiles and portraits'. Here was a showcase for their talent in front of an unusual concentration of their peers (who also took turns in the presidential chair), proprietors and agents. After successful bens the pros would be seen in handsome new togs, treating themselves and others to 'big feeds' and drinks at the Oxford matinee or betting heavily at the Victoria Club. For the stars, who regularly held benefits at the end of an engagement or before provincial tours, financial returns were often handsome. At the Cambridge one night, Walter Laburnum was said to have taken £70 at the door, 'while the private sale of tickets was something fabulous'. At a sell-out at another East End hall, Jenny Hill was reported 'like the king of the nursery story, counting out her money'.[38] But in return the system made heavy demands on performers of any prominence. Writing to the *Entr'acte*, a successful pro declared the 'bespeak' system a nuisance, for he claimed to be pestered to contribute his services on average twice a week.[39] Mutuality had its price, most obviously for the performers, whose services were of course central to the operation.

The anxieties and abuses of the benefit system were more problematical for the lesser performer. A financial profit was far from assured. The stars could command a 'full clear' or genuinely 'complimentary' benefit with the proprietor waiving all house costs (such gestures were compensated by his monopoly on drink profits) but the minor artist was lucky to secure the remission of even a fraction of these, and might have to foot all running expenses. Some managers demanded their prepayment and there were in any case the additional costs of advertising. The first call on friends therefore might be for cash to float the benefit 'granted' by the proprietor, after which they would, if performers, be solicited for their services on the programme. The appearance of a big name was crucial for success but attracting the services of artists outside the circle of one's intimates was tricky. It was customary to approach an artist and ask his or her terms for an appearance, hoping that any fee would be waived. Paying for services, however big the name, might wreck the budget; but with no fees involved, the guest might not turn up, to the great embarrassment of the beneficiary who would have given the star top billing and ran the risk of charges of misrepresentation. And in the final accounting, the beneficiary had to beware of the unscrupulous proprietor who would falsify the figures or pad the costs. For the small fry then, the benefit might 'increase their vanity, without assisting their pocket'.[40] Overall, too, it was the rank and file who could least afford to forgo a night's salary in providing their services free in what were becoming in many cases involuntary levies rather than a mutual exchange of services.

Although criticisms of the music hall benefit system grew among artists, they continued to give it their support. *In extremis*, the benefit was still the most reliable source of relief and one which avoided the stigma of direct charity. For the greenhorn the benefit afforded a chance for exposure to the big time as a fill-in during the 'waits' (the turns system complicated the scheduling, and benefit programmes often defied efficient stage management). But, as one pro remonstrated with his fellows, such eagerness was soon converted into toadyism and ignobility:

> You would like to be associated, even in ever so small a way, with influential people, and will nearly cringe to them to be allowed to take an unpaid part in a performance under good patronage, though you would shrink from allowing your name to be used on behalf of a distressed brother to whom you might be of real service.

According to another critic, even 'the Great Guns' solicited for appearance and would rather be out of pocket than absent from the benefit programmes of the 'men of power'.[41]

If the real benefits of this exercise in collective self-help seemed to be made to flow more readily upwards, the system did have some redistributive effect, not only across but downwards to the 'small people' of the halls. Not so small people such as the chairman might have an annual benefit in their terms of engagement, but the privilege was rapidly extended in the 1860s to cover a wide range of minor functionaries and service staff — under-managers, cashiers, money- and check-takers, carpenters, machinists and waiters. In a marginal business such benefits may have been important in meeting running costs, easing the problem of cash flow in a money-poor operation by functioning as a supplement to or in lieu of wages. But the more likely function was that of building the proprietor's local reputation through his benevolent manipulation of the gift relationship. Again benevolences had to be paid for, and staff might find their annual bonanza and the brief glory of a summons on stage small compensation for their involuntary 'assistance' at other bens throughout the year. Musicians seem to have suffered most (which may have accounted for their reputation as particularly importunate demanders of tips or 'prossers') for their only return seems to have been a putative share in the conductor's benefit.

Music halls were also common venues for benefits held by or in aid of local societies. We get a glimpse of this underrecorded function from John Wilton, who was proud 'that during the last twelve months no less than eighty nights have been set apart for some philanthropic purpose or another — either for benefitting the funds of a friendly society or improving the conditions of some distressed private individual'.[42] Wilton meant this as a tribute to his working-class clientele, but proprietors also derived credit for throwing their halls open to such use, as well as from other forms of relief. Holland, who brewed up soup for the unemployed in 1886, was applauded for holding a benefit for the Newcastle workers who struck for the nine-hour day in 1871, and Crowder was commended by the unions for 'allowing the workingmen free use of his hall for the ventilation of their trade and labour grievances'.[43] The profession as a whole, together with its public, were ever ready with benefits and subscriptions for the victims of local and national calamities — the painter who broke his leg, the victims of colliery disasters and shipwrecks, the unemployed Lancashire workers in the cotton famine.

In all of these variations on the benefit, the proprietor played his part, made his contribution, and took his credit. To a degree he was servant as well as master of the system, and it may be argued that the nexus of custom and mutuality exemplified in the good fellowship of the benefit night was part of a traditional ideology and practice on the halls that muted and diffused the rationalising thrust of modern capitalism. (It is significant that Morton, with his austere personal style and early use of written contracts, rarely held a personal bespeak and thus would seem to have avoided its clinging mesh of obligations.) But in the overall arithmetic of its reciprocities we may rightly suspect that by fair means or foul it was the big man who derived the greatest returns from the benefit.

By the 1880s the benefit system was badly overloaded and more actively resisted. Its occasions became fewer, and its forms changed. It was less the conflict of interests that brought about its decline than the increasing scale and bureaucratisation of music hall that made the rituals of friendship and mutuality a cosmetic rather than an essential way of doing business.

The top men of the new syndicated halls were directors rather than proprietors, and more often accountants than publicans. They raised capital on the stock market, not from their cronies, and were more concerned to advertise their probity to a board and shareholders than impress their good fellowship on the local butcher in the stalls bar. They had less direct contact with artists, who were hired by agents and booking managers, and who were themselves now more concerned to formalise contracts and business dealings. The profession also increasingly withheld its services from the benefit, setting up its own autonomous welfare institutions which relieved some of its dependence both on management and public.[44]

The surviving forms of the benefit bore the mark of this more rational and distanced mode of business. Personal benefits were mostly restricted to long-serving unit managers in the combines whose local standing reproduced something of the substance of the early owner-proprietors.[45] Benefit performances for other staff were long gone, and though the annual paternalist beanfeast remained, the new big men were rarely there to play their role. At a staff outing from the South London in 1902, an official apologised for the directors' absence: 'Mr. Payne is on holiday, Mr. Tozer has gout, Mr. Newson-Smith has a very arkward day . . .'.[46] Charitable benefits found a new form in the special matinée. Held more for national than local causes, they attracted more distinguished patronage, which flattered the industry's leaders into attendance (though it renewed performers' accusations of exploitation).[47] The combines reduced their favours to the local community in other ways. After Crowder's Paragon incorporated with the Canterbury, working-class societies reported that charges for holding their annual benefit had doubled, a percentage was charged on the take, and various restrictions were now imposed by 'the none too courteous management'.[48] By this time, in the mid-1890s, free orders had also been cut back in most London halls (though one of the dispossessed pulled a revolver at the affront!).

From the turn of the century, the industry looked back indulgently on the old style personal proprietor. The syndicate director Henry Tozer recalled:

'They all in their youth loved and admired him, his glossy hat, his substantial jewellery, his glowing affability, and his habitual spoof.' But now, in the words of another of the new men, 'the old blatant music hall manager . . . has given place to the sharp but courteous business man'. Even so, the type they romanticised, with his affability and spoof, had been no less of a businessman.[49]

IV

Friendship — 'a voluntary, close and enduring relationship' — is a ubiquitous and self-evident phenomenon, yet its history and sociology are still waiting to be written.[50] In terms of its own particular history, music hall friendship would seem to be a descendant of two observable eighteenth-century forms. The first is that institutionalised in the popular and numerous Friendly Societies.[51] Friendship here was collective in sentiment and purpose. Within a rule-bound body, members (mostly artisanal and petty bourgeois) gathered to promote conviviality (ritualised and ceremonial), while pooling their resources to protect the welfare and security of the individuals within the group. The second form was more middle- or upper-class.[52] Similar in its combination of the affective and instrumental, it was less institutionalised, sociable in a different style, and based on personal contact within looser and more extensive networks of family, kin and other dependents and associates. 'Friend' meant specifically one with whom to exchange favours, in the form of goods, services and, in an age of patronage, place. The use of the word in this context is particularly interesting, for its implicit equality elides the social discriminations of rank through which patronage was mediated.

Music hall friendship was both a derivation and a reworking of the two strands with their complementary yet also divergent ideologies. Music hall's direct descent from the pub as provident club and the popular theatre as 're-public of players' made for a tighter, less differentiated sense of mutuality in the tradition of the friendly societies. But at the same time, the rivalrous vanities of the performers and the palpable ambition of the caterers in a singularly competitive and insecure business made for a more self-conscious individualism within the common nexus of regard that seems to derive from the other, more bourgeois strand. Thus part separated, part integrated, a process of as it were individual mutuality was always in negotiation amid the larger collective mutuality that constituted music hall friendship.

Characteristically fulsome in sentiment, music hall friendship was none the less explicit in its demands, as the transactions of the benefit night make plain. Then, as Holland declared, you found out who your friends really were; then you called them to account for the debts and credits in the ledger — the metaphor came to life in the name of one East End pub music hall, The Bank of Friendship. The system, though less rule-bound than a Friendly Society, was none the less highly normative. But for all its candour on some occasions, the language of friendship was often more slippery. As in the exchanges of patronage in a previous era it was a useful fiction in the exercise of discriminatory power, for its sentiments flattered inferiors, and appeased or bemused the exploited. Thus its equalising rhetoric obscured the asymmetrical distribution of advantage in the gift relationship of the benefit system. Moreover, in a time of transition between relationships of place and service on the one hand, and contract and employment on the other, 'friend' was likely to be an even more useful term to cover confusion and ignorance, or simply to evade.

The rhetoric of music hall friendship was all-inclusive, promising universal membership. In this we can recognise a genial cognate of other omnibus and ideal categories of Victorian Britain as a liberal democracy — associationism, social citizenship, respectability — combining the properties of voluntarism, equality, dignity and earned inclusion.[53] Of particular importance to the halls in this respect was that friendship included women. Again the usage may well have been hegemonic and a cloak or lever in economic and emotional exploitation, but it may also have served to defuse or elide tensions of gender and sexuality. Though there are notable ambiguities in this context, early nineteenth-century literature suggests that friendship could denote a sexually disinterested protective function.[54]

But there can be no inclusion without exclusion, no friends without enemies, or at least non-friends — the 'chums and rotters' of one account — and music hall friendship was both all-embracing and select. One appropriate analogy here might be freemasonry (much practised in the profession) with its ideals of universal brotherhood and its practice of exclusion. The halls, however, were not a closed institution on this model but a more fluid, sub-cultural world which for all the density of its local ties was also, particularly in London, a mobile and ever recomposing community. Music hall was both parochial and cosmopolitan in a way which generated chronic tensions in relationships. The tightness of the neighbourhood connexion intensified rather than ventilated differences of interest, while the growth of industry, the ready flow of recruits, entrepreneurial and artistic, and the particular pattern of production in the turns system brought constant shifts and intensification in rivalry and competition. The device and rhetoric of friendship were thus probably the more extensively invoked in direct proportion to the growth in the dynamic and fissionable properties of the music hall world. Colin MacInnes, in his study of the songs of the halls, noted that 'there are more invocations of friendship after a row has happened, than among friends who've never much quarrelled at all'.[55]

Again in a wider context, that of a modern urbanising and arguably more impersonal society, friendship was a complex metaphor of recognition and identity, a free order or 'face pass' as it were to membership of a community, or in Victor Turner's less structured sense, '*communitas*'.[56] Sociological definitions leave out the property of trust which is part of the ideal of friendship, and which promised stability and certitude in music hall's slippery and capricious microcosm of a larger world. The deceits and emptiness of many relationships in contrast to the ideal could be desolating. 'Friends, what friends? I have none', was the despairing cry of the great star George

Leybourne, and the authentic voice of alienation in a business that was as abrasive as it was emollient.[57] That friendship was often an illusion, a fragile membrane of good intentions, made its desirability all the more intense.

Friendship in the halls was in any case being redefined in this period as the industry was rationalised and the extension of the sub-culture diluted intimacy. It became more a private than a public interchange, a matter of withdrawal rather than display. Indeed, a distinction not only of degree but of kind creeps into music hall discourse from the 1870s. The *Era* saw the audience at one of Syer's benefits as comprising the 'general public and particular friends' and the sense of a divergent if complementary set of categories became more common.[58] At a benefit for Villiers, the paper distinguished between 'an inner circle and the public in general'. 'Privately his social qualifications may render him an object deserving homage from his friends; publicly his management may have been conducted with energy, with talent and with success; and the two sections of the public actuated by different desires, unite to do honour to the occasion.'[59] This is more than a differentiation between a proprietor's cronies and the rest; it represents the lapsing of friendship as an instrument of everyday business and music hall community. Friendship was replaced by civility.

Yet it would be too simplistic to see in this line of development the almost inevitable triumph of the rational and contractual in social relationships, the victory of *Gesellschaft* over *Gemeinschaft*. Friendship remained a common theme in the music hall canon and popular literature, and the language of pals and chums ('Thank God, for a trusty one', wrote Kipling), was translated from sentiment into action in the pals' battalions of 1914. *Gemeinschaft* and *Gesellschaft* are in any case not necessarily specific historical and mutually exclusive conditions, but co-existing states of experience.[60] People fashion affective relationships within the most depersonalised social systems; conversely, the appeal of amiable inclusion is likely to be a necessary interpellation or hook in any scheme that seeks to make a business out of pleasure. This was certainly true for Billy Holland and the other big men of London music hall who made friendship a powerful engine of a new form of capitalism — capitalism with a beaming human face.

Notes

(Place of publication is London unless stated otherwise.)

1. *Era*, 5 December 1869. On Holland himself, see *Era*, 13 December 1890; 4 January 1896; *Blackpool Gazette*, 3 December 1895.
2. Morton dominates the record with the 'official' biography by his brother William and H. C. Newton, *Sixty Years Stage Service*, 1905. H. Scott, *The Early Doors*, Wakefield, 1977, pp. 220–5, offers correctives on the Morton myth, and useful notes on other leading London managers. L. Senelick, D. F. Cheshire and U. Schneider, *British Music Hall, 1840–1923: A Bibliography and Guide to Sources*, Hamden, CT, 1981 provides some bibliographical references, but there are no

entries for managers in R. Busby, *British Music Hall: An Illustrated Who's Who*, 1976. The best source remains the trade press, from which most of the material for this piece was drawn, though it cannot all be referenced here. For a useful account of a provincial caterer, see K. Barker, 'Thomas Youdan of Sheffield', *Theatrephile*, Spring 1985, pp. 9–12.

3. *Era*, 25 February 1866.
4. *Entr'acte*, 13 June 1874.
5. Besant and J. Rice, *Ready Money Mortiboy*, 1872, vol. 2, pp. 159–66, 260–76. I owe this reference to Anna Davin.
6. *Musician and Music Hall Times*, 19 July 1862.
7. *Era*, 5 July 1866; 31 March 1872.
8. *Music Hall & Theatre Review*, 28 February 1908. For the concept of 'the big man' in anthropology and its application here, see P. Bailey, 'Custom, Capital and Culture in the Victorian Music Hall', in R. Storch (ed.), *Popular Culture and Custom in Nineteenth Century England*, 1982, p. 192.
9. *Era*, 13 December 1890.
10. See H. Powdermaker, *The Dream Factory: An Anthropologist Looks at Movie Making*, Boston, 1950, pp. 92–7.
11. There is no satisfactory history of London music hall for the period. C. D. Stuart and A. J. Park, *The Variety Stage: A History of the Music Halls*, 1895, Chapters 4–6, records the heightened activity of the 1860s but probably underestimate the industry's continuing vigour in the 1870s. D. Howard, *London Theatres and Music Halls, 1850–1950*, 1970, is an invaluable source and reference book. My figures leave out the smaller pub concert rooms.
12. *Entr'acte*, 12 July 1879; 24 January 1880; *Era*, 14 September 1879.
13. Select Committee on Theatrical Licences, *Parliamentary Papers*, House of Commons, HC 1866 (373) XVI, app. 3, p. 313.
14. *Entr'acte*, 9 October 1880. Morton mortgaged his premises to Combe & Delafield for £600 in 1854; see J. Earl and J. Stanton, *The Canterbury Hall and Theatre of Varieties*, Cambridge, 1982, p. 15. By this time, breweries owned or helped in the mortgage of more than half of London's pubs as well as being an important source of investment capital in other businesses, including the theatre. Hard data for involvement in the halls is scarce.
15. Holland started in partnership with his publican uncle, Morton joined with his solicitor brother-in-law. A number of early directors were surgeons or officers, no doubt prolonging their student or cadet enthusiasms.
16. B. H. Harrison, *Drink and the Victorians*, 1971, p. 250. For Payne, see L. Rutherford, Chapter 5, this volume.
17. 'One of the Old Brigade', *London in the Sixties*, 1908, p. 78.
18. *Entr'acte*, 9 October 1880; 'The Music Hall Business', *St James Gazette*, 10 February 1885.
19. *Era*, 20 June, 1 August 1869; 3 February 1870.
20. Ibid., 7 March 1875; 12 September 1869.
21. *Music Hall and Theatre Review*, 28 February 1908. See also Rutherford, Chapter 5.
22. *Era*, 5 December 1869.
23. *Entr'acte*, 24 September 1870.
24. *Era*, 24 and 31 March, 7 April 1867; W. H. Boardman, *Vaudeville Days*, London, 1935, pp. 117–18.
25. *Era*, 23 August 1874.
26. 'The Cost of Amusing the Public', *London Society*, vol. 1, 1862, pp. 193–8.

27. Proprietors experimented with mechanical turnstiles in the 1870s, to eradicate the peculations of the money and check takers.

28. *Entr'acte*, 18 December 1880.

29. *Figaro*, 22 April 1874, provides a good account of the in-crowd, though it provoked an action for libel.

30. For background, see T. St V. Troubridge, *The Benefit System in the British Theatre*, 1967. See also E. Dutton Cook, *A Book of the Play*, 1876, vol. 2, pp. 123–46; C. W. Scott, 'Charity on Crutches', *Era Almanack*, 1877.

31. *Era*, 20 October 1883, 7 November 1885.

32. *Entr'acte*, 9 April 1870.

33. Mrs Poole was one of the few women music hall proprietors, having taken over on her husband's death. Wives often played a major role in a business which routinely exploited family, though some proprietors withdrew their womenfolk in classic bourgeois manner and the widow's succession was less common in music hall than in the licensed trade.

34. *Era*, 16 February 1862.

35. Ibid., 25 August 1872.

36. Ibid., 10 June 1877; 25 November 1866; 11 November 1860.

37. See, for example, A. Rosman and P. C. Rubel, *Feasting With Mine Enemy: Rank and Exchange among North West Coast Societies*, New York, 1971; R. Firth, *Symbols Public and Private*, 1973, pp. 368–402.

38. *Entr'acte*, 8 May 1875, thought £30 a good return for the established artist.

39. Ibid., 6 December 1873.

40. *Era*, 24 April 1875.

41. *Entr'acte*, 16 December 1873; 8 May 1875.

42. *Era*, 16 February 1862.

43. For a general commendation of music hall's service to the working-class community, see Select Committee on Theatres, *Parliamentary Papers*, HC, 1892, XVIII, q. 5177.

44. For the crucial changes in the 1880s, see Bailey, 'Custom, Capital and Culture', pp. 191–3.

45. See J. Crump, Chapter 3, this volume.

46. *Era*, 2 August 1902.

47. For renewed complaints in the profession, see *Performer Annual*, 1908; *Stage Year Book*, 1909, pp. 71–2.

48. *Eastern Argus*, 20 October 1894, 19 October 1895.

49. *Era*, 26 April 1902; 21 February 1903. For the parallel persistence of traditional styles of authority in industry see H. Newby, 'Paternalism and Capitalism' in R. Scase (ed.), *Industrial Society: Class, Clearage and Control*, 1977, pp. 59–73; P. Joyce, *Work, Society and Politics: The Culture of the Factory in Later Victorian England*, 1980, Chapter 5.

50. The quote is from O. Ramsoy, 'Friendship', *International Encyclopaedia of Social Science*, New York, 1968. See also G. A. Allan, *A Sociology of Friendship and Kinship*, 1979, and the suggestive essay by G. Simmel, 'The Sociology of Sociability' (what he calls 'the art or play form of association'), *American Journal of Sociology*, November 1949, pp. 254–61. T. Zeldin, *France, 1848–1945: Intellect, Taste and Anxiety*, Cambridge, 1977, pp. 651–6, speaks of the need for a history of sociability; see also R. Holt, *Sport and Society in Modern France*, 1981, pp. 150–68. There are, of course, distinctions to be made between friendship and sociability.

51. E. P. Thompson, *The Making of the English Working Class*, New York, 1963,

pp. 418–29; T. R. Tholfsen, *Working-Class Radicalism in Mid-Victorian England*, 1976, pp. 288–305.

52. H. Perkin, *Origins of Modern English Society*, 1969, pp. 45–9. I am grateful to Leonore Davidoff for letting me read an unpublished paper on her work with Catherine Hall on middle-class networks in Birmingham of the period.

53. See Tholfsen, *Working-Class Radicalism*; H. Meller, *Leisure and the Changing City*, 1976; S. Yeo, *Religion and Voluntary Organisations in Crisis*, 1976.

54. I owe this point to J. S. Bratton.

55. C. MacInnes, *Sweet Saturday Night*, 1969, p. 150.

56. V. Turner, *The Ritual Process: Structure and Anti-Structure*, 1969, Chapter 3.

57. The story is told in H. G. Hibbert, *Fifty Years of a Londoner's Life*, 1916, p. 230. For the commercially promoted sociability of Leybourne's career see P. Bailey, 'Champagne Charlie: Performance and Ideology in the Music Hall Swell Song' in the companion volume by J. S. Bratton, *Music Hall: Performance and Style*.

58. *Era*, 14 July 1872.

59. Ibid., 15 July 1882.

60. R. Dennis, *English Industrial Cities of the Nineteenth Century: A Social Geography*, Cambridge, 1984, p. 9.

3 Provincial Music Hall: Promoters and Public in Leicester, 1863–1929

JEREMY CRUMP

The study of the development of music hall and related institutions in a single provincial town offers valuable comparison with the largely metropolitan work which has hitherto dominated the field. Where provincial studies have been undertaken, they have tended to focus on areas where strong traditions of popular song and literature have made music hall to a greater extent resistant to the domination of London. Both the concert halls of the North-East and Lancashire music hall fit this pattern. Leicester had no such strong local identity, and while music hall flourished in Nottingham and Birmingham, its success there needs to be located in the context of early integration into a national circuit based in London rather than a regional tradition. A local study such as the present one shows the intensity of the relationship between proprietors and their clientele, but it does not follow inevitably that this depended upon distinctive forms of local song and humour. There were local favourites among touring stars, but there is no evidence of a Leicester school of performers or songwriters comparable to that of Tyneside.

An attempt at a comprehensive survey of provincial music hall must await further local studies, but those produced hitherto suggest a broad chronological framework. The Star Music Hall, Bolton, opened in 1832, a date which suggested to Robert Poole that it was 'arguably Britain's first music hall'. Generally, though, provincial music hall emerged from a range of public house entertainment from the 1840s. Kathleen Barker dates early singing saloons to 1842 in Newcastle and Nottingham, 1843 in Sheffield and 1844 in Bristol. Purpose-built halls, or major conversions of existing facilities, such as lecture halls, took place in two waves in the early 1850s and in the 1860s. Newcastle and Nottingham acquired prestigious, well-financed halls at this time, at the same time as Leicester's first music halls opened. What is striking in Leicester is the apparent weakness of the proto-music hall phase, which the present essay seeks to explain in terms of the blighted state of the town's main industry well into the 1850s. Barker describes the 1850s and 1860s as a period of 'one or two continued successes and many failures'. This aptly describes music hall in Leicester throughout the nineteenth century, and it is argued here that music hall was financially unstable beyond the first injection of capital from outside the town in the 1890s and up to the arrival of Stoll's national chain.[1]

The local context

Two elements in the wider society acted as constraints on the development of commercial forms of entertainment in Leicester during the mid-nineteenth century. Liberal newspapers, the *Leicester Chronicle* and *Leicester Mercury*, rejoiced in the town's reputation as a metropolis of nonconformity. The town's middle class, its politics and its council were dominated by nonconformists much as in the Birmingham of Dixon and Chamberlain. Merchant hosiers rather than manufacturers, the town's élite had tenuous links with the bulk of the working population. Collective institutions were set up to try to improve public behaviour, notably the Leicester Domestic Mission (1846), the Town Museum (1849), the Free Library (1869) and the Abbey Park (1882). There was also a severe licensing regime, and Leicester was the base of a strong temperance lobby.[2]

The work experience of much of the population was determined by the late growth of factory production in its two major industries. Hosiery, the staple until the 1860s, was largely based on outwork production, and suffered chronic depression from the 1830s until the 1860s. The industry and its fortunes were the basis of a radical working-class movement which made Leicester a prominent centre of Chartism.[3] Boot and shoe production, which came to rival hosiery as a source of male employment, was similarly reliant on domestic and workshop production until the 1890s. The susceptibility of British markets to American competition in the 1890s and 1900s meant that unemployment was again high in Leicester at that time, although there was no general economic collapse as had occurred under the conditions of monoculture in the 1840s. Only with the revival of the British boot trade after 1905 did all sectors of the local economy share in prosperity which was to last for over half a century.

Workshop production and economic insecurity made for independence from employer-imposed discipline on the part of Leicester workers which perturbed the middle class and enabled the late survival of traditions of irregular work.[4] This may in part account for the relatively late development of modern spectator sport in the town and the financial insecurity of Leicester theatre and music hall.

It is necessary to place the development of music hall in the context not only of broad economic trends, but also of other musical traditions in the town. Prior to the worst of the depression of the 1840s, Leicester supported a thriving musical life, extending beyond the gentry who patronised subscription concerts. A choral society was founded in 1826, a. Mechanics' Institute established a choir in 1837. William Gardiner, a leading figure in local concert life and an advocate of the music of Beethoven from the 1790s, taught instrumental and vocal music to people of all classes. Both formal ventures collapsed in 1840–1.[5]

Alongside popular enthusiasm for 'high' musical culture were public house entertainments of a less rational kind. In 1869, a blind fiddler unsuccessfully brought an action against a man who, during a dance at the Green Man, was pushed over by a woman and fell on the fiddle.[6] This report supports a recollection by the temperance advocate, William Stanyon, who in 1900 remembered how in the 1830s his family had lived next door but one to a public house where at holiday time the working men and 'well known bad girls' began early in the day dancing to the fiddle, 'and as they were poisoned and befuddled with drink they dropped away by twos and more, openly into a yard devoted exclusively for brothels'.[7]

The early music hall of the 1860s drew on both the self-improving interest in concert music and on the hedonism of public house entertainments. During the 1850s, the former received renewed institutional expression. In 1853, the band-leader Henry Nicholson announced the first of a series of promenade concerts on the Wharf Street Cricket Ground.[8] Four years later, a former member of Nicholson's band, one Herr Ptacek, undertook open-air concerts on behalf of the middle-class Public Music Committee. The press reported that 'the bands are attended by increasing numbers, and evidently afford rational enjoyment to people of all classes'.[9]

At this time, Samuel Cleaver, later a councillor, Poor Law Guardian, President of the Licensed Victuallers Defence League and local representative for Bass, became landlord of the Rainbow and Dove. The pub achieved a reputation as 'the most celebrated of all rooms for classical music established in the town'. Members of all classes were said to have attended.[10] In the late 1850s, too, such factory-based paternalism as there was in Leicester contributed to the development of brass bands. George Stevenson, a Liberal councillor, told the Literary and Philosophical Society in 1862 that 'factory hands . . . have supplanted many low habits and created a means of recreation and a taste for classical music'.[11] Band contests were first held on the cricket ground in 1857.

In 1853, the opening of the Temperance Hall, among whose shareholders were prominent teetotallers such as Thomas Cook and Radical politicians including William and John Biggs, provided Leicester with its first major concert hall. During the 1850s and 1860s, it was used for drawing room and operatic entertainments, concerts and recitals by touring artistes such as Jenny Lind and Charles Dickens, and sixpenny 'hops' on Monday nights. The Temperance Hall became a respectable alternative to the music halls, presenting negro entertainments and operatic selections in a drink-free environment. That this involved considerable hypocrisy on the part of members of the middle class who, often on religious grounds, deplored the town's legitimate theatre almost as much as public house entertainments, did not go unnoticed. The *Leicester Chronicle* noted on the occasion of a concert performance of two operattas by Eliot Galer's company in 1863 that 'the entertainment will be popular with that large and influential class who strive to satisfy their desire for theatrical entertainments without incurring the contamination of a theatre'.[12]

Nor were the entertainments there restricted to such obviously respectable forms as operetta. William Paul, the music hall proprietor, tried to put on Mackney and Edward Marshall in 1865 during the town's annual Race Week, only to be frustrated as the hall was already booked. Vance performed there in 1873, while Thomas Cook himself had promoted a musical entertainment including resident artistes from local music halls in 1865. While the town's music halls suffered in the trade depression of 1866, respectable families filled the Temperance Hall to watch Lumbard's Christy Minstrels.[13]

Such entertainments, while they did not provide the bulk of the hall's income, which was derived chiefly from lettings for meetings, lectures and bazaars, show that there was sizeable middle-class and respectable working-class demand for variety entertainments. This included an interest in established music hall performers, and was further exploited by Stoll in the 1900s. It was also a tempting potential market for Paul from the 1860s, and it was in the hope of attracting such an audience that caterers protested the classlessness of their appeal and the respectability of their calling. The important distinction between Paul's Concert Hall and the Temperance Hall was the availability of drink and the physical proximity of the working class. Matcham's designs and Stoll's exclusion of drink from the auditorium were to overcome both barriers to a greater middle-class presence in the Palace Theatre of Varieties, built in 1901.

Local proprietors: music halls, free and easies and clubs, 1863–1890

When music halls finally opened in Leicester, significantly after the worst of the depression of the hosiery industry in the 1840s and 1850s, it was thus against a background of widely varying types of public entertainment. The immediate impulse came from yet another source. The circus clown, Dan Cook, returned to Leicester in September 1862 and reopened Stevens's wooden circus building at the Fleur de Lis, Belgrave Gate, as a concert hall. With an acting manager, company of 14 and performances by visiting favourites such as Mr and Mrs Howard Paul, this venture, known as the Alhambra Music Hall, represents the relatively late beginning of music hall proper in Leicester. The *Leicester Journal* noted that 'demand for this kind of entertainment is still a growing one, and seems to satisfy a certain class of person who, although not caring to visit a theatre, are desirous of witnessing an entertainment akin to it. Leicester has as yet been without an amusement of this character . . .'.[14]

By early November, low prices, with the gallery at twopence, were bringing in packed audiences, but there was an abrupt falling off and termination of the season at the end of the month, probably due to seasonal unemployment in the hosiery trade. Apart from a brief Christmas season, Cook did not carry on with music hall promotion.[15]

By this time, too, public houses were providing musical entertainment in increasingly elaborate settings, including the first purpose-built saloons. While this phase started late in Leicester in comparison with other provincial towns such as Birmingham, Bolton or Nottingham, the origins of the capital on which it was founded were by no means exceptional. The 1860s was, after all, a decade in which the number of provincial music halls doubled. What distinguishes Leicester from the general picture given by Peter Bailey and others, but which may be more typical of many lesser centres of the music hall, is the endemic precariousness of music hall finances, with caterers striving to present nationally-known artists in expensively refurbished halls before audiences whose economic well-being was itself uncertain. It was not only the audience which needed to seek consolation and security against the harsh realities of a market economy in a state of cyclical fluctuation.

Leicester had two major halls for much of the period from 1863 to 1901, both located in the densely populated district of working-class housing half a mile north of the town centre. In addition there was a fluctuating but relatively small number of lesser halls, free and easies and, later, musical clubs. Paul's music hall in Belgrave Gate continued to exist under a single family's management until 1889, when it was replaced by a variety theatre. Sweeney's, Wharf Street, on the other hand, experienced many vicissitudes, short-lived managements and periods of closure or use for other purposes. Examination of the development of these two institutions illustrates the ambition and scope of provincial caterers, as well as the limits which economic factors set to the nature of music hall entertainment.

Cooper's Music Hall, as Sweeney's was first known, was located on public house premises on a corner of Wharf Street. Plans for extension were soon under way. When Samuel Sweeney reopened it as the New Oxford Music Hall in 1864, it had new galleries and a refurbished stage. At the time of its sale by auction in 1885, the pub and hall had a wholesale wine and spirits department, smoke-room, concert hall with gallery and two bars, seating over 500. There were grounds behind the hall which could accommodate 3,000 for dancing, foot racing, circuses and promenade concerts.[16] Dancing was a major attraction at first but Sweeney discontinued it soon after taking over. In 1866, his licence was held over at the Brewster Sessions while the conduct of the hall was scrutinised. Sweeney told the magistrates that dancing on the green had been stopped two years previously. Dancing was deplored by moralists as encouraging the mixing of young people of both sexes. Joseph Dare, a Unitarian missionary, complained in 1862 that 'Necessary amusements are rendered demoralising by promiscuous gatherings of the young and neglected, by the vicious excitement of the tavern dance, by the morbid exhibitions of the circus, and the disgusting orgies of the viler "bal masqué"'.[17]

The ban on dancing did not put a stop to 'promiscuous gatherings' at

Sweeney's though. In 1865 the *Era* reported that the hall was 'crowded every Saturday and Monday, and often inconveniently so, for young people of both sexes do not always observe such strict order as a more moderate attendance commands'.[18] Sweeney made considerable efforts to reform the hall and establish it as an orderly house. He told magistrates in 1866 that at one point he had closed for seven weeks in order to rid himself of 'bad characters', that unaccompanied girls were not admitted, and that those under 17 had to be accompanied by an adult.[19] Sweeney's enterprise did not survive the general slump in working-class income in the depression of 1866, and the scenery and fittings were sold in November under a bill of sale and distress for rent. The building was bought the following year by a manufacturer, Charles Smith of Charles Street, Leicester for £1,400, presumably as a warehouse. by 1873, it was used by the Yeoman Lane Ragged School for classes for children and adults.[20] The building was restored to its original use by 1882, when Sam Torr, a Nottingham-born comedian who had been successful on the London stage and who had managed the freakshow career of the Elephant Man, moved to the hall from the nearby Green Man public house. Torr was evidently willing to invest considerably in the hall, which opened as the Gaiety in August 1883, bringing in a Nottingham painter and a furnisher from Basford to assist with fitting it out. The hall had a proscenium arch and a fixed stage, but also featured what the *Leicester Daily Post* described as 'a select area' for 50 friends of the chairman near the orchestra and the chairman's seat.[21] Building plans indicate that this was the greatest prominence given to the chairman's seat in any of the Leicester halls. Possibly it was a feature favoured by the much travelled Torr, but not indigenous to Leicester halls. The contrast with Paul's is striking, implying a wish to assert the status of the chairman of the new hall in such a way that he could rival Paul, who was a prominent figure in the local community.

Torr was personally well-liked in Leicester and his song 'Daddy-O' is one of the few perennial favourites in the town mentioned in the sources. He could rely on bringing in stars such as Vesta Tilley, who appeared on his second bill. The venture was not a success though, and lasted only three years. Torr's wish to raise the standard and tone of the hall was not compatible with its role as a decidedly down-market institution located in a lesser thoroughfare. According to a biographical article in *The Music Hall* in 1889, 'business was not so good as anticipated after a while, and it became evident that the town did not contain enough of the class he catered for to support Mr Torr'. This epitaph on Torr's career as a music hall promoter in Leicester reads much like the apologia of the town's many failed theatre directors. Their inability to identify and satisfy popular demand was similarly attributed to the audience's unpreparedness for their improvements. After Torr left, prices were reduced and a large working-class audience returned, at least for a short time.[22]

Opening at the Prince of Wales public house in Belgrave Gate in 1863, Paul's Theatre of Varieties remained in the family of William Paul until 1888. Paul (1821–82) achieved greater financial success than did Sweeney or his successors, although failure was narrowly avoided on a number of occasions. Reports in 1865, for example, that Paul could not pay his company were denied with suspicious vehemence, and the general slackness of trade of 1886 had its effect, too. Only in 1870 could the *Era* report that 'The wavering fortunes of the Midland seem to have taken a new lease of life'.[23]

Paul fitted the model of the caterer as local popular dignitary, as established by Morton and others in London. He gave benefit performances for the lunatic asylum, the aged poor and, in 1875, for striking elastic web weavers. Paul's claimed sufficient attention from the local press to suggest that the hall was well regarded in the town as a whole. By 1880, Paul had achieved enough respectability for Canon Burfield of St Mark's to attend the New Year treat for the aged poor in order to show his support for the caterer.[24]

Paul's theatre attracted a largely working-class audience. In 1863, the *Era* admitted that 'From its distance from the heart of the town, the Hall has scarcely gained that amount of patronage among the better classes which it will certainly have as it becomes widely known'. It does not seem that the hall ever did become a resort of the 'better classes', although there is no doubt that Paul's was always an orderly and highly respectable house. At the 1866 Brewster Sessions, it was asserted by one of the magistrates, Edward Shipley Ellis, also a director of the Midland Railway Company, Quaker and prominent supporter of the temperance cause, that 'the reputation of the house was very bad'. Paul was able to withstand this accusation, and Ellis was unable to give any specific examples of bad behaviour. At the hearing Paul outlined the rules of the hall, which showed that the management was anxious to impose strict order on the proceedings. None were admitted who showed signs of 'being in liquor' and no 'rude or boisterous behaviour' was tolerated. No unaccompanied girls were allowed in, nor indeed was anybody under the age of 20. The scale of charges was in line with Sweeney's, and cheaper than the Theatre Royal. Discipline extended to the stage as well; professionals were 'not allowed to sing anything on the stage tending to immorality'.[25]

Like the Gaiety, Paul's always had a chairman, for many years William Paul himself, but the lack of any special rostrum in the plans of the hall suggests that the role was performed from the stage itself. In an incident between Paul and the duettists William and Caroline Horbury, Paul made his presence felt from the centre of the hall.[26] Whatever his place in the hall, he intended to stamp his authority on the proceedings, so that his intervention became a part of the entertainment. On one occasion, he told the young Vesta Tilley, appearing in boy's clothes, to leave the stage and not return until properly dressed.[27] Like a father to favoured performers, his rule was at times patriarchal, and this informed his insistence on maintaining sobriety and decorum in the hall.

Further evidence of William Paul's domineering managerial style, and also of early links with the London music hall world, is to be found in the report of the court case in which he was prosecuted by the Horburys in 1868. They had been engaged by his agent in London, and they were evidently also acquainted with George Day, the Birmingham proprietor. While Paul's motivation is not easy to discover from the report — he was evidently offended by their warm reception, but claimed that they had compromised the respectability of the entertainment — he is shown taking a very direct role in controlling what went on.

The programmes at Paul's were initially very varied. Joseph Dare, who visited the hall in 1865, said that the performance consisted of three-sixths negro entertainments, two-sixths comic and one-sixth sentimental, suggesting an unusually high proportion of black-face acts.[28] But this was not all that Paul provided. The house soprano, Mme Bosanneck, gave selections of classical pieces. Spectacles such as Pepper's ghost and a mechanical display of the Siege of Sebastopol ran for extended peiods, and there was a tableau on the death of Nelson and a ballet, 'The Village in Uproar'. In 1868, Paul put on a can-can ballet, much to Dare's dismay.[29]

When William Paul was ill in the mid-1870s, his family found the running of the hall burdensome, and tried to sell up in 1875. The property was withdrawn from sale at £3,200, however, and William Paul returned to management later in the year.[30] The business continued to prosper until his death (by choking on a piece of tripe) in November 1882. By that time Paul, with the ostentation customary to his calling, had moved to the prosperous suburb of Belgrave with his son. The funeral was marked in a way which indicated his standing in the local community. Thousands watched the cortège, and many shops in Belgrave Gate closed.[31]

On the death of William Paul Jr in 1888, the hall was sold by auction to A. F. Lovejoy of the Peckham Music Hall for £6,100. At that time, the hall had seating for 800, a proscenium stage, four dressing rooms and two bars.[32] Considerable alterations were needed to meet safety regulations, but destruction by fire the following year saved Lovejoy the expense. In August 1890, a new building in renaissance style, known as the Prince of Wales's Theatre of Varieties, was opened.

The passing of Paul's marked the end of the phase in which local capital alone was sufficient to sustain a business in the highly competitive music hall industry. Lovejoy, mobilising London capital, was able to meet fire regulations and build a hall capable of exploiting more fully popular demand for variety.[33]

If Paul's and Sweeney's represent the more influential mainstream of music hall within the town, there persisted a tradition of less highly capitalised popular music-making and entertainment in the form of free and easies. At its upper end, this tradition sought the status of the established halls, but the enforcement of a bylaw for music licensing in 1884 rigidly divided the halls from lesser ventures. The result was to force much informal entertainment into bogus clubs, while at the same time creating the legal circumstances for the rise of entertainments as a central feature of working men's clubs. Monopolising tendencies in the late nineteenth-century entertainment industry were furthered as the very strict control of music licences enhanced the value of the few which the magistrates were willing to issue. Commercial pressure encouraged halls to be operated with a keener eye to profit maximisation than hitherto, and Leicester's halls attracted the attention of speculators from outside the town eager to invest in such property. These twin pressures of magisterial opposition to small halls and pub entertainment and the deployment of much larger sums of money than hitherto for the purchase and redevelopment of the major sites were to determine the general nature of the development of music hall entertainment in the town from the mid-1880s.

In his annual report for 1882–3, Leicester's Chief Constable, Duns, noted that musical entertainments in pubs were greatly increasing in number, and that there was no law with which to control them. He asked for, and in 1884 received, a clause concerning music licensing in the local act of that year. By 1885, pub music halls had been virtually abolished in Leicester, leaving only Paul's and the Gaiety.[34] In the 1880s, there had been a number of Leicester halls, such as Noble's Magazine Palace of Varieties, Illsley's Varieties and the White Swan, which employed professional acts. Although smaller than Paul's, these purpose-built saloons represented considerable investments in the industry. Illsley's Black Lion Hotel in Belgrave Gate, including outbuildings and three adjacent houses, was withdrawn from sale in May 1885 at £7,500.[35]

At the same time, less formal pub entertainments flourished. The *Leicester Town Crier* observed in 1882 that public house music was 'one of the methods which is being largely adopted to bolster up the fall off of the liquor trade', adding that 'What would be inadmissible in a music hall is the "correct card" here. . . . All over the town pianos are being hammered where pianos were never hammered before.' It was claimed that parents took their children to free and easies.[36] Such entertainments had a long pedigree. Tom Barclay recalled the attraction of drink to adolescents in the 1860s and 1870s, and how 'we went to the "Free and Easy" and heard "Old Mother Glum" sung, and "After the Opera's over" and "Not for Joe" and "It's Naughty but it's Nice"'.[37] Joseph Dare had a less enthusiastic view of such activity in the 1870s, and thought the lure of free and easies, in back rooms of pubs, was partly responsible for the failure of many working-class girls to develop domestic skills. 'These rooms', he wrote, 'are filled with boys and girls, the boys are smoking and the girls are drinking . . . Here they learn songs of a very low order.' As usual, Monday and Saturday evenings were the most popular nights, although some pubs held musical evenings more frequently.[38]

The free and easy was to have few public supporters in 1884. Among those active in mobilising opinion against them was Councillor Samuel Lennard, a lieutenant of the censorious Baptist minister F. B. Meyer. The solicitor representing the Licensed Victuallers' Society and the Beerhouse Keepers' Association asked the bench to lay down a general principle which would avoid establishing a new monopoly in music licences. Most licencees, he claimed, did not want music anyway, especially given the declining tone of popular songs. The magistrates accepted the views of the organised parts of the trade. Fifty-three pubs were licensed for informal music in semi-private rooms, and casual performances on the piano were not objected to. But 34 applications were refused, including all those for music and dancing licences.[39]

The strict enforcement of the music licensing by-law was only a further aspect of a long-term campaign by the Leicester licensing bench, a body dominated for long periods by prominent temperance supporters. The bench aimed to suppress activities, some legal, others not, which increased the salience of the public house in neighbourhood culture. There were concerted efforts against Sunday drinking (1869), the use of pubs as meeting places for prostitutes (1872), and by-occupations such as milk-selling (1873). In 1872, hours were reduced by national legislation, while in 1875 the principle was established that structural changes were subject to magisterial consent, giving the bench a veto over publicans wishing to increase the capacity of their houses. From 1875, there were a series of cases in which the bench refused to licence sports grounds and specific outdoor events. The effect of much of this was to drive the activities concerned elsewhere, and pub music and late-night and Sunday drinking took refuge in working men's clubs. These in turn became the subject of police attention and a series of prosecutions in 1901, in advance of the Licensing Act 1902.[40]

One such club was the Vocal and Instrumental Club, Brunswick Street, started by local amateur singers who had been entertainers at other clubs. It flourished around 1900 in a disused factory, converted to provide a concert room which could hold 500, skittle alley and reading room. In several particulars, it resembled singing saloons of 40 years previously — except that it was not run by the licensed trade. The *Leicester Guardian* commented that 'only for the absence of galleries and string band, curtains and gilding, you would say you were in a slightly reduced Tivoli or Empire'.[41]

There was a chairman, keeping order with a hammer, beer and lemonade were served at tables during the performance, and there were five turns, all but one done for drinks only. The paid artist received 5 or 6 shillings. It is particularly striking that artists and audience were young. The Leicester United Trades Club provided similar entertainments, receiving all its income from drink sales. Both were viewed favourably by the *Leicester Guardian*'s correspondent, whereas the East Leicester Working Men's Club represented all that was worst in the tradition of informal public house entertainment. The newspaper commented that even for members, 'this drinking late into the night, and this congregating of both sexes to listen to vulgar comic songs . . . must be demoralising to themselves. We long ago put down the old fashioned "free and easy" . . .'.[42]

Most of the clubs broke the law by admitting non-members, and such 'bogus' clubs were suppressed in 1901, often by the use of informers or plainclothes police who sought admission as non-members. Variety entertainment was increasingly a staple of more respectable working men's clubs, which did not break the law, from the 1860s, and remained so after 1902. These clubs developed their own performance conventions and circuits which marked them off from the less formal entertainments of the saloons and lesser pub music halls, dependent as these had been on local talent.

Changing patterns of ownership, 1890–1959

The boom in demand for music hall property in the late 1880s and 1890s has been discussed elsewhere largely in terms of the emergence of major national chains, notably those of Stoll, Moss and MacNaughten. But the Leicester case shows that there were a large number of unsuccessful speculations in the provinces at the time, and the dominant circuits of the Edwardian period were constructed amidst the ruin of others' efforts at aggrandisement. While the monopolistic position of Leicester's two halls after 1884 made them attractive investments for theatrical speculators, the decade between the demise of Torr's and Paul's family businesses and the take-over of the Pavilion and the Palace by MacNaughten and Stoll respectively in 1901 was marked by frequent changes in management and ownership in the Leicester halls. Financial instability was not the only continuity between the two phases of the halls' development. There also remained a marked difference in the relative social standing of the rival halls.

Torr's old premises in Wharf Street were, by the late 1880s, old and unlikely to pass more stringent safety regulations imposed by the Borough after the Exeter fire disaster of 1887. Rebuilding was planned by Messrs Reeves and Verdo in 1892, but it was under the ownership of Wesbrook Bros that the New Empire Theatre was opened in 1894, at a cost of £6,000. Although it was built with a three-tiered auditorium, building plans reveal several archaic features. There was a chairman's seat, tables and bars in each part of the hall. The stage was located in a corner.[43]

By 1901, the hall was in the hands of the official receiver, and, in 1903, it was relicensed as a public house. Its owner had been offered £5,000 for it in 1901, such was the attraction of a licensed town-centre property to asset-strippers, who could hope to exchange it for a new licence in the suburbs. Four years later, the Empire was owned by the New Bioscope Trading Co., and was one of the first buildings in Leicester to be used wholly as a cinema. But it was the advent of Stoll's Palace, rather than the bioscope, which finally drove it out of use as a music hall.[44]

Lovejoy's Prince of Wales Theatre of Varieties, the successor to Paul's, was opened in August 1890, at a cost of £10,000 and accommodating 1,260 people.[45] Yet while Lovejoy may have been successful in mobilising capital from outside on a scale beyond the means of local leisure entrepreneurs he had not bargained for the weak demand for such entertainment in Leicester at a time of worsening trade. The venture failed within a year of opening and by 1894 was in the hands of Captain Orr Grey, who ran it as the Tivoli Theatre of Varieties, later the Pavilion Theatre of Varieties (popularly known as the 'Pav'). In the face of competition from Stoll, he sold out to MacNaughten in 1901.[46] It was run as part of a chain which included halls in

nearby Lincoln and Nottingham. Lovejoy's building included a formal position for the chairman, apparently absent at Paul's as it was to be at the Palace.
With the Empire's demise, the Pavilion was left as the less prestigious of the
town's halls, and the last resort of a wholly working-class audience. The
Pavilion was demolished in 1929 in a road widening scheme. It is likely that
it would otherwise have been converted into a cinema.

In 1899, Oswald Stoll bought the Floral Hall, a large building in Belgrave
Gate used for exhibitions, political rallies and religious services. The theatre
architect, Frank Matcham, incorporated it into the structure of a massive
new Palace Theatre of Varieties which was opened with a cast led by Charles
Coborn in June 1901.[47] The description of the building given in the
shareholder's prospectus indicates how far this building surpassed its
rivals.[48] The three-tiered auditorium seated over 3,000, with separate
entrances and exits permitting rapid changes of audience necessitated
by the twice-nightly system. There was to be no drinking in the auditorium
so that it would be a place where 'the respectable man [could] take his
wife and family without risk of contamination'. There were, nevertheless,
ample refreshment facilities, with restaurant, buffet, café and billiard
saloon, as well as bars on each floor. Matcham, who was involved in seven
other theatre-building and reconstruction projects in 1900 and 1901,
was employed by Stoll specifically for his ability to create buildings giving a
high degree of safety, comfort and good ventilation, rigid but unobtrusive
class division and an environment which allowed variety theatres to extend
their appeal to people who would earlier have regarded music halls with
abhorrence.[49]

At the Palace, Stoll was able to present the full range of stars who toured
his circuit. The biograph was introduced in the opening performance and
remained an important part of the programme. In the last years before the
First World War, there was an increasing number of reviews. The spoken
word and music largely edged out the circus element which was still in evidence in 1901, and, according to the *Leicester Daily Post* even comedians were
less prominent.[50]

The Palace returned a 10 per cent profit throughout the 1920s, and evidently withstood the competition of the silent cinema. The Floral Hall
cinema run in conjunction with it was more seriously threatened by the
purpose-built cinemas of the mid-1920s. Stoll complained that the coal
strike depressed local industry, bringing about a fall in his profits in
1926–7, and that high rates and taxes made it necessary to employ greater
economy in running the hall.[51] It is unfortunate that company records
have been destroyed, so that analysis of the state of business between
1930 and the demolition of the hall in 1959 is not possible.[52] Reminiscences
of interviewees and correspondents to the *Leicester Mercury* are largely
anecdotal, recalling visiting stars and major productions such as pan-
tomimes, but they do at least suggest that the theatre avoided the worst of the
decline into seediness which beset variety at the onset of competition from
television.

The Audience

What, though, of the audience which caterers, managers and speculators alike hoped to attract? The evidence is, as ever, fragmentary, but allows certain conclusions to be drawn concerning age, class and behaviour. Moralists were quick to deplore the youth of many music hall patrons, and Barclay's account confirms the popularity of this type of entertainment with adolescents. Dare was appalled by the mixing of the sexes there, but his 1865 account of a Friday night at Paul's suggests that we should not be misled by this stress on the more lurid aspects of the dangers of seduction and prostitution to overlook the truly heterogenous nature of the crowd. Dare observed a large audience, of all classes, from sweated labourers in shoe-finishing to professional gentlemen. The age range was wide, from 16 to 70, with many mothers nursing children. Dare did not see this as a way to control youthful excesses, though, and deplored the degeneracy of home life which the sight of a whole family out together implied. Prominent among the crowd were shoe-hands employed by firms which paid on Friday. In a later report, Dare noted that the most objectionable characters were youths in the casual parts of the shoe trade who enjoyed a brief prosperity in good times, unburdened as they were by family commitments. These, he said, 'assume either a flashy exterior, or shirk about in slovenly attire. The throng the low dancing or music halls, and fill our public promenades with obscenity.'[53]

By comparison with the theatre in the 1860s, the good order at Paul's is striking.[54] The presence of the chairman was partly responsible, and the performance conventions of music halls permitted more direct manipulation of the audience. The latter were not just spectators, and their enthusiasm could find more creative expression than the catcall, witticism or missile. The music halls, for all their cultivation or respectability, were free from the aristocratic and artistic pretensions of the theatre which invited the ridicule of alienated sections of the audience. There is no hint in the sources of a group of gallery roughs intent on rowdyism in the music halls.

In the early twentieth century, the Pavilion remained a wholly working-class hall, while the Palace offered the middle class the opportunity to enjoy variety entertainment in sumptuous surroundings without loss of caste or contamination from the working class. The Pavilion, like the Palace, had a wide range of prices, from fourpence in the gallery to one pound for the best box,[55] but there remained a hint of 'Darkest England' in the tone adopted by journalists who ventured there. In 1900, Arthur Stevens disguised himself in cloth cap, old overcoat and bristles to spend 'A Night with the Gods in the Empire', as his report was entitled. He found the crowd attentive, the songs decent. There was much smoking and many drinks were ordered. Stevens sat next to a man who told him, 'I never miss a Friday night at a 'all, and haven't done these 15 years, I gets paid on a Friday, and I allus reckons a tanner for amusement, threepence to come and the other for two drinks when I gets out'. He preferred to attend the second house, since the first left him too much time for drinking after it. It is also evident that the gallery was a place for eating fish and chips or pigs' trotters during the performance.[56]

The Pav's position as a working-class hall left it open to the attention of moralists such as members of the Leicester Citizen's Vigilance Association. In 1912, they objected to the renewal of its licences — the first such case involving a music hall since 1866, and sought to protray it as a den of iniquity, but their evidence was largely discredited in court.[57] A shoe-hand who they claimed to have been seen dead drunk at the hall told the court that he was a teetotaller prone to severe headaches. Police evidence that good order was maintained, and MacNaughten's personal appearance in court, denying that drink was a major source of profit at the hall, convinced the magistrates that there were no grounds for objection. They did however, finally put a stop to consumption of drink in the auditorium, and refused permission to sell drink to under-15s.[58] That such young people frequented the hall is further indication of continuities with the free and easies of the 1860s, and one suspects that much of the audience for lesser halls at all times was young. That the bench was able to take a calm view of the phenomenon contrasts with the moral panic felt by Joseph Dare. In 1912, the lobby was itself far less influential, and the municipal authorities more confident in their own ability to control this aspect of popular culture.

Observers were generally unconcerned about the gallery audience at the Palace. In common with the East End audiences who expressed disapproval of Marie Lloyd's more risqué material, the Palace audience was thought to have rejected licentiousness. The *Leicester Guardian* observed in 1901 that

> one of the most encouraging features about the audiences who flock to the Palace is the fact that they almost invariably appreciate the best things best. When some hard voiced 'comedienne' sings meaningless song with many smirks and a little dancing, she rarely gets many hands to applaude her, but let a really good vocalist sing a really good song and applause breaks forth spontaneously from every part of the building.[59]

The late nineteenth- and early twentieth-century audience was morally dependable, and did not represent a political threat. Contemporaries often described the entertainment as a refuge from the world, not a place for comment on it. In January 1910, the *Leicester Daily Post* observed that 'There were many people at the Palace last night who were glad to escape the stress and turmoil of a political election and enjoy a programme of mirth, song and music'.[60] The trivial, escapist nature of what was offered at the Palace was as much a source of exasperation to some socialists at the time as it has been to socialist historians since. The local ILP paper, the *Leicester Pioneer*, commented at the time of the Palace's opening, that while the entertainments were not vicious, 'a place such as this should exert greater powers of refining and elevation, by stimulating the imagination, and aiding the higher faculties'.[61] F. J. Gould, secularist and ILP member of the Leicester School Board, made his first visit to a hall in 30 years (his only previous one had been to the Alhambra in London) shortly afterwards. He found the piecemeal nature of entertainments analogous to the alienated nature of modern life in which he said 'we live in bits — our work, our play, our religion, are partitioned and divided'. Regrettably, he thought, 'thousands of people prefer the scattered items of a music hall to the connected thought of an epic or the sustained intent of the classical drama'.[62]

Some light is shed on the political awareness of the audience by the reaction of the crowd at the Palace to a picket of the hall by members of the Amalgamated Musicians Union in 1914. Stoll was in dispute with the union in Manchester and London, but not in Leicester, where only half the orchestra was unionised. Nevertheless, the union sought to enforce a sympathetic action by discouraging working-class attendance at the Palace. A picket was organised by the secrerary of the town's no. 1 branch of the National Union of Boot and Shoe Operatives. Houses were poor as a result, men staying away in larger numbers than women, due presumably to trade union affiliation. Stoll responded with a series of very expensive acts, including the statuesque Australian poseuse, La Milo, and Vesta Tilley, for whom crossing a picket-line could be seen as a prelude to her later involvement in Tory politics. The Palace also began to give free gifts to attract its audience.[63] The incident, which lasted until Stoll made concessions in July 1914, suggests that, for all the denunciation of the halls by Labour speakers and journalists, a sizeable part of the usual audience were working-class Labour supporters and trade unionists, for whom politics and entertainment were usually quite distinct spheres of their lives. Nevertheless, many were not willing to ignore Stoll's anti-unionism on this occasion. There is, however, no evidence that any radical alternative to the Palace sprang up during the strike. Indeed, the *Pioneer's* theatrical critic continued to review the acts there as though nothing unusual was happening. News of the strike was confined to the paper's industrial columns.

Conclusion: What difference did ownership really make?

Music hall was a relatively late arrival in Leicester, and a sickly growth for much of the time before 1900. Both features arose directly from the insecurity of working-class incomes and the hostility of the middle-class. There is little trace of a bohemian sub-culture focusing on the halls in this most respectable of bourgeois communities. Starting when it did, Leicester music hall was at once able to become part of a national entertainment industry, access to London-based artists limited only by the ability to pay, not by communications. From the beginning, Paul's, and later the Gaiety, cultivated respectability and formality in their programmes which suggests that the dichotomy of hall and palace of variety can be overdrawn. Paul's severe regime pre-dated the local licensing act of 1884. Parallel to this major tradition were those of lesser music halls, generally seeking to emulate the established halls by employing professional artists in purpose-built saloons, and free and easies, driven into illegality and the bogus clubs by the local act. The latter seem to have been particularly a focus of sociability among the young working class. By 1910, this was centred on the Pavilion, and was no longer the cause of moral panic.

Alone of Leicester music halls, Stoll's Palace Theatre was able to show healthy profits consistently over a long period. This must be attributed both to the calculatedly efficient use of resources in the Stoll halls, notably the two-house system, and to the Palace's success in exploiting middle-class taste for variety entertainments, previously catered for at the Temperance Hall. But the transition from locally-owned halls to chains was not a sudden one. During the 1890s, Leicester halls were run by a series of unsuccessful lesser chains, able to mobilise more capital than local entrepreneurs, but unable to present entertainment as lavish as Stoll's or MacNaughten's.

It remains to consider what light this case study throws on the relationship between music hall managers and caterers and the local community. In Peter Bailey's account, leading caterers became 'big men', centres of local patronage networks, acquiring the status of cultural leaders in their neighbourhood. William Paul fits the pattern closely.[64] The funeral procession, comparable to that of civic leaders and prominent clergymen, was a suitable end to a career in which he had cultivated regal authority within the hall, characterful to the point of eccentricity, the subject of legend in the profession and the town alike. The suburban residence served further to distinguish him, and permitted the same ostentatious display as that available to large employers driving in to visit their factories and warehouses in the town. But Paul was not typical of Leicester music hall proprietors. No other music hall owner achieved Paul's longevity in the profession — indeed, most of the others, like their stars and the capital supporting their ventures, came from outside the town. Dan Cook and Sam Toor had previously achieved success on Leicester stages, but carpet-bagging speculators were as much a feature of the halls as they were of the town's legitimate theatre.

The social distance between such outsiders and the audience should not be exaggerated. Torr's failure was wilful, in that he refused to acknowledge the strength of local tradition and taste, raising prices in an effort to elevate the status of the Gaiety. Others, and in particular Stoll's managers at the Palace, were careful to cultivate local affection by charitable benefaction. Then George F. Reynolds left the Palace in 1914 after three years as manager (to take over at the Manchester Hippodrome), the *Leicester Pioneer* reported that 'he has gained the esteem of everyone with whom he has come into contact by his geniality and unfailing courtesy'. His successor, Truman Towers, was manager until his death in 1926, a length of service which allowed him to achieve popularity with patrons and to judge local taste as well. His passing was, according to Stoll, a cause of decreased profitability.[65] Like Paul, charitable gifts and free letting of the hall to be used for benefits helped enmesh it in local society. Support for established town charities, the Royal Infirmary and the Poor Boys' and Girls' Summer Camp in 1914, and sports clubs, notably the County Cricket Club, achieved wide publicity and were wholly uncontroversial. The organisation by C. Finch-Hatton, Stoll's manager in

1909, of the Palace Unemployment Fund appears to have been more daring, especially in the light of the Unemployment March to London from Leicester in 1905. But the fund, amassed from collecting boxes, was managed by the ILP leader, Alderman William Banton, and was distributed in the form of one-shilling grocery tickets, giving it an aura of respectability, good intention and implicit intervention in working-class family budgets.[66] Without wishing to impute cynical motives to the Palace's management, it was an astute means of appealing to the hall's working-class constituency, at the same time alleviating the distress of its own potential audience and giving aid in a paternalistic manner. Such elements were present in all philanthropy, and in Paul's as much as others', but his charitable acts seem to have been a regular part of community life in a way in which those of the Palace were not. Moreover, as the boycott of 1914 shows, the working-class audience was well aware of the real social attitude of the Palace's management.

Music hall achieved a significant place in working-class entertainment in Leicester, although not a dominant one. It came to rival, but did not displace, popular legitimate theatre. The town's Theatre Royal thrived as a house for melodrama until the First World War, a major resort on Saturday nights and bank holidays, and a focus for youth culture. Music hall nevertheless lacked strong local traditions of performance and genre. Favourites were generally outsiders resident in Leicester or, later, recurrent visitors. Again, there is little indication of an organic relationship between what was performed at the halls and the working-class community. Such identifications could be generated by an audience of regulars, but, as in contemporary professional football, that allegiance had to be won by managements who were often not of that audience, presenting entertainers who were also outsiders. It is a further example of the modernity of music hall as commercial entertainment that it offered the local audience not a mirror of themselves, but of a generalised working-class culture.

Finally, what conclusions can be drawn from this study of music hall in a single town, which may be indicative of broader trends in the provinces? Most strikingly, it is clear that music hall, far from being a focus of local and regional popular cultural expression, served as a conduit for the further permeation of national standards of performance and national imagery. The Leicester example suggests that this was not simply a process of coercion, alienation or the imposition of a hegemonistic culture. Local artists were already of only secondary importance when music halls were first opened in Leicester in the 1860s. Apart from Paul, there are no notable examples of caterers with strong local connections beyond the stage successes of Dan Cook and Sam Torr. There is little sign that local content was predominant in what was sung or spoken on stage, and no evidence exists of local songwriting or dialect comedy. In so far as the provincial music hall was central to a local popular culture, it was as a place for sociability among its audience. The importance of this is perhaps acknowledged by the concern shown for the moral effects of music hall attendance by Joseph Dare and, less directly, by the magistrates and police. As Tom Barclay's memoirs suggest, the halls are likely also to have been a source of songs and types of humour popular in the working-class community. It seems rash, though, to assume that the audience perceived the increasing dominance of the local halls by outsiders to the town as a loss. We may recoil before the replacement of intimate pub entertainments by the slick professionalism of Oswald Stoll, but it is surely the case that the audience appreciated the greater accomplishment of nationally known performers. It is in any case impossible to construe development in Leicester in terms of an indigenous tradition of entertainment being driven out by proprietors of the great chains of palaces of variety.[67]

It is indisputable that the character of music hall changed fundamentally between 1860 and 1900. On the evidence presented here, it is preferable to see this in terms of changes in the nature of the working-class community, notably in the structure of employment and the position of youth, which greatly modified its audience's patterns of sociability, rather than as an unmediated imposition of new forms of commercial exploitation from outside the community. Nevertheless, the political intervention of local authorities could play a major role in restricting certain aspects of working-class culture and in creating circumstances favourable to particular forms of commercial development. That this conclusion remains so tentative reflects the complex nature of the process of cultural changes which is illustrated by the case of provincial music hall.

Notes

(Place of publication is London except where stated otherwise.)

1. On music hall in the North-East, see David Harker, 'The Making of Tyneside Concert Hall', *Popular Music*, vol. 1, 1981, pp. 27–56; and, for a different approach to its culture, Robert Colls, *The Collier's Rant*, 1977. Dialect poetry and song from Lancashire is discussed in Martha Vicinus, *The Industrial Muse*, 1974. For the growth of music hall in Bolton, see Peter Bailey, *Leisure and Class in Victorian England*, 1978, and Robert Poole, *Popular Leisure and the Music hall in Nineteenth Century Bolton*, Lancaster, 1982. G. J. Mellor's *The Northern Music Hall*, Gateshead, 1970, is a starting point for further research. It indicates some of the major developments in various towns, but lacks adequate documentation. Provincial music hall in southern England has received less attention, but see Kathleen Barker, 'The Performing Arts in Five Provincial Towns, 1840–1870', unpublished PhD thesis, University of Leicester, 1982.
2. Jeremy Crump, 'Amusements of the People; Recreational Provision in Leicester, 1850–1914', unpublished PhD thesis, University of Warwick, 1985.
3. J. F. C. Harrison, 'Chartism in Leicester', in Asa Briggs (ed.), *Chartist Studies*, 1959.
4. W. Lancaster, 'Radicalism to Socialism. The Leicester Working Class, 1860–1914', unpublished PhD thesis, University of Warwick, 1982.
5. William Gardiner, *Music and Friends*, Leicester, 1878, vol. II, p. 85; A. Temple Patterson, *Radical Leicester*, Leicester, 1954, p. 13.

6. *Leicester Chronicle (LC)*, 1 May 1869.
7. *Leicester Guardian (LG)* 29 May 1900.
8. *LC*, 28 March 1853.
9. *LC*, 20 June 1857.
10. Robert Head, *Modern Leicester*, Leicester, 1882. *Leicester Daily Post (LDP)*, 1 July 1892.
11. George Stevenson, *Book Friends and Tastes; and Free Libraries*, Leicester, 1862.
12. *LC*, 26 December 1863.
13. *Era*, 3 September, 16 April 1865; 2 December 1866; *LC*, 9 August 1873.
14. *Leicester Journal, (LJ)*, 19 September 1862.
15. *Era*, 18 August, 1 September, 29 December 1861; 19 September 1862. For audiences elsewhere, see Dagmar Höher, Chapter 4 this volume.
16. *Era*, 31 May, 12 July, 22 November, 1863; 20 November 1864; *LC*, 9 May 1883.
17. Leicester Domestic Mission, *Annual Report (LDM)*, 1862.
18. *Era*, 27 August 1866.
19. *LJ*, 31 August 1866.
20. *Era*, 2 December 1866, 25 August 1867; *LC*, 4 January, 18 January 1873.
21. *LDP*, 1 September 1883.
22. *The Music Hall*, 22 February 1889; *LJ*, 3 October 1890.
23. *Era*, 19 February 1865; 21 November 1866; 14 August 1870.
24. *Era*, 2 August 1863; 5 March 1865; 31 January 1875; 11 January 1880.
25. *LJ*, 31 August 1866.
26. *LJ*, 20 June 1868.
27. Lady de Frece (Vesta Tilley), *Recollections of Vesta Tilley*, 1934.
28. *LDM*, 1865.
29. *Era*, 8 January, 2 April, 21 May, 16 October 1865; *LDM*, 1868.
30. *Era*, 7 March, 21 March, 27 June 1875.
31. *LJ*, 24 November 1882.
32. *LC*, 9 June 1888; *Leicester Era*, 9 March 1889.
33. *LJ*, 8 August 1890; *LDP*, 5 August 1890.
34. *LC*, 1 September 1883, 22 November 1884.
35. *LC*, 9 May 1885.
36. *Leicester Town Crier*, 6 January, 11 February, 17 February 1882.
37. Tom Barclay, *Memoirs and Medleys*, Leicester, 1934, p. 16. Barclay, a working-class autodidact from Leicester's Irish community, comments elsewhere that 'My scientific studies did not prevent me from having a few drinks of beer and whisky, and from singing in pubs and at "Free and Easies"'. The titles he lists show that many of the songs were Irish (ibid., p. 43).
38. *LDM*, 1864.
39. *LC*, 22 November 1884; 14 February, 17 June 1888. A comparable act had been passed for Bradford in 1882. By 1900, several towns had made the same provision, although Liverpool and Derby (1901) were among the exceptions. *LC*, 17 August 1901, gave the following table showing numbers of music and dancing (i.e. music hall) licences:

Derby	176	Wolverhampton	12	Lincoln	0
Liverpool	106	Leicester	2		
Birmingham	46	Plymouth	0		

Such legislation need not be so strictly enforced, however. Bolton's Improvement Act of 1872 provided similar powers, but magistrates were willing to grant 'about a dozen' licences for music and dancing in 1880 (Poole, *Popular Leisure*, p. 72).

40. Crump, 'Amusements of the People', Chapter 5; *LG*, 22 June 1901.
41. *LG*, 16 December 1899.
42. *LG*, 30 December 1899; 7 April 1900.
43. Leicestershire Record Office (LRO) Plan, Wharf St. 358/1892/L and B. Detailed studies of the architecture of Leicestershire halls are to be published by Richard and Helen Leacroft in a forthcoming book, together with reconstructed perspective drawings. I am grateful to them for guiding me to the plans of halls in the LRO.
44. Mellor, *Northern Music Hall* op. cit; *LG*, 12 January, 5 October 1901; 7 February 1903.
45. *LDP*, 5 August 1890.
46. Programme for the Pavilion Theatre, LRO DE2156.
47. *LG*, 22 June 1901.
48. Shareholders' Prospectus, LRO DE1936/51.
49. Brian Mercer Walker (ed.), *Frank Matcham: Theatre Architect*, Belfast, 1980.
50. *LDP*, 6 January 1914.
51. *The Times*, 9 March 1927.
52. Records of sale of contents, LRO misc. 392. The catalogue entry for the Leicester Palace Theatre of Varieties in Companies House notes that the records have been destroyed.
53. *LDM*, 1865.
54. Jeremy Crump, 'Patronage, Pleasure and Profit; a Study of the Theatre Royal, Leicester 1847–1900', *Theatre Notebook*, vol. 28, no. 2, 1984. It is clear that, by the 1860s, efforts by successive managers to maintain respectability and good order had failed. Indeed, theatre in Leicester was only to regain a regular middle-class following after 1880.
55. *LRO*, DE2156.
56. *LG*, 8 December 1900; Kathryn Gent, 'Leisure Activities in Leicester, 1870–1901', unpublished MA thesis, University of Leicester, 1976.
57. *Leicester Pioneer* (*LP*), 17 February 1912.
58. *LDP*, 16 March 1912.
59. *LG*, 10 August 1901.
60. *LDP*, 11 January 1910.
61. *LP*, 22 June 1901.
62. *LP*, 14 September 1901.
63. *LP*, 23 January, 27 February, 3 April 1914.
64. See Bailey, Chapter 2, this volume, and his 'Custom, Capital and Culture', in R. Storch (ed.), *Popular Culture and Custom in Nineteenth Century England*, 1982, pp. 180–208.
65. *LP*, 27 March 1914; *The Times*, 17 March 1926.
66. *LP*, 13 March 1909.
67. In this respect, I would dissent from Poole's portrayal of a residual, unchanging popular culture which endured from the early nineteenth century until at least the early twentieth. Such a view is expressed in Poole, *Popular Leisure*, p. 73: 'The commercial success of the late nineteenth century music hall mirrored an economic change rather than a cultural one . . . Popular culture in Bolton was far longer lasting and had far deeper roots than did the passing glitter of the extravagantly unlikely variety theatres which, over a few decades, gave the people a little space to play in.'

4 The Composition of Music Hall Audiences 1850–1900

DAGMAR HÖHER

When, in the late 1890s and early decades of the twentieth century, the first articles and books on the history of the music hall were being published, they not only created a particular historiography of the development of the halls, but also of their audiences. Informed by a predominantly romantic and — especially after the First World War — nostalgic view of the 'heyday of the Music Hall' in the London of the 1890s, they depicted the history of the halls as a development 'from pot house to palace' with a corresponding change in the make-up of the audience from an all-male gathering of roughs (both plebeian and patrician) to a respectable assembly of all classes and both sexes.[1] As *The Times* put it in 1910:

> Today, in place of the obscure supper-room or the hall attached to the tavern, we have a large number of comfortable, handsome buildings, . . . [and] in place of an audience of men only, or of men accompanied by the least creditable of their female acquaintances, we see among the audience the family . . .[2]

Recent historians of the music hall have, by and large, corroborated this scheme as far as the change towards increasing respectability and mass audience is concerned, although the composition of the pre-1890 audiences has become a subject of confusion, being described, alternatively, as working-class, lower middle-class and labour aristocracy, as working and lower middle-class, as probably not class-based at all, as purely male as well as generally mixed and, finally, as 'far too mixed to be easily characterised at all'.[3] Such assessments are, however, not the result of an extensive debate on audience composition, for the subject has not been treated in its own right either comprehensively or in its historical development.[4]

This essay will attempt to fill some of the gaps in our knowledge by looking at metropolitan and provincial music hall audiences between 1850 and 1900 in terms of residence, class, gender, age and visiting patterns. I will try to reach more precise conclusions as to the composition, character and practices of these audiences by drawing mainly on quantitative data from music hall disasters rather than contemporary descriptive sources.

The latter are frequently either impressionistic articles by middle class explorers on their ventures into 'music hall land', or anti-music hall pamphlets and articles by social reformers denouncing the halls as 'low, vulgar, disreputable taprooms on a large scale, where men go and drink bad beer, smoke vile cigars . . . and stare at a stupid, senseless entertainment, to their intellectual detriment . . .' and moral corruption.[5] Although both groups differed in their attitudes towards the halls, their perception was commonly informed by a nineteenth-century middle-class moral discourse on popular amusements, which classified the halls — due to their public house origins — as somewhat disreputable places, describing their audiences accordingly as roughs and women of morally dubious character.

The presence of women in particular, whose proper place according to the dominant code of values was the home and certainly not the pub, furnished one of the most fevered public controversies about the halls, which illustrates quite strikingly the tendentiousness of many descriptive sources. This is exemplified by the Parliamentary Reports on the halls and the reports on the annual London licensing sessions, where two questions recur time and time again.[6] What is the nature of the women in the audience? And how can they be anything but prostitutes? Such was the reasoning of the music hall opponents and frequently of the authorities as well. In 1874 the police opposed the granting of a licence to the Oxford in London because, as they put it, 'women had been admitted without men'.[7] Equally, in 1891, the Theatres and Music Halls' Committee of the London County Council refused to grant two licences on the assumption that the women visitors to the halls were prostitutes.[8] Prostitutes did, of course, form part of many a music hall audience and some people, including Sir Richard Mayne, Chief Commissioner of the Metropolitan Police in the 1850s and 1860s, were willing to tolerate this on the grounds that prostitutes were to be found in all public places and that barring them from the halls would in no way contribute to solving the problem.[9] Most arguments in the reports, however, tended to be apologetic rather than aggressive. For obvious reasons music hall owners and managers were reluctant to get involved in discussions as to the relative merits of admitting or excluding prostitutes. Instead they preferred to divert attention to an entirely different group of women: the wives. Married women, they argued, had formed a regular part of the audience from the time Charles Morton had opened the Canterbury to the wives of his patrons, and his policy, soon to be adopted by other music hall owners, had proved to be immensely beneficial. For did not the wife keep a watchful eye on the husband and restrain him from 'committing any excess'?[10] Thus the idea of the 'wife' was put forward as a respectable counterpart to the prostitute. The 'wife' not only embodied a necessary control factor, more importantly she gave the whole institution an aura of respectability. It is noteworthy that respectable single unaccompanied women hardly ever figure in these reports, nor, as we have seen, in the early music hall historiography — despite the fact that they formed, as I shall show, a considerable part of many a music hall audience.

By examining audience composition and visiting patterns I shall argue that the early halls were not the sole preserve of the disreputable. They addressed men and women alike, the rough and the respectable. By providing social space and entertainment both for the family and for people who worked together, they catered for all members of the urban working class and also for some sections of the lower middle class, with the middle classes joining hesitatingly only towards the turn of the century. Nineteenth-century music hall attendance was determined by the social calendar of work and leisure and, for women in particular, by their changing cycles of life and work, It has been argued that music hall culture replaced an earlier culture which was centred on the home, the work-place and the local pub.[11] Geographically this is true, but not so socially and culturally. For the halls played a cohesive part in helping people to counter the divisive effects of the Industrial Revolution.

The geographical scope of the article will comprise metropolitan and provincial audiences, and here I will argue that London was rather the exception than the prototype.

I

Since most music hall researchers have concentrated their efforts on London the term 'London music hall' has almost always been used as a synonym for the 'English music hall'. Undoubtedly London, as the political and cultural centre, did set tones and fashions which were followed in the rest of the country. It was precisely this 'metropolitan' factor, however, together with London's size, diversity of population and its specific industrial and occupational structure based on administration, commerce and small-scale production, which set the capital apart from the rest of the country, especially from the economically and socially more homogeneous industrial and factory towns of the North.[12] Consequently the London music halls developed features and audiences which were exclusive to the metropolis.

When F. Anstey wrote about these features in the 1890s he was describing a social and geographical phenomenon which had to some extent been present from the very beginnings. 'London music halls might be roughly grouped into four classes — first, the aristocratic variety theatre of the West End, chiefly found in the immediate neighbourhood of Leicester Square; then the smaller and less aristocratic West End halls; next, the large bourgeois music halls of the less fashionable parts and in the suburbs; last the minor music halls of the poor and squalid districts.'[13] The more expensive sections of the first two categories, the West End halls, had always attracted an audience of bohemians, aristocrats and students; the sort of audience which had formerly frequented such institutions as Evans's Song-and-Supper Rooms.[14] The third category of hall, which Anstey rather euphemistically described as 'bourgeois' included the Metropolitan in Edgware Road, the Canterbury in Lambeth, the Winchester in Southwark, Wilton's in the East End and, more centrally situated, the Middlesex in Holborn. They catered for a predominantly local audience of small tradesmen, shopkeepers and their assistants, mechanics and labourers, as well as soldiers and sailors.[15] The top range of admission prices underlines this social segregation (see Table 4.1).[16]

Table 4.1: Admission prices in some London music halls

Decade	Music Hall (category according to Anstey)	Price range Seats	Boxes
1860s 1870s	Alhambra (1)	6d.–4s. 6d.–5s.	1gn. 1gn.–2gn.
1870s	Oxford (2)	6d.–1s.6d.	10s.6d.–1gn.
1860s 1870s	Canterbury (3)	6d.–1s. 6d.–1s.6d.	none none
1860s	Wilton's (3)	4d.–8d.	1s.
1860s	Boro' Music Hall (4)	3d.–6d.	1s.

The bottom range, however, indicates that the overwhelming majority of London music hall patrons came from the working and lower middle class, especially when one considers that there existed a great number of local pub-based halls and singing saloons in addition to the purpose-built music halls.[17]

Certain suburban music hall proprietors such as James Robinson of the Eastern, John Wilton of Wilton's and Charles Morton of the Canterbury tried to broaden their audiences from time to time. Not only did they broadcast their newly-acquired respectability with a view to attracting the middle classes, their advertisements included train and bus connections to and from the centre of London in order to win the patronage of those who would normally only frequent West End establishments. But by and large these audiences failed to materialise, and press campaigns to draw them into the suburbs tended to be rather sporadic before the 1890s.[18]

In the provinces the situation was entirely different. Here, despite residential segregation, there were no distinct classes of music hall in different areas of the towns. In fact almost all provincial music halls were situated in or near the town centres, even in cities with large suburban areas such as Manchester, Liverpool and Glasgow. It was only towards the end of the century that the majority of halls began to be built outside the city centre (see Figure 4.1).[19] This is not to say that the poorer districts were completely devoid of musical entertainment: they too had their singing saloons and free and easies. Leeds magistrates issued roughly 160 music and dancing licences in 1867 and more than three times that number in 1871.[20] But the majority of the major saloons were in the centre and both they and the music halls drew their audiences from all areas of the town.

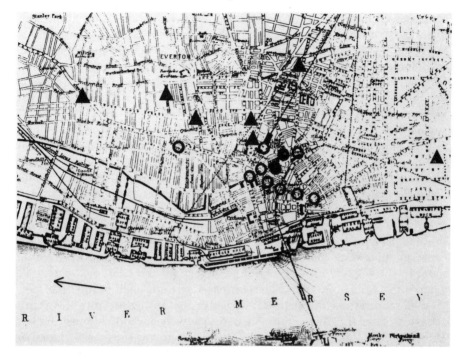

Figure 4.1: Music halls in Liverpool
○ in 1878; ● in 1878 and 1898; ▲ in 1898.

II

Invaluable information on provincial audiences is provided by the reports on and casualty lists of fires and panics. These sources are, admittedly, not written by members of the audience themselves, but rather stem from coroners and their juries, the police and newspaper reporters. They do, however, provide hard personal data on 203 individuals (in most cases name, age, residence and occupation) and give the people concerned the opportunity and space to speak for themselves. At the inquests and in interviews with the press the survivors talked about themselves, the victims and their music hall visiting patterns — why they went to the halls, why they went on particular days, who they went with, and where they sat.[21]

There were, in the United Kingdom between 1850 and 1900, 87 fires and ten panics, the latter commonly occurring after false alarms. Of the fires, only one — at the People's Palace of Varieties in Aberdeen in 1896 — resulted in considerable casualties; by contrast, precisely half the panics gave rise to injuries and fatalities. These five panics were at the Surrey in Sheffield in 1858, at Springthorpe's in Dundee in 1865, at the Victoria in Manchester in 1868, at the Colosseum in Liverpool in 1878 and at the Star Theatre of Varieties in Glasgow in 1884. The ensuing injuries and casualties occurred when those people trying to escape met with inadequate exits, narrow staircases and steep and worn-out stairs. Of the six music halls in question five were structurally unsafe. Local authorities were, as a rule, aware of this, but could do nothing about it owing to a lack of local licensing regulations; on the other hand, they made little effort to ameliorate matters by applying for such regulations, even after the music hall disasters. But, as the case of the Surrey in Sheffield demonstrates, panics could and did also lead to fatalities in structurally safer buildings.

That staircases were the scene of most accidents points to the fact that the victims came from specific area of the halls — apart from Springthorpe's in Dundee which had no internal divisions. In Liverpool, Manchester and Aberdeen the victims were situated in the galleries, in Sheffield in one of the two galleries and in Glasgow in one gallery and the pit. None the less, the evidence provided by witnesses at the inquests and the differing admission prices allow us to make an overall assessment of the audience composition in those halls. The Sheffield, Dundee and Aberdeen halls can be regarded as representative since there were few, if any, other halls in these towns at the time. In the big towns — Manchester, Liverpool and Glasgow — the halls where the panics occurred will be compared to other halls of the time.

In all six disasters, the victims invariably came from the poorer, working-class districts of the town. Figures 4.2–4.4 show the location of music halls in Manchester in 1868, Liverpool in 1878 and Glasgow in 1884 and — based on the lists of victims and witnesses – the catchment areas of the halls where the panics occurred.[22]

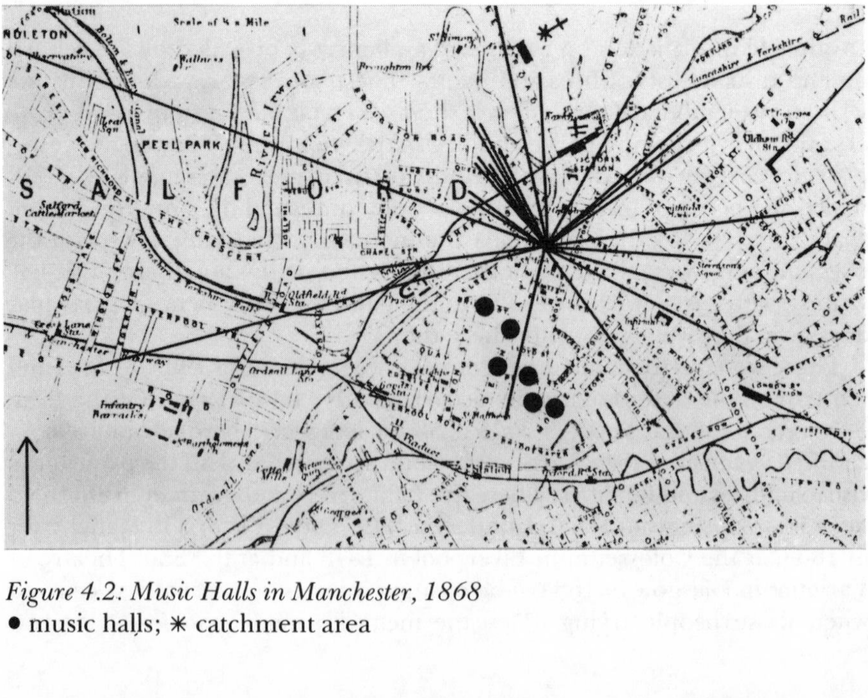

Figure 4.2: Music Halls in Manchester, 1868
● music halls; ✳ catchment area

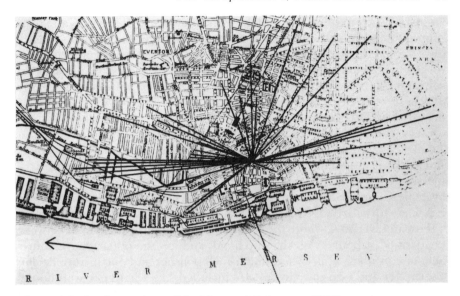

Figure 4.3: Catchment Area of the Liverpool Colosseum, 1878

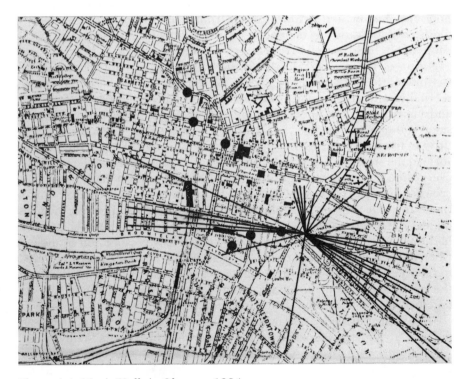

Figure 4.4: Music Halls in Glasgow, 1884
● music halls; ✳ catchment area

The majority of the victims and the witnesses were working-class and their composition reflects the occupational structure of the work-forces in each town. In Sheffield, 75 per cent of all those whose occupation was given worked in the cutlery trades, as grinders, filesmiths and razorsmiths, as scissor filers, filecutters and edge-tool fitters; in Dundee, 11 out of 13 and in Manchester two-fifths of those whose occupation was given were textile-factory workers; victims and witnesses in Liverpool and Aberdeen include workers from seafaring trades and allied industries: in Liverpool a quarter and in Aberdeen a third of those whose occupation was given were seamen, ropeworkers and shore-labourers. Large towns with a complex industrial structure such as Manchester, Liverpool and Glasgow naturally had more diversified music hall audiences. Thus workers in building and heavy industries made up a further third of the Manchester victims and another quarter of those in Liverpool, where the remainder was almost equally split between (unspecified) labourers on the one hand, and, on the other, drovers, firemen, one printer's apprentice, one french polisher and one picture dealer. Manchester and Glasgow victims also included street hawkers, warehousemen and message boys and girls. It can thus be seen that these audiences comprised a broad section of working people from every economic and industrial sphere. They range from labourers to skilled factory workers and artisans (small masters in Sheffield as well as printers in Manchester, Liverpool and Glasgow) and include workers from industries in different stages of industrialisation and mechanisation, from the domestic industries and workshops of Sheffield as well as the factories of Manchester.

For all of them, a visit to the music hall was closely integrated in the rhythms of the working week and even the working day, as one of the witnesses of the panic at the Liverpool Colosseum explained: 'I work in a foundry, and sometimes I and others go to the Colosseum just as we leave work. We stand at the rear of the pit . . . [since] the pit is more convenient for us just to drop in for a little during the "first house".'[23] Visitors like him might have formed the stock of the everyday audience. The mass of the audience, however, came in on the new and traditional holidays. Music halls were most crowded on Saturdays, in Manchester additionally on Fridays (pay-day in the cotton mills) and on 'St Monday'. In Bolton, miners would visit the halls on Monday afternoons.[24] Miners in another (unspecified) Lancashire town had established a different pattern, as Vesta Tilley recalled: on Mondays, when the new programme started, 'gaffers' from each mine were delegated to report on its quality before the mineworkers themselves attended later in the week.[25] The miners, textile and foundry workers not only worked together, they also enjoyed their leisure time collectively.

Music hall visits were social events: people tended to go there in groups, if not with workmates, then with neighbours or members of the family.

Children, who formed a considerable part of music hall audiences, attended in the company of siblings and friends, as did many of the victims in Dundee, where the panic occurred on the 'chief holiday in the year, when most young people are absent from home and in search of enjoyment'. They often got in at half-price or even for nothing — by sneaking in unseen.[26]

Other family groups were young couples, often with babies. In Pullan's in Bradford 'children in arms are freely admitted, and cackle, and laugh, and cry at their own sweet will — the crying, if I must speak the truth, being the predominant baby sound'.[27] In the pit of the Glasgow Star special provision was made for women with children.[28] Such family groups existed even in the early days of the singing saloons. Angus B. Reach, visiting the textile districts on behalf of the *Morning Chronicle* in the late 1840s, described the audience of a Manchester singing saloon thus:

> two thirds might be men: the others were women — young and old — a few of them with children seated in their laps, and several with babies at their breasts. The class of the assembly was that of artisans and mill-hands. Almost without an exception, men and women were decently dressed, and it was quite evident that several of the groups formed family parties.[29]

From the early days, women formed as integral a part of the audience as men. What set them apart was rather their pattern of attendance, a pattern closely coinciding with their changing cycles of life and work.

Most women frequenting the halls were young, single and employed. According to the victims' lists such women worked in textile factories or as domestic servants, message girls or in shops and offices. The more employment facilities for women a town offered, the higher was the percentage of women attending the halls. Thus Liverpool audiences contained relatively few women, whereas in strongholds of the textile industry such as Manchester, and in industrial areas like Sheffield where the domestic and workshop system meant that there tended to be a high proportion of female workers, the situation was entirely different.

The young women would visit the halls with their neighbours or friends from work, and in groups rather than alone or accompanied by men. Writing of Pullan's Music Hall in Bradford in 1872, James Burnley observed that 'the weaker sex shows itself much stronger than I expected. Some have evidently come with husbands or lovers, but most of them are unaccompanied by male companions.'[30] Indeed young men and women, with the exception of the occasional courting couple, seem to have gone to the halls separately, although contacts between them could and did develop once they were inside the halls. One observer noted that the young female visitors to the Alhambra in Liverpool in 1877 'did not resent any offers to enter into conversation with chance admirers of the masculine gender, for "false modesty" in no wise seemed to be their most distinguished characteristic. Upon the whole, nevertheless, I noticed nothing in their conduct to which special exception could be taken.'[31]

Next to the young single women the most important section of the female audience consisted of young wives and mothers. Annie Whitworth, a witness to the 1868 disaster in Manchester, was 21 and married to a shoemaker; and Sarah Godwin, a victim of the Glasgow panic in 1884, was 22 and a married mother. One journalist who visited a Bradford music hall in 1887 estimated that about a quarter of the audience consisted of husbands and wives.[32]

Even after marriage, young couples frequently stuck to their habits of visiting the halls in the company of friends or relatives. Alexander Bertram went to Springthorpe's Hall in Dundee with his wife and a friend of hers. Fred Ward visited the Surrey in Sheffield with his brother and his wife's sister.[33] That his wife was not present as well might have been due to the fact that she had to remain at home to look after a growing family. This, of course, was a factor which affected both a woman's leisure activities and her opportunities for employment. A single child in the family tended to make very little difference: female textile workers with one child would continue to work in the factories since they could earn enough money to pay another woman to mind their child, and often have a little money over to spend on leisure.[34] But with two or more children, child care became too expensive and women were forced to give up their employment, with a subsequent fall in the family income and a corresponding rise in the demands of child care and housework. Music hall visits thus became the privilege of husbands and fathers, and, later, of the elder children, many of whom were possibly earning their own keep. Amongst the victims of the Liverpool disaster of 1878 there were five family fathers with a total of seventeen children; their wives and children had not been present at the hall.

The situation changed again once the children had grown up and started working themselves. Women were then able to take up their old leisure habits once more. One such woman was a Mrs Cooper, aged 58, who visited the People's Palace in Aberdeen in 1896 with her husband and who was one of the victims of the fire disaster.

Once inside the halls, each group had 'its' seating area, according to age and income. The galleries were usually occupied by the children and young people, provided they were the cheapest areas.[35] This is ilustrated by comparison of the ages of the victims in the Manchester Victoria in 1868 and the Liverpool Colosseum in 1878, both halls with panics originating in the galleries (see Table 4.2), which shows the varying age distribution in differently priced seating areas. The table also shows that 10–14-year-olds comprise a considerable subgroup within the under-20s. This is true for the other music halls where the victims were seated in the cheapest areas.

The attendance of young people and children in large numbers provided yet another pretext for the reforming lobby to demand restriction, or even abolition, of the halls and singing saloons on the grounds that they destroyed what 'Day or Sunday School' had so laboriously built up.[36] Although this tactic enjoyed a measure of success in Bolton in the 1850s, on the whole it proved fruitless.[37] When, in 1877, the Chief Constable of Liverpool launched an attack on the city's singing saloons because of their 'most pernicious effect upon young people of both sexes', he failed to win any effective public support. An evening newspaper, the *Liverpool Albion* responded with a series of favourable, if not entirely uncritical, articles on the various

Table 4.2: Age distribution of victims

Victoria Music Hall
gallery: 2*d.*

Colosseum
gallery: 6*d.*

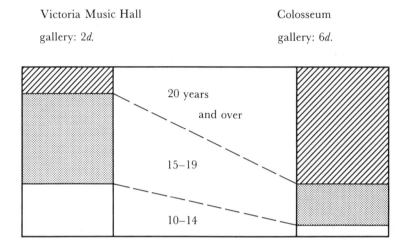

establishments.[38] More importantly, the majority of people were not concerned by the fact that young people visited the halls. One witness — referring to boys — put it to the Select Committee on Public Houses in 1852–3 that if they were allowed to earn their living in mills and factories and 'made premature men of in that way, I submit to this Committee the gross injustice of excluding them from their amusement in the evening'.[36] Only gradually did a rise in the standard of living in some sections of the working class and a series of Acts reducing children's employment and enforcing school attendance begin to create the idea of 'childhood' and 'youth' as distinct periods of life in spheres set apart from that of adulthoold.[40] But even this did not seem to have changed music hall visiting patterns amongst young people: of the 28 dead and injured in the Aberdeen disaster in 1896, 15 were aged between 15 and 19 and eight between 10 and 14.

Just as age formed one factor of the internal distribution of a music hall audience, class formed another and can to some extent be related to admission prices. In Liverpool's Colosseum, where the admission prices were 1*d.* for the pit and 6*d.* for the gallery, the pit 'was made up of working men of the lower class . . . [i.e.] working men other than high-class mechanics — dock labourers and labourers engaged in the varied labour of this great port' and the gallery contained the higher-class workers and sailors.[41] A similar internal distribution might also have prevailed in other halls where panics occurred. But how valid is this for all halls at the time?

In Manchester in 1868 and in Liverpool in 1878 the halls where the panics occurred were the cheapest in town. However, as Table 4.3 shows, admission prices at other establishments were not much higher, nor was the composition of their audiences noticeably different.[42] Like the Colosseum, the

Metropolitan and the Alhambra also catered mainly for members of the working class — the one shilling seats of the latter remaining for the most part unsold. Where the shilling seats were occupied, such as in the Parthenon, the audience was 'not wholly composed of the working or labouring class', but included a 'fair sprinkling' of commercial travellers, clerks and shopmen, as in the case of the London and the Alexandra in Manchester.[43] In this respect the relationship of price to audience composition was similar to that of the London suburban halls of Anstey's third category.

Table 4.3: Admission prices in Manchester and Liverpool Music Halls

Manchester 1868 (capacity)		Liverpool 1878	
Victoria	2d.–3d. (2,000)	Colosseum	1d.–6d.
People's	2d.–6d. (3,000)	Alhambra	1d.–1s.
London	6d.–1s. (2,000)	Gaiety	2d.–1s.
Alexandra	6d.–1s. (1,500)	Parthenon	6d.–1s.
		Star	6d.–1s.6d.
		Constellation	free
		Crystal Palace	free
		Griffith's	free
		Metropolitan	free

Of all the music halls in Manchester and Liverpool during the 1860s and 1870s, only the Star in Liverpool deliberately set out to attract an audience which went beyond the working and lower middle class. Modelled on the London West End halls, it used its somewhat metropolitan ambience to distinguish itself from the ordinary provincial hall, and it was the only hall which advertised in nearly all the Liverpool literary weeklies and middle class entertainment guides throughout the 1870s. None the less, it remains questionable whether the middle class — given their attitude towards the halls in general — did in fact patronise the Star. Indeed, clerks seem to have been more in evidence there than their employers.[44] Manchester's Alexandra did attract the 'sons of wealthy merchants and manufacturers', but their presence can be attributed less to a desire to share in working-class culture than to enjoy the company of the prostitutes for which this hall was renowned in the 1870s.[45] In general, however, the middle class tended to leave the halls to the working class and those sections of the lower middle class (artisans, tradesmen and shopkeepers, as well as their assistants and clerks) who continued to share a common cultural context with them.

The extent to which members of the lower middle class participated in music hall culture depended very much on the local industrial and commercial structure. When the manager of Day's Music Hall in Birmingham stated before the Select Committee of 1866 that his audience consisted mainly of manufacturers, tradesmen, artisans and even the occasional magistrate, his comments were not only meant for their publicity effect but also reflected the occupational structure of Birmingham, which was indeed dominated by artisans and small masters.[46] On the other hand, such statements underline the fact that for many members of the lower middle class, music hall visits did not necessarily carry a taint of unrespectability with them.[47]

It has been suggested that during the nineteenth century the lower middle class increasingly separated and protected itself geographically, economically, socially and ideologically from the working class. However, this is not equally true for all sections of this class, and becomes more valid only towards the turn of the century, by which time the lower middle class as a whole had already become an integral part of music hall audiences. Although enjoying a somewhat 'better' status and income, many members of the old lower middle class — shopkeepers and artisans — continued to share their living quarters with the working class during the early decades, and remained close to their style of life, especially since there was still a certain amount of social mobility between artisans and (skilled) workers, and between workers and traders. Geographical, social and economic proximity to the working class equally applied to many members of the new lower middle class, the clerks and shop assistants. Consequently, both groups chose to participate in working-class rather than exclusively in middle-class culture.[48] They did, however, not share the same seating areas: in Manchester's Alexandra the workers sat in the galleries, and the body of the hall was occupied by shopkeepers, clerks and artisans.[49]

III

It has been suggested that the middle class finally took to visiting the halls in the 1890s as a result of the attempts of owners and managers to break with the public house tradition of the halls and turn them into variety theatres — by banning the sale of drink in the auditorium, by replacing tables with rows of seats, by cleaning up the artistes' material and by taking measures to control the behaviour of the audience.[50] The most prominent role in this process was played by the owners of the large music hall syndicates, Moss, Thornton and Stoll. Similar policies were also pursued by smaller impresarios and major local caterers.[51] Their opening ceremonies tended to start with a rendering of the National Anthem followed by speeches from the managers who would vow to banish any objectionable features from their programmes, presenting instead variety entertainments 'that the most fastidious man in this city can safely bring his wife and family to witness'.[52] By this time the middle class itself had begun to have some closer contact with music hall culture. An increasing number of middle-class children were learning music hall songs from their nurses and nannies, and music hall song sheets were to be seen on drawing-room pianos. Furthermore, from the 1880s onwards the annual Christmas pantomime had been a source of direct contact with music hall stars.[53] This change in audience composition is documented in the early histories of the halls and the numerous reminiscences of those who lived through the time. Likewise, the presence of town dignitaries now became a regular feature at the opening ceremonies of new music halls.[54]

However, the middle class did not take to the music hall as easily as it might appear. The 1890s were also a particular time of conflict, and members of this class inspired and led a considerable number of anti-music hall campaigns, most notably that of Mrs Ormiston Chant against the London Empire. The conflicts were not confined to the capital. In Manchester, pressure groups comprising 'many of the religious, temperance, educational, and social improvement bodies' combined to oppose the granting of a licence to the city's new variety theatre, the Palace.[55] And in Liverpool there were disputes over music hall licences which were conducted very much on class lines. When, in 1892, the police opposed the granting of a licence to the Liverpool Grand, the Federation of Trades Unions held a meeting and unanimously issued a resolution in support of the Grand and its manager. In this they were supported by Liverpool's first working-class Justice of the Peace, William Matkin.[56] In many of these disputes the anti-music hall lobby received backing from the newly-elected town councils which had replaced the magistrates after the Local Government Act of 1888. As elected bodies susceptible to public pressure and frequently containing a reforming element, they played a forceful role in furthering the development of and improvements to the halls which the major music hall owners and managers had instigated. Although not all of them became as rigid as the notorious London County Council, they were all factors which music hall owners had to reckon with.[57]

Although the attitude of the middle class towards the music hall during the 1890s was by no means uniform, it did become more favourable during the decade as a result of the changes introduced by the owners and promoted by the authorities. The new character of the entertainment, the rejection of the old tavern atmosphere, the visual presentation of the halls, the style of the advertisements and the rhetoric of the opening speeches all contributed to a new language of representation on the part of the music hall owners: now 'healthy' entertainment went along with 'elegance' in outfit and 'style' in architecture; and 'safety' did not only refer to the adequate provision of staircases and exits but symbolically included both form and content. Such language, emphasising themes and concepts familiar to the middle classes, helped to break down resistance to the halls and alter the way in which they were perceived by outside observers. Health, elegance, style and safety were the keywords in their aesthetic and ethical vocabulary.

This is not to deny that before the 1890s certain owners like Charles Morton had always claimed to be providing the public with the most beautiful hall and the most rational amusement in the kingdom. In the main, however, links with the pub tradition remained strong and the entertainment offered was neither entirely rational nor free from objectionable features, so that it was somewhat difficult to convince the public at large of such claims. It was not in fact style which predominated, but the spectacular; this applying not only to the entertainment but also to a lesser extent to the architecture and amenities. Sensations, novelties and exotic curiosities were the order of the day rather than safety and elegance.[58] Nor were all music hall owners disposed to curry favour with the middle classes. Thomas Sharples of the Bolton Star, who narrowly survived a campaign against him in the early 1840s by the Bolton 'Anti-Singing Saloon Association', retorted by inserting the words '*Honi soit qui mal y pense*' within the emblem of the Star which appeared in the advertisements in the *Bolton Chronicle*. The hall itself he proudly proclaimed as being 'under the patronage of the working classes', indicating that he was quite content with the make-up of the audience as it was. In Leeds, Joe Hobson showed a similar pride in his advertisements for the Princess's Concert Hall in the 1860s, calling it 'the greatest Sixpennyworth in the World', fashionable, magnificent and combining 'the comfort of a Club and Amusements for the Million'.[59] These expressions of proletarian culture uttered with all the self-confidence of the aristocracy were also exemplified in the title 'People's Palace' which was to be found on many halls throughout the country. By the 1890s a more moderate and conciliatory attitude had set in as the owners strove to gain the approval of the middle class. New halls tended now to receive the title 'Empire'.

The new language of representation was, on the whole, convincing since both rhetoric and fact, form and content were finally congruent. But how large was middle-class participation in music hall culture in reality? In London, halls such as the Coliseum and the Hippodrome were addressed to and patronised by the middle class.[60] Likewise, in the provinces a few halls in the city centres began to cater for an audience upwards of the lower middle class. In Manchester the Tivoli (formerly the Alexandra) and the Palace, and in Liverpool the Star, all held their bottom price at 6*d*., but the top prices went well beyond the traditional norm in the provinces. At the Tivoli they rose from 1*s*. in the 1860s to 3*s*. in the 1890s, with boxes at 10*s*. 6*d*. and £2; and at the newly-built Palace the top price was 5*s*., with boxes at 1gn and 2gns. The rise in prices at the Liverpool Star was less, from 1*s*. 6*d*. in the 1870s to 2*s*. two decades later, but its more expensive seating areas were by then also being occupied by 'employers . . . well-to-do tradesmen . . . excursionists and visitors to the city'.[61] But all other music halls in these two cities (that is, the overwhelming majority) remained the resort of the working and lower middle class. Their admission prices and location indicate this quite clearly. Of the old halls in Liverpool only the Star and the Parthenon survived into the 1890s. The price range of the latter had not changed over the years and remained at 3*d*. to 1*s*. Significantly all the city's new music halls in this decade were uniformly cheaper. The Roscommon charged between 3*d*. and 6*d*., and the Royal Palace 6*d*.; Kiernan's three music halls, the new Park Palace and the Tivoli (formerly St. James's Hall) also fell within this price range.[62] Furthermore all the new halls in Liverpool were built in densely populated working-class districts, as were Broadhead's new chain of music halls in Manchester.[63] The fact is that the middle classes still did not visit the halls in great numbers, and where they did, class segregation was maintained. This can be seen in the class-based division of the provincial music hall scene which, in the 1890s, developed similar features to those in London prior to 1890, and also in those music halls which catered for all classes of society. Here, although they assembled under the same roof, the classes were kept well apart from each other in different seating areas and by the use of separate entrances. Manchester's Alexandra had, for example, two seating areas in the 1860s. Renamed the Tivoli in the 1890s, it had six — similar to most variety theatres of the time. Although it is true to say that middle-class hostility to the music hall was on the decrease from the late 1890s onwards, it still took nearly two decades until general social acceptance came about, culminating in the Royal Command Performances which began in 1912.

IV

Thus far I have looked at audiences in the music halls in the nineteenth century and, by following them from their homes and work-places to the halls, I have tried to establish their visiting patterns and to discover the social and cultural role the music hall played in their everyday life. For reasons of space I have not been able to look at audience behaviour inside the halls and shall instead conclude with a summary of some recent research on the subject and suggestions for further areas of study.

As in the case of audience composition, long established stereotypes have distorted our perception of audience behaviour. The music hall audience has been depicted as a rowdy crowd, either participating vigorously in the choruses when they liked the performance or barracking the performer when they did not. Although this did happen, the picture is far from complete.

Recent studies by Bailey (on music hall) and Reid (on the theatre) have tried to give a clearer definition of the audience's 'participatory or regulatory role'. [64] Both have focused their attention on 'disturbances' among certain sections of the audience, identifying different modes of performer–audience communication and forms of popular control. Placing the various forms of audience behaviour in their historical and cultural context, they have redeemed them as the custom of the day rather than as offence. Such forms of popular control included the territorial appropriation of certain seating areas in the 'gods', and the levying of a *taxe populaire* on the wealthier members of the audience, the rituals of the claqueurs, the blackmailing of artistes, and the traditions of riotous behaviour. Bailey, especially, has pointed out how what 'once may have been tolerated as custom was ... redefined as deliquency' in the 1880s as managements increasingly tried to impose tighter measures of control upon their audiences. [65]

Reid and Bailey have drawn on research on youth culture and popular protest in order to base their approach on a reinterpretation of forms of disruptive behaviour amongst certain sections of the audience. Dickinson, using oral evidence, has looked at everyday experience of audiences in terms of their 'needs' and 'functions', that is, their expectations regarding the evening's entertainment, and how they were used by performers and management to test the quality of the entertainment, how performers sometimes engaged the sympathies of the audience in pay disputes, and how management used the audience to control the tone of the performance.[66]

A comprehensive study of audience behaviour has yet to come. By placing audience behaviour in a context of social relationships and popular customs, it should examine both 'disruption' and 'normal behaviour' and the borderline between the two. Reports in the *Era* on disturbances indicate that audiences had a very clear idea of what they ought to get for their money and felt perfectly justified in demanding their rights in ways in which the outside observer tended to classify as offensive.[67] The dynamics of the audience's relationship with both management and performers will also have to be examined. As Dickinson has pointed out, audiences took side with managements on some issues and with performers on others. Sometimes they fought both, as in the dispute over the encore system.[68] Such a study should further include the relationship of the audience to the programme in terms of participation as well as reception. Audience participation could include amateur groups performing on stage as well as contests such as clog-dancing, comic singing and sack racing which featured regularly on the provincial music hall stage.[69] An analysis of the reception of the programme should address itself to the symbolism, metaphors and emotions which were being conveyed, and how they were coveyed to and received by the audience. That there was a complex relationship between the 'lion comique' and the aristocratic 'swell' on the one hand and the lower-middle-class or working-class 'dandy' on the other was always clear to the contemporary music hall observer.[70] This relationship was informed by mutual imitation and parody and contained in itself multifarious social comments.[71] But, again, the exchange between stage and audience comprised more than one part of either. Therefore, study of audience behaviour should try to differentiate equally between various sections of the audience, those in the pit as well as those in the gallery, adults as well as young people, and women as well as men, thus fruitfully combining research into composition with research on behaviour.

Notes

(Place of publication is London unless stated otherwise.)

1. See, for example, C. G. Stuart and A. J. Park, *The Variety Stage*, 1895, and the numerous memoirs of journalists, critics and 'men about town' such as H. G. Hibbert, *Fifty Year of a Londoner's Life*, 1916; H. Chance Newton, *Idols of the 'Halls'*, 1928; J. B. Booth, *London Town*, 1929; and J. B. Booth, *'Master' and Men*, 1927.
2. *The Times*, 24 January 1910.
3. L. Senelick, 'Politics as Entertainment: Victorian Music-Hall Songs', *Victorian Studies*, vol. 19, 1975–6, p. 150; see also C. Barker, 'The Chartists, Theatre, Reform and Research', *Theatre Quarterly*, vol. 1, no. 4, 1971, pp. 3–10. For a more class-orientated audience composition, see D. F. Cheshire, *Music Hall in Britain*, Newton Abbot, 1974, Chapter 6; G. Stedman Jones, 'Working-Class Culture and

Working-Class Politics in London, 1870–1900', *Journal of Social History*, vol. 7, 1974, p. 478; and P. Bailey, *Leisure and Class in Victorian England*, 1978, Chapter 7, pp. 154–6 – all arguing that the audience was predominantly working- and lower middle-class. Local research on leisure has pointed to an even more proletarian clientele: see G. E. Wewiora, 'Manchester Music-Hall Audiences in the 1880s', *Manchester Review*, vol. 12, no. 4, 1973, pp. 124–8; M. B. Smith, 'Victorian Entertainment in the Lancashire Cotton Towns' in S. P. Bell (ed.), *Victorian Lancashire*, Newton Abbot, 1974, pp. 169–185; and R. Poole, *Popular Leisure and the Music Hall in Nineteenth Century Bolton*, Lancaster, 1982. E. Voigt, *Die Music-Hall-Songs und das öffentliche Leben Englands*, Greifswald, 1929, on the other hand, argues that the music hall was basically a resort for the lower middle class (p. 24), and S. Pollard, 'Englische Arbeiterkultur im Zeitalter der Industrialisierung', *Geschichte und Gesellschaft*, vol. 5, 1979, p. 165, maintains that it was frequented by the labour aristocracy. For the trend towards mass audiences see M. Vicinus, *The Industrial Muse*, 1974, Chapter 6; and P. Summerfield, 'The Effingham Arms and the Empire: Deliberate Selection in the Evolution of Music Hall in London' in E. and S. Yeo (eds), *Popular Culture and Class Conflict 1590–1914*, Hassocks, 1981, pp. 209–40.

4. More comprehensive studies on audiences have so far been done mainly on the theatre. See C. Barker, 'The Audiences of the Britannia Theatre, Hoxton', *Theatre Quarterly*, vol. 9, no. 34, 1979, pp. 27–41; and D. Reid, 'Popular Theatre in Victorian Birmingham', in D. Bradby *et al.* (eds), *Performance and Politics in Popular Drama*, Cambridge, 1980, pp. 65–89.

5. Quoted in *Free Lance*, 29 May 1874, p. 173.

6. See *Parliamentary Papers*, Select Committee on Theatrical Licences, HC 1866 (373) XVI and Select Committee on Theatres and Places of Entertainment, HC 1892 (240) XVIII. On London licensing see the annual reports in *The Times*, at the beginning of October.

7. *The Times*, 10 October 1874.

8. See *Parliamentary Papers*, HC 1892 (240) XVIII, pp. 492–3.

9. See *Parliamentary Papers*, HC 1866 (373) XVI, p. 45.

10. See ibid., pp. 4, 255, 306.

11. See Stedman Jones, 'Working-Class Culture', pp. 485–6.

12. For the differences between London and the northern industrial towns see A. Briggs, *Victorian Cities*, Harmondsworth, 1977, pp. 311–12; G. Stedman Jones, *Outcast London*, Oxford, 1971, pp. 27–32; and P. Waller, *Town, City and Nation*, Oxford, 1983, p. 24.

13. F. Anstey, 'London Music Hall', *Harper's Monthly Magazine*, vol. 91, 1891, p. 190.

14. See *Parliamentary Papers*, HC 1866 (373) XVI, p. 201.

15. See J. S. Bratton, *Wilton's Music Hall*, Cambridge, 1980, p. 17 and U. Schneider, *Die Londoner Music Hall und ihre Songs*, Tübingen, 1984, p. 40–1.

16. Admission prices come from *Parliamentary Papers*, HC 1866 (373) XVI and from advertisements in the *Era Almanack*, 1868–72.

17. See *Parliamentary Papers*, HC 1866 (373) XVI, pp. 21, 313; and J. Greenwood, *The Wilds of London*, 1874, p. 90.

18. See the advertisement in the *Era Almanack*, 1868; see also Bailey, *Leisure and Class*, pp. 155–6 and Bratton, *Wilton's Music Hall*, p. 14.

19. Information on provincial music halls comes from the yearly lists of British music halls published in the *Era Almanack* and their addresses are from local directories or advertisements in the papers.

20. See *Leeds Licensing Records*,LC/J/6, Special Sessions 1864–76.
21. Reports on fires, panics and inquests come from *The Times*, the *Era*, local newspapers and the lists of music hall fires in *Parliamentary Papers*, HC 1892 (240) XVIII, pp. 519–20. For the lists of victims see *Supplement to the Sheffield and Rotherham Independent*, 18 and 25 September 1858; *Dundee Advertiser*, 4 January 1865, and *The Times*, 5 January 1865; *Manchester Courier and Lancashire General Advertiser*, 3 and 13 August 1868; *Liverpool Weekly Albion*, 19 October 1878; *Glasgow Weekly Herald*, 8 November 1884; *Aberdeen Evening Express*, 1 October 1896; and *Aberdeen Weekly Journal*, 7 October 1896.
22. I have been able to establish the addresses of most of the listed halls in the *Era Almanack* of the year in question, and of the majority of victims – but not the precise location of either within the given streets.
23. *Liverpool Weekly Albion*, 19 October 1878.
24. See 'Depositions Relating to the Star in Bolton', Bolton Reference Library.
25. See V. Tilley, 'Concerning Audiences', *Era Almanack*, 1899, p. 67.
26. See *Scotsman*, 4 January 1865.
27. *Bradford Observer*, 4 January 1886.
28. See (Glasgow) *Evening News and Star*, 3 November 1884.
29. A. Aspin (ed.), *A. B. Reach: Manchester and the Textile Districts in 1849*, Helmshore, 1972, p. 59; see also J. Crump on Leicester audiences in the 1860s, Chapter 3, this volume.
30. J. Burnley, *Phases of Bradford Life*, 1872, p. 55.
31. *Liverpool Albion*, 8 December 1877.
32. See *Bradford Observer Budget*, 12 February 1887.
33. See *Sheffield Times*, 14 September 1858.
34. See *Parliamentary Papers*, First Report of the Commissioners on the Employment of Children in Factories, HC 1833, (450) XX C2, p. 6. See also M. Anderson, *Family Structure in Nineteenth Century Lancashire*, Cambridge, 1971, p. 71.
35. In the People's Palace in Aberdeen and in the Colosseum in Liverpool young people tended to be found in the pit.
36. See J. Hole, *The Working Classes of Leeds*, 1863, pp. 113–14.
37. See Poole, *Popular Leisure*, pp. 58–9.
38. See *Liverpool Albion*, 23 November 1877, and subsequent articles in December 1877 and January 1878.
39. See *Parliamentary Papers*, Select Committee in Public Houses, HC 1852–3 (855) XXXVII, p. 454.
40. On the history of youth see J. Gillis, *Youth and History*, 1974.
41. See *Liverpool Albion*, 3 December 1877.
42. I have included all institutions which contemporary journalists classified as music halls and whose prices I have been able to find. Admission prices and seating capacity come from *Free Lance*, 25 January 1868, p. 236 (People's) and 22 April 1871, p. 125 (Alexandra); *Manchester Courier*, 13 August 1868 (Victoria); and *Bolton Chronicle*, 14 February 1863 (London). For Liverpool, see note 38.
43. See *Liverpool Review*, 17 November 1883, p. 10; and *Free Lance*, 22 November 1866, p. 5.
44. See B. G. Orchard, *The Clerks of Liverpool*, Liverpool, 1871, p. 16.
45. See *City Jackdaw*, 5 May 1876, p. 226; and *City Lantern*, 1 December 1876, p. 79.
46. See *Parliamentary Papers*, HC 1866 (373) XVI, p. 260.
47. On the concept of 'respectability' and its varying meanings see P. Bailey, '"Will the Real Bill Banks Please Stand Up?" Towards a Role Analysis of Mid-Victorian

Working-Class Respectability', *Journal of Social History*, vol. 12, 1978–9, pp. 336–53.

48. For the debate on lower middle class and labour aristocracy see G. Crossick (ed.), *The Lower Middle Class in Britain 1870–1914*, 1977.

49. See *City Lantern*, 1 December 1876, p. 79.

50. See Bailey, *Leisure*, pp. 165–8.

51. See *Era*, 1 August 1896; and *Liverpool Review*, 5 and 19 December 1896, pp. 4 and 5.

52. *Era*, 3 September 1898.

53. See R. Mander and J. Mitchenson, *British Music Hall*, 1965, p. 26. As J. Crump points out (see his article on Leicester, Chapter 3, this volume) there had been a tradition of middle-class demand for variety entertainment long before the 1890s and catered for by the temperance halls.

54. See *Era*, 11 October 1890 and 27 August 1892, and *Bradford Observer*, 31 January 1899, on openings in Bootle, Brighton and Bradford.

55. *Manchester Courier*, 18 February 1891. See also the article by C. Waters, Chapter 7, this volume.

56. See (Liverpool) *Evening Express*, 27 and 28 October 1892.

57. See Bailey, *Leisure*, p. 162; Summerfield, 'Effingham Arms', and the article by S. Pennybacker, Chapter 6, this volume, on the LCC.

58. See, for example, the adverts of the Bolton Star in the *Bolton Chronicle* during the 1840s.

59. See his adverts in the *Yorkshire Post*, 1866.

60. See Booth, *London Town*, p. 165.

61. *Liverpool Review*, 15 October 1892, p. 14.

62. See ibid. and 21 May 1892; and *Parliamentary Papers*, HC 1892 (240) XVIII, p. 244. For Manchester see *Manchester Amusements*, March 1893 and music hall programmes of the time in the Theatre Collection of Manchester Central Library. For a similar division of local music hall patronage, although on a smaller scale, see J. Crump on the difference between the Leicester Pavilion and the Palace in the early twentieth century, Chapter 3, this volume.

63. See Figure 4.1 for Liverpool; and B. Dickinson, 'The Magic of Music Hall', *Manchester Evening News*, 17 January 1983.

64. P. Bailey, 'Custom, Capital and Culture in the Victorian Music Hall', in R. D. Storch (ed.), *Popular Culture and Custom in Nineteenth Century England*, 1982, p. 193; and Reid, 'Popular Theatre'.

65. See Bailey, *Custom*, p. 193.

66. See B. Dickinson, 'In the Audience', *Oral History Journal*, vol. 11, 1983, pp. 52–61.

67. See *Era*, 16 August 1874; 31 March 1875; and 28 November 1891.

68. See *Era*, 13 January 1878.

69. See *Era*, 23 October 1897.

70. See *Dublin University Magazine*, August 1874, p. 235; Burnley, *Phases*, pp. 56–7; the *Yorkshire Busy Bee*, 22 October 1881, p. 151; and R. T. McDonald, *Swings and Roundabouts*, 1919, p. 160.

71. For a detailed analysis of the persona of the 'lion comique' and its social implications see P. Bailey, 'Champagne Charlie: Performance and Ideology in the Music Hall Swell Song' in the companion volume to this, J. S. Bratton (ed.), *Music Hall: Performance and Style*.

5 'Managers in a small way'[1]: The Professionalisation of Variety Artistes, 1860–1914

LOIS RUTHERFORD

When Edward Moss, 'popular chairman' of Moss Empires, received his knighthood in December 1905, the *Stage* editorial commented that 'the honour is Royal recognition of the music hall profession'. It continued with a glowing picture of the vaudeville profession's reaction:

> A chorus of congratulations to Sir Edward has reached him from all grades of the profession, and artistes realize that in honouring him the King has honoured the calling to which they belong. In recent years members of the music hall 'profession' have been 'commanded' to appear before His Majesty, notably the late Dan Leno, Mr Bransby Williams, and Mr Horace Goldin, a fact which eloquently testifies to the advance in character and general popularity of the lighter side of stage entertainment. It is to such men as Sir Edward that this happy result is chiefly attributable, though it must be allowed that a ready response has been made by the artistes themselves.[2]

This superficial appraisal gives the impression, so common in the music hall press, that artistes were subordinate but co-operative instruments of managerial initiatives. From the 1860s to the early 1900s proprietors and artistes institutionalised their professional aspiration in a succession of organisations (see Appendix 5.1). The mutuality of interest that characterised the music hall societies before 1880 was rarely to be found in the later variety theatre. The economic changes implemented by managements from the mid-1880s onwards increasingly brought artistes and proprietors into commercial conflict. By 1906, just a few months after Sir Edward's knighthood, a trade union for variety artistes was formed and early in 1907 an extraordinary strike in London music halls drew the nation's attention to grave dissensions between variety artistes and the magnates who headed the corporate managements of the variety theatre. Echoing grievances that had surfaced in the 1880s, artistes objected to being 'used simply as a pawn in the game between managers'. They felt that their position was reduced to that of a 'chattel and a machine that can be turned on and off, ordered here or there according to the fancy of the managers'.[3]

The main theme of this essay is to explore the links between the performers' efforts to enhance their own status as a professional, businesslike occupational group, and their resistance of the abuses of paternalistic commercialisation. Although the institutional policies of music hall artistes were to a large extent conditioned by economic initiatives implemented by their employers, it would be inaccurate to interpret their collective action in a wholly defensive light. Moreover, it is misleading to regard artistes as a homogeneous or class-specific group, who were 'not fundamentally different from other workers'.[4] Music hall artistes, and the later generation of variety performers, relished belonging to a world apart from ordinary manual or white-collar workers. They do not conform completely to the model of a deviant sub-culture, yet their social aspirations and their economic ideology reveal them to be in an ambivalent and subcultural relationship towards the respectability of the dominant Victorian class culture. They called themselves 'pros', with what one artiste typified as their 'spirit of joking exaggeration', yet when they wanted to command more serious notice they chose to use the proper label, 'professional'.[5] The focus of this argument rests upon the role of formal organisations as a means of countering market conflict. It is therefore impractical to discuss the related theme of the significance of artistes' organisations in so far as they helped to subdue the disreputable and flamboyant public image attached to 'pros' before the 1890s. Rather, I shall concentrate upon the connection between the performer's social and occupational background, the changing economic climate in which they were employed, and the aims of the organisations they consequently formed. The nature and range of extant published sources provide a disproportionate amount of information about the leaders of the profession, both in terms of those artistes who were leaders by virtue of popular notoriety, and those who were the activists and journalists involved in music hall societies. Invariably they were not 'stars', but medium-rank or 'middle-class' performers whose expectations were frustrated by their working conditions. That emphasis is no disadvantage to the argument because it is important to identify the occupational ideology of the performers who acted as spokesmen for the profession as a whole. I have not approached the question of professional women in this discussion: their role appears to have been one of supportive attendance and membership rather than participation in the leadership of organisations in the male-dominated music hall profession.

The Occupational Status of Leaders of the Profession

The term 'professional' referred to anyone earning a living within the halls, but colloquially it applied most usually to performers. Census figures are of little use in estimating the rise in recruitment of music hall artistes, and trade directories are decidedly biased towards the metropolitan acts. Nevertheless, the *Era Almanack* does reveal a boom from 862 acts listed in 1868, to 1,896 in 1878. The *Music Hall Directory and Variety ABC*, edited by Albert Voyce, listed only 1,606 acts in 1899, but a more accurate index of the variety artistes seeking work may be found in the 3,300 strong membership of the Music Hall Artistes Railway Association in 1899, which rose to 6,000 in 1906. Similarly, the Variety Artistes Federation enrolled 4,500 members in 1907, settling at 2,600 to 3,300 during 1910–14. In order to identify patterns of change in recruitment, this analysis looks primarily at comic singers and comedians, the leading 'branch' of the profession. They figure most prominently in newspapers, music hall directories and autobiographies. They were the largest single 'branch' numerically, and the most highly paid 'star comics' enjoyed 'considerable prominence' on the bill.[6] A popularity poll taken in 1906 showed that many comedians were amongst the most favoured and respected members of the profession.[7] There does not appear to be any direct correlation between social origins and occupational succcess. Therefore, generalisations about recruitment to the ranks of the comedians may be valid for other 'branches', and possibly for the occupational group as a whole.

I have identified the occupational origins of 42 top-ranking vocalists who made their debuts on the pub music hall stage, and who were active from the 1860s until the 1880s or 1890s.[8] This is the generation that included George Leybourne, Alfred Vance, Herbert Campbell, G. H. Chirgwin, Harry Randall, Arthur Roberts and Charles Coborn. Less than one-third reveal details of parental occupation: three fathers were businessmen, eight were tradesmen or skilled workers, and two were publicans. Comic singers were more willing to describe their own occupational history. It emerges that seven began their working lives in commercial, white-collar or clerical jobs; twelve were artisans or skilled workers; six were in casual labour or 'boy' odd-jobs; five went straight into entertainment, and overall six went through a period on the legitimate stage as actors. I have used the same sources to compare the occupational history of 34 leading variety comedians who made their debuts after 1890. This date was chosen as the most convenient to demonstrate the new type of aspirant attracted to the variety theatre, rather than the pub music hall, and such changes gathered momentum after the mid-1880s. Some of the better known names of this generation include Gus Elen, Albert Chevalier, Will Evans, Harry Lauder, George Robey, and Harry Tate. Again, there are few details about their fathers' occupations. Five were tradesmen or skilled workers, four were artistes themselves, and one a publican. The former backgrounds of the comedians can be enumerated as follows: two from 'semi-professional' jobs in journalism and the civil service, 16 from clerical or trade jobs, 11 from skilled artisan or factory labour, three from stage families or no previous occupation and two were former legitimate actors.

Although the sample is small numerically, and may overstate the proportion of newcomers to the profession, it does show the strength of solidly artisan, white-collar and casual working-class origins among recruits, with a progressive trend towards the increased inclusion of artisans with lower-middle-class, or latterly middle-class, backgrounds. The most substantial contemporary analysis came from the *St James Gazette* in 1892, describing how artistes came from 'everywhere and nearly all classes'. But, it was thought that the real divisions were between those 'out of the shops, factories, offices and what not — sometimes out of the gutter' and the other 'class' who had 'the thing in their blood' and were trained for 'muscular' and 'mental' self-possession by 'regular courses' from relatives.[9]

The social reputation of the profession also depended upon its internal composition. The proportion of comic singers and comedians serves as a barometer of occupational respectability, because they earned their living creating the *risqué* and vulgar attitudes and images which the public mind indentified with the music hall. The *Era Almanack* provides classifications of established acts in the 1860s and 1870s, and these can be compared with the lists in the 1899 *Variety ABC*. The breakdowns are given in full in Appendix 5.2. The most important comment to make is that comic singers constituted around 20 per cent from 1868 to 1899, but their pre-eminence was challenged after 1880 by more respectable types of act. The proportion of all 'comic' acts rose in the 1870s, from 59 per cent in 1868 to 64 per cent in 1878. Comic singers were closely followed by their female counterparts, the 'serio-comic', forming 14 per cent in 1868 and 20 per cent in 1878. With the steady decline in sentimental and ballad singers (from 20 per cent in 1868 to 8 per cent in 1899) managers began a policy of 'diversification', which was still the corner-stone of booking practices in the 1900s.[10] As a result, the proportion of 'comic' acts had fallen to 54 per cent by 1899. 'Speciality' and 'Continental' acts, first listed in 1878, grew steadily towards the end of the century. These included the broadly defined 'society entertainers'; conjurors, jugglers, illusionists and ventriloquists rose from 36 acts, or 4 per cent in 1868, to 173 (9 per cent) in 1878, and to 302 acts, or 20 per cent in 1899. In addition to these 'high-class' acts, there was a steady, substantial increase in the numbers of semi-dramatic and theatrical acts. By 1899 comic duos, trios and pantomimists had been replaced by 'comedy pairs', comic teams and sketch troupes, forming 21 per cent of all comic-dramatic acts by the end of the century.

The social significance of these trends lay in the fact that society entertainers and sketch artistes cultivated an air of middle class refinement rather alien to music hall circles. Theatrical sketch artistes reminded 'pros' of the 'great social gulf' between the halls and the legitimate theatre, and managerial preference for a 'more educated type of performer' could understandably cause resentment.[11] Society entertainers were traditionally associated with drawing room, salon and concert hall venues, and they basked in the reflected glory of their superior patrons and audiences. Also, judging from potted biographies in *Magic*, many of them were formerly businessmen or journalists, and had risen from the genteel status of 'amateur entertainers'.[12]

The artistes with political ambitions who became leaders of music hall societies repeatedly came from the ranks of the comic singers, comedians, sketch artistes and society entertainers. Collectively they were the most literate and wealthy performers, responsible for setting the tone of the profession. Mirroring trends noticeable among managers, they often had previous experience in the professional theatre, or had worked in a clerical, journalistic or trading capacity, euphemistically called 'commerce'. For instance, the Music Hall Sick Fund and Provident Society was conceived by Dion Boucicault, a dramatic author; Pat Corri, conductor at Weston's Music Hall; 'Jolly' John Nash, said to be a failed businessman and amateur entertainer from Gloucester; and Arthur Lloyd, a former actor, concert party artiste and sometime manager; their Committee also included Harry Liston, a former commercial traveller and drawing-room entertainer, and other leading comiques. The Secretary was G. W. Hunt, a songwriter who was also a dedicated music hall administrator. The Music Hall Artistes Association (1885) was formally headed by ex-theatrical Lloyd and pantomime dame Herbert Campbell, and Charles Coborn, a former clerk, was Treasurer. The Committee of Management consisted largely of leading metropolitan comic singers.[13] The Sketch Artistes Association (1889) had two spokesmen, namely Joe Keegan, former gold-beater and actor, and Cecil Merrie, an insurance manager and member of the Terriers Association.[14] The Music Hall Artistes Railway Association (MHARA) (1896) relied upon extra-professional guidance, from C. D. Stuart, theatrical journalist and secretary, a Kennington publican for its host and treasurer, and there were other 'friends' and patrons with MP or JP status to petition along with occasional support from star comedians like Dan Leno.[15] Another Terrier with a commercial background became President of the MHARA, and later Chairman of the Variety Artistes Federation. This was Albert Voyce, a scena artiste; his turn was then worth £12, and with his well-oiled hair and high starched collars, he exemplified the image of the typical refined 'pro'.[16] The leaders of the Variety Artistes Federation were likewise medium-salary acts, but they were not all new recruits of the 1890s. Joe O'Gorman, the first Chairman, was an 'Irish comedian' with 27 years' experience, a £20 turn; Wal Pink, reputedly a gasfitter turned song and sketch writer for 20 years; Fred Russell, formerly a London journalist who made his ventriloquial debut in the West End in 1896; William Herbert (never a 'Bill') Clemart, son of a Mancunian doctor and JP (Dr Cartmell, whence his stage name) had a commercial and society entertaining background, and made his debut as a ventriloquist in 1894, but was a static £9 turn by 1906. Other influential ex-MHARA members of the VAF were George Gray ('the Fighting Parson'), a former solicitor's clerk and melodramatic sketch actor, and Frank Gerald, son of a Liverpool Mayor, ex-public school boy and touring actor. It would seem, therefore, that the VAF Chairman was reasonably correct in 1911 when he welcomed the influx of a 'more intelligent and more refined element amongst performers'.[17] This shift towards a more bourgeois tone in leadership would have important implications for the institutionalisation of professional societies.

Professional Societies and Music Hall Paternalism 1860–80

Music hall paternalism was a forceful, dynamic determinant of relations between artistes and managers, both before and after 1880. Broadly speaking, the paternalism of the mid-Victorian period may be conceptualised as a kind of convivial, father-like dependence. By comparison, that of the late Victorian years was proudly, deliberately commercial, an overt expression of the balance of economic power in the business. The paternalism of the earlier period was revealed in a 'professional' language of reciprocity; it sustained the ethos of *bonhomie*, and expectations of friendly concern and mutual obligations so assiduously cultivated by metropolitan and provincial proprietors. There was essentially a downward flow of largess and sociability from managers to artistes, typified in loans, outings, dinners and speeches. In return 'pros' participated in ceremonial benefits and presentations expressing the gratitude and appreciation they owed to proprietors.[18]

The music hall societies that were formed between 1860 and 1880 were not only influenced by paternalism; to a lesser extent, they bore some marks of 'pros' trying to emulate initiatives taken by the actors in the legitimate theatre who were striving to institutionalise respectability and professionalism. Music hall artistes were never a profession in the strict sense of the word. Although Stuart and Park were claiming that they constituted a 'recognised profession' in the mid-1890s, the frequent use of inverted commas indicates considerable scepticism among other contemporaries. In retrospect, it seems that their occupational development bears more resemblance to groups who have been assessed as 'semi-' or 'para-professionals'. 'Semi-professionals' are noted for not achieving 'cohesion, commitment to norms of service . . . homogeneity of membership, control over occupational violations'.[19] There were, for instance, certain quasi-corrupt practices aimed at extorting money through blackmail or direct begging.[20] In terms of the role of casual generosity in the business, and in light of the enormous disparities in income levels, such habits were relatively 'fair', and proved almost impossible to eradicate. Another occupational category, 'para-professionals', are described as a 'species' who are closely influenced by another profession yet only achieve partial autonomy and exclusivity to justify their claims.[21] Such a model encompasses the music hall artiste's 'spirit of proper emulation' of the actors of the legitimate stage.[22] Recent publications have systematically revealed how actors compensated for the lack of a coherent professional structure before 1914, by creating and maintaining an overwhelmingly middle-class image. The variety theatre could never match the legitimate in terms of the social and educational status of its recruits, nor the pretensions of 'the Drama' as stage entertainment. However, many of the social and institutional initiatives which contributed to the respectability of the acting profession were belatedly adopted by variety artistes.[23]

The professional aspirations of music hall artistes also stemmed from their economic ideology and status within the paternalistic structure of the publican-proprietor's business. It seems clear from statements issued by artistes meeting at times of duress that their belief in free enterprise and freedom of contract was well entrenched by the 1870s. The music hall business evolved on the basis of individual 'agreements' between performers and proprietors, agreements made on a one-to-one basis, in London and the provinces. In practice, the only artistes who ever had genuine bargaining power were 'stars' whose performances had an impact on box-office takings. But all artistes could be committed to the notion of freedom of contract because it focused on contractual status rather than wage levels as such. As P. S. Atiyah has argued, freedom of contract as a common economic ideology outlived the conditions in which it first flourished, persisting among 'minorities or eccentrics'.[24] Nevertheless, in the 1860s and 1870s artistes were theoretically free to appear as 'turns' for different managers, often acting in three or more halls in each evening. This practice was probably more established and profitable in London, where there were many halls in close proximity to each other. It seems to have been less common in the provinces, where artistes would travel to perform for one manager at a time. Performers were jealously protective of their salary value, conceptualising their worth in terms of refusing to work 'under price' in order to obtain engagements.[25] Thus, the more turns worked, the higher the actual salary the artiste created for himself: and professional self-respect was inextricably linked to the right to be independent to maximise one's own income.

The two most important objectives of these early organisations were to protect the mutual interest of proprietors and artistes, and to defend the professional status of artistes. Proprietors, music hall and theatrical businessmen sat on the Committee of the Music Hall Sick Fund and Provident Society in 1866, and provincial managers participated in the anti-agency agitation of 1872.[26] Reciprocally, artistes lent support to the proprietor's anti-agency society in 1861, to their Defence Fund in 1871 and for copyright prosecutions in 1876. Press sources indicate that these early societies were relatively élitist in leadership and membership. For instance, the MHSF was apparently open to any one of 19 'branches' of professional, but it required a doctor's certificate, two years' experience and a 5s. entry fee to gain membership. Even though this was reduced to 2s.6d. in 1874, the Fund had only 40 members in 1879. The Music Hall Artistes Protection Society and the Cooperative Anti-Agency Union in 1872 were reported to have nearly 1,200 members, but since enrolment depended on personal and word-of-mouth recommendations from Committee members, this figure is questionable.

Respectability was one recurrent aim common to all music hall artistes' societies, particularly in their initial stages of organising in the 1860s. It was often expressed in terms of acquiring a respectful independence by means of providential collective self-help, typically associated with upwardly mobile artisans and skilled workers. The emphasis upon respectability in private life and social life off-stage also mirrored the priorities of the legitimate stage. The MHSF evolved because elderly music hall artistes were excluded from the almshouse benefits of the Dramatic Equestrian and Music Sick Fund Association (1856) even though they contributed to that Fund. Indeed, the playwright Dion Boucicault was among the first to sum up the connection between self-help, respectability and professionalisation, telling Sick Fund members that

> any profession respecting itself, and desiring to be respected by other profes-
> sions in the community takes the first and earliest step . . . to provide that none
> of its members, when in sickness, or subsequently, in age, or their children,
> shall ever fall as a burden on the rest of the community.[27]

Self-help benefits remained central to the aims of all the later societies seeking to attract a wide and general membership. In the 1880s, the Music Hall Artistes Association (MHAA) extended benefits to include legal and insurance costs, although it was left to the MHARA a decade later to bring these into effect.[28] At the core of the trade unionism of the Variety Artistes Federation (VAF) in 1906 were several objectives designed to uphold the performer's independence, 'the very essence of his existence'. To protect the 'position and status' of variety artistes, the VAF instituted a charitable fund, death benefits, legal assistance and pensions, all intended to encourage the 'steady, sober and reliable performer'.[29]

The outbreak of organisational activity in 1872, in London and the northern provinces, was the first attempt by artistes to influence the commercial structure of the business. In so far as this was a political gesture, it was less 'militant trade union activity' than a desire to enhance the status of an artiste as a 'professional man', who, as one activist said, ought to be 'an ornament to society'.[30] There were several probable factors contributing to unrest among performers in the early 1870s. According to *Era Almanack* lists, the number of recognised acts rose from 1,292 in 1870 to 1,416 in 1872. This increase was unmatched by a corresponding growth in halls. In fact, the number of halls listed fell from 416 in 1870, to 219 in 1871 and 248 in 1872. At that time there was no regular seasonal practice of touring the provinces to relieve pressure in the metropolis. However, in so far as *Era* reports the angry tone of Music Hall Artistes Protection Society (MHAPS) meetings, most of the resentment was directed against agents, for their unreasonable rates of commission, and the 'favouritism' operated by London agencies. They also complained bitterly about 'encroachments' upon their 'liberties and salaries' which were reducing them 'below the level of a bricklayer's labourer', because some agents were trying to prevent artistes from transacting business with another agent. They proposed to elect a 'gentleman' to represent their interests, subscribe to a supplementary employment agency, and it was also suggested that a 'loan fund' would enable artistes to build their own concert halls, to bypass agents altogether.

The Shift towards Commercial Paternalism in the Variety Theatre, 1879–1906

The late 1870s may be seen as a watershed period in the music hall business, preceding the conscious development of business-like reform and refinement in the 1880s and 1890s. Managerial paternalism progressively relinquished vestiges of the bohemian camaraderie of exchanging mutual favours, relying more upon specified obligations and accepting that loyalty had to be adequately, and formally, recompensed. To some extent, professionalisation of managerial practices and performer's conduct was stimulated by external pressures. The Metropolitan Building Act 1878 imposed unprecedented fire and safety regulations upon proprietors in London. As this legislation was haphazardly adopted in the provinces the number of pub music halls was drastically cut and the future of the business lay in the hands of the proprietors of 'variety theatres'. Around the same time, professionals began to debate the issue of internal self-reform, and its potential effect upon the profitability of the business. The immediate impetus came from an attack by the Middlesex magistrates upon proprietors in the spring of 1879. The magistrates had complained to the Home Secretary about the moral atmosphere of the music hall, and particularly of the laxity of the police officers who did not prosecute the main offenders, that is, comic singers on stage and prostitutes in the body of the halls. London proprietors reacted by reviving the 1860 Music Hall Protection Society, newly reconstituted as the Entertainments Protection Association. Led by the former theatrical proprietor, Edwin Villiers, they petitioned the Home Secretary, asking for governmental supervision, and making the leading comic singers the scapegoats for the immoral tone of their entertainment. The episode revealed that the profession was ready to change its public image, in the belief that future prosperity lay in proving their respectability and legitimacy, in order to attract what Villiers called a 'better class audience . . . than that which now supports them'. If they were supervised, he argued, 'they would hold a better position in society, their licenses would be more safe, and it would tend to increase their profits'.[31]

The moral panic also exposed the proprietor's determination to reduce their economic and cultural dependence upon star comic singers as the major box-office attractions. The managers' mouthpiece, *Entr'acte* warned that 'comic singers must not put the forebearance of the proprietors to too severe a tension, or possibly, the latter may try to show the world that an attractive music hall entertainment may be framed without the assistance of the comique'. It cannot be entirely coincidental that a few years later *Entr'acte* was noting that continental acts and speciality acts were indeed releasing managers from their reliance upon the comic singers as the main top-of-the-bill attractions.[32] From the point of view of artistes collaborating with proprietors, such expressions of policy against those performers who were still regarded as *de facto* leaders of the profession, inevitably hastened the demise of the mutual interest paternalism of the previous generation. Furthermore, the anger vented against comic singers and 'lions comiques' was not confined to prorietorial circles. As managers gradually withdrew from all except the sociable or charitable societies for artistes, so new spokemen emerged from the performers' own ranks. By 1879 it seems clear that some artistes, possibly only a minority who had not been born into the music hall, identified with the proprietors' aspirations of drawing a higher-class clientele into the variety theatre. This was not just another manifestation of residual paternalism, but rather, the realisation that respectability could be remunerative for their interests, and achieved on their terms. As Charles Coborn, the most cogent exponent of the refined artiste's outlook, wrote:

> it would be more to our credit as a profession if the necessary reforms could be accomplished by ourselves, and not . . . forced upon us from outside. This can never be, however, while those who hold the highest positions amongst us continue to exhibit themselves as models of ignorance and vulgarity.
>   . . . and speaking in more sordid tones, I want to see my salary considerably raised. There are many rich crops awaiting the sickle; why therefore waste valuable time on fields which are every year becoming more unproductive?[33]

However, proprietors and managers took the most visible initiatives to attract a wider and more reputable public. The elements of 'judgement and liberality' described by Bailey of the earlier generation, persisted in the 1880s in the notion of 'liberal catering'. In this period, however, liberal management advocated even greater beautification, visual delight and physical comfort in the refurbishing and rebuilding of the halls. As *Entr'acte* put it, 'as the caterer sows, so shall he reap'.[34] The sheer size and scale of the variety theatres, properly equipped with theatrical apparatus backstage, and regulated seating in the auditorium, revived and reinforced the proprietor's dual commitment to generous expenditure and public service. Consequently, more extensive sources of capital and more rational, efficiency-orientated modes of management were required than in the years of the single proprietor and partnerships. Swift capitalisation began in the 1880s and was facilitated by the amalgamation of managements into mutually protective booking circuits, and also by the formation of public companies, in which the shares of predominantly middle-class investors financed the expansion of variety theatre circuits in London and the provinces. The combined effect of these two trends was towards the institutionalisation of a hierarchical industry, monopolised by a handful of wealthy managements enjoying 'first class' status in the profession. By 1907, for instance, the *Green Room Book* calculated that there was £10 million invested in the variety theatre, approximately 20 per cent of which was represented by the Moss and Stoll combine. By that time, too, the calls listed in the *Performer* showed 123 halls, 74 of which were in one of seven leading circuits, and 34 of these were Moss and Stoll halls. The rush towards creating companies on the Stock Exchange also gained momentum from the mid-1880s onwards, for according to the lists of 35 registered companies given in the *Music Hall* in the mid-1890s, there was one in the 1850s, three in the 1860s, four in the 1870s, eight between 1886 and 1890 ten between 1890 and 1893 and nine between 1894 and 1896.

It was the onset of managerial collaboration and protectionism in booking policies in the mid-1880s which occasioned one of the shortest-lived but significant outbreaks of unrest among artistes. The costs of liberal catering and concern for performance standards encouraged proprietors to insist upon a less casual approach towards the artistes' filling their bills. Gradually 'agreements' and 'engagements' began to be replaced by 'contracts', and by 1882 *Era* observed that 'contract law' had already become central to the 'general interests' of both actors and singers.[35] Contracts quickly became the instrument both for disciplining and expressing ownership of performers, who, understandably, began to perceive proprietors' actions as an 'aggressive policy'. The summer months of 1885 were said to be 'bad times' for performers, with demand lagging behind supply. Proprietors began to combine to hold down salaries and prevent performers working in rival institutions, such as the 'Saturday Pops' concerts in town halls. From the artistes' viewpoint, these were opportunities for them to supplement their music hall salaries, but managers now assumed their right to the legitimate returns on their investments. Although they argued in terms of professional prestige and specialisation, they were actually objecting to artiste's taking audiences away from the halls. As *Entr'acte* put it, 'it seems rather rough on them that singers who have made whatever reputation they have at the music hall should help to take money out of their pockets on the very best night of the week'. Artistes' leaders argued vehemently in *Era* that they were subject to 'dictation or coercion', as proprietors sat in 'conclave' over a 'glass and cigar', considering them as a 'huckster would merchandise', speaking of their '"market price" as a butcher would of cattle'.[36]

Although there was a slight reference to the need for trades unionism, the Music Hall Artistes Association came into existence without a stated policy. This appeared six months later in August 1886, in their *MHAA Gazette*. Despite the radical rhetoric of Coborn and other anonymous writers in the press, the Association sought to promote their own 'social and business interests'. It was said to embody the 'healthy desire for self management', and the *MHAA Gazette* also appealed for more businesslike and professional practices. It was still relatively expensive to join, the entry fee costing 10s. 6d. At its height, the Association only claimed between 500 and 600 members. Although some comic singers acted as figureheads, it seems that the Association's facilities were most valued by new artistes. For instance, an alternative agency was set up, and of the acts which advertised their availability in the *Gazette*, the majority were acts who had joined the profession after 1880, not having been listed in the *Era Almanack* of the 1860s and 1870s. A club was established in Russell Street, London, in order to 'foster friendship and good understanding' with proprietors — a recognition, perhaps of the growing social and commercial gulf between even the stars and the managers. Failing to be floated as a company, however, the whole enterprise collapsed in 1887.

The late 1880s and 1890s were apparently fairly quiescent years within the music hall profession. Attacks on proprietors from the Metropolitan Board and the London County Council contributed towards reviving a sense of mutual interest amongst professionals. The failure of the MHAA and fear of blacklisting discouraged successful and rising 'pros' from political activity. Instead, artistes turned to forming social and charitable clubs and associations. The privatisation of their convivial activity both preserved their sub-cultural habits and facilitated a degree of occupational respectability. Beforehand, artistes used a network of recognised 'pros' pubs', and had no share in the financially and culturally exclusive theatrical clubs like the Garrick or the Savage. But in 1889, two semi-masonic, prestigious societies were formed for established variety artistes. The most exclusive was the Grand Order of Water Rats, for 'good fellows' rather than stars. Their Sunday meetings were a mixture of 'fast and furious fun', interspersed with 'inspiring and dignified' ceremonial. They had their own Vaudeville Club from 1901 onwards; this was, as Fred Russell said, 'more instrumental in raising the status of artistes than using the "local" for meetings'.[37] The Terriers Association was for artistes of lesser rank and less bohemian temperament, with more sedate socialising and a greater concern to involve managers in their activities. Neither were as conventionally respectable as the Music Hall Ladies Guild, the one and only music hall society organised by wives of pros and female artistes. Women had been technically eligible as members of all other societies, but their presence was rarely reported in any significant terms. In the MHLG, by contrast, female pros cultivated a genteel and philanthropic image, helping wives and orphans, gaining the patronage of Their Majesties, and also in building up links with the Actor's Church Union.[38]

The Music Hall Artistes Railway Association was very much the product of the appeasement that characterised professional relations in the 1890s. The MHARA was officially apolitical, concentrating rather upon self-help benefits and rail-travel concessions. It was partly an attempt by music hall pros to follow the lead taken by actors, who, with the help of the *Stage* newspaper, first secured reductions from railway companies for parties of touring theatrical companies.[39] The MHARA was also the first, and possibly only, mass music hall organisation. It was unprecedently cheap, entry costing only 1*s.* in the first year, 5*s.* thereafter. It recruited widely, being open to circus, music hall and variety artistes. Thus, membership increased steadily from 1896, to reach between 6,000 and 7,000 in 1907. This was potentially the most powerful political body ever formed by variety artistes, yet before 1900, the majority of its leaders, typical of contemporary white-collar associations, were moderate and conciliatory almost to the point of obsequiousness.[40] Not only were leading artistes discouraged from antagonising proprietors in the 1890s, but many were actively engaged in proving their identification with managements by purchasing shares in new variety theatre companies. Appendix 5.3 gives a list compiled from the company records at the Public Record Office. There were fewer artistes than managers, but of those who subscribe, it is worth noting that nearly all the names were performers who were also involved in the MHARA and VAF Executive Committee.

With hindsight, the economic climate of the 1890s and early 1900s appears much less healthy than the accumulation of capital and expansion of theatres might suggest. Managerial combinations did not prevent the business from being prey to fluctuations, insecure profitability and 'scandalous liquidations'.[41] This is not the place for a full discussion of the proprietors' financial headaches, but several sources of evidence verify the impression of an unstable, risky business in which profits were increasingly being squeezed after 1900. The lists of companies in the *Green Room* and *Stage Year Book* indicate that dividends were definitely falling in the early 1900s; many companies were short-lived, with only approximately a quarter of those listed in 1896 surviving until 1906. Alfred Butt of the Palace claimed that 'the tendency is for cheaper amusement but the expenses are the whole time on the increase'.[42] His argument is borne out by the salary and takings book of the London Music Hall, Shoreditch. In 1906, salaries cost over £150 on 21 weeks and takings rose over £500 in 12 weeks: but by 1911, salaries cost over £150 on 45 weeks and only seven weeks yielded over £500 takings. Managers conceded that their industry was 'most difficult to manage . . . highly speculative, and . . . exceedingly sensitive'.[43] Because of these conditions, they asked for 'entire freedom of contract for everything' for themselves, seemingly impervious to the way that they were progressively encroaching upon the artistes' contractual liberties. For instance, in order to maximise admissions whilst holding down seat prices, proprietors doubled the number of performances, institutionalising twice nightly schedules and matinees, activating dormant clauses in contracts that demanded these performances 'as required'. Clearly, such a schedule bound the artistes to one house for more hours, hindering their chances of acting a turn elsewhere, but worst of all, performers rarely received extra payments for these 'extra' shows.

The most controversial area of conflict in contractual rights remained the barring clauses, and the proprietor's assumption that they could 'in effect buy the output' of artistes 'for a certain number of years'. All proprietors were inclined to be possessive of artistes in whom they invested, barring 'their' performers from rivals within a certain radius, for specific periods before an engagement. To this extent artistes were victims of managerial competition, but in return for the erosion of their freedom to contract at will they were progressively being offered a higher salary level, and a kind of job security based upon multiple bookings and return engagements. Managers frequently asserted that if barring and advance booking were relinquished, the profession's status would sink again:

> It would be a return to the old days and methods, when a crowd of anxious artistes could be seen at the corner of Waterloo Road waiting for the chance of an engagement . . . the freedom of negotiation, the present high salaries, the permanence of employment now enjoyed by artistes would be a thing of the past.[44]

The exercise of paternalistic authority in the variety theatre was far from homogeneous. In broad terms, the dominant trend among managers was away from the bohemian informality of the music hall generation and towards a more businesslike, impersonal style of relationship based less upon familiarity than upon properly understood contracts. George Adney Payne of the Pavilion, Tivoli, Canterbury and Paragon syndicate is a good example of the former type of music hall 'guv'nor'. On the one hand Payne was an astute businessman, a licensed victualler later trained in accountancy. On the other, he designated himself the 'father of the profession', after the death of 'old Morton'. One of the VAF leaders offered a somewhat different perspective upon Payne's paternalism, perceiving it rather as his patronising 'sit down little boy style'. Instead of insisting upon more rigorous standards of conduct, Payne preferred to acknowledge that his artistes were likely to be unreliable, so he made allowances for their 'tricks', and the temperamental behaviour expected of pros suffering from the professional syndrome of the 'swollen head'. He completely rejected the notion of a trade union or conciliation board intervening in the business. His syndicate issued complicated 'compound exclusive contracts', which were a blend of the 'traditional' turn system, and the newer trend towards exclusivity. They offered performers several turns a night in both his West End and suburban halls, and, as he said himself, he often got into a 'nice difficulty' with their datebooks.[45]

By comparison, Oswald Stoll typified the new breed of forward-looking, provincial manager who valued efficiency more than personal niceties. He had no patience with artistes' protestations regarding the complexity and terminology of their contracts, and he had concluded that 'the more considerate you are the greater fool they think you'. By nature a rather autocratic and intellectual figure, he and Moss built up a provincial circuit into a professional 'hallmark' based upon Stoll's belief that 'it does not pay managers to grind down salaries . . . an intelligent man can earn money in any profession. We do not want to drive intelligent people out of the profession. We want good performances and we pay the necessary amount to get those good performances.'[46] Thus £5 was the Stoll minimum wage, and other proprietors acknowledged that this was becoming the expected 'commencement' pay, replacing the 'older idea' of £2 or £3 a week. In order to maintain the exclusivity and 'freshness' of 'Stoll artistes', he did not pay turn money, but offered various kinds of 'exclusive' contracts at the higher rate normally reserved for engagements in provincial theatres.[47] The introduction of these rates in Stoll's metropolitan halls exacerbated the use of barring clauses, and helped to undercut the remaining single-house proprietors who could no longer afford the artistes who were touring these first-class circuits. Stoll also broke ranks with other proprietors by stopping his booking offices from deducting an extra 2½ per cent commission for agents, a practice which was especially galling for artistes who negotiated their own fees without an agent. It is significant that when variety artistes went on strike, not one of Stoll's halls was affected.[48]

But his standards were not typical throughout the business. As one industrial relations expert observed, the industry grew up 'without mutual understanding between employers as to any common rules suitable for the industry as a whole and without guidance or cohesion on any suitable relations between employers and employed'.[49] After 1900 some artistes began to acknowledge that these conditions were unnecessarily intolerable. The MHARA Sub-Committee on Contracts became the base for a Progressive party led by Frank Gerald to politicise a minority of the organisation. Convinced that contract reform was essential, they concluded that it was foolish to 'limit the usefulness' of the MHARA any longer to merely seeking concessionary measures.[50]

The Variety Artistes Federation and the Music Hall Strike

The Variety Artistes Federation was conceived, according to its official organ, the *Performer*, with a mission to 'abolish or at least to alleviate' commercial injustices. Around the turn of the century it became acceptable to discuss the potential role of trade unionism in the music hall business, recognising from experience that no other form of organisation could reasonably aspire to protect the economic interests of the average performer. No other method of action could confront the exploitative paternalism of the variety syndicates. There were no other channels for formal negotiations between proprietors and artistes: the MHARA was unsuitable as it was feared that rail concessions would be threatened if the Association became identified with any form of trade unionism.

There was a consensus in the trade press that performers' leaders turned to trade unionism because of the malfunctioning of the barring clause. As the *Stage* enthused, they were 'addressing themselves to the task of moulding their profession on sound and beneficial lines'.[51] Between 1903 and 1906 at least three schemes for structural and contractual reform were put before the MHARA, amounting to bids for personal power by Messrs Gerald, Gray and Coborn.[52] However, the mood within the music hall was against one individual holding a personal charismatic and political influence akin to that of Sir Henry Irving over actors. In the event, the formation of the VAF owed much to the interaction of convivial and political activity among artistes. A group of Water Rats (Russell, Pink, O'Gorman and Clemart) manoeuvred a take-over of the MHARA in 1905, and invited representatives from the Rats, Terriers, MHARA and International Artistes Lodge to combine in a Federation to protect the interest of all variety performers.[53]

The VAF has been cast in rather too radical a mould largely because the infamous music hall strike broke out in London within a year of its formation.[54] The Entertainments Protection Association and the most powerful managements refused to acknowledge the Federation, its Charter of grievances, and proposals for contract reform. The stalemate could only be broken by radical measures, but the conduct of the strike and the militancy of its propaganda were not typical of the predominantly moderate ideology of the union. From December 1906 until the spring of 1907 the union's affairs were largely directed by the sketch actors Frank Gerald, General Secretary of the VAF, and his close friend Harry Mountford, a member of the International Artistes Lodge. Both were educated, persuasive speakers, and passionately committed to socialist ideas.[55] It was they who drafted in the aid of Ben Tillett, Labour MPs and Trades Council members. They used the language of battle on behalf of the exploited workers of the variety business, and were frustrated to find that some artistes misunderstood their attack on the system as a personal attack on individual proprietors.

The dispute erupted in December 1906, when Walter Gibbons, son-in-law and business partner of George Adney Payne, was refused the renewal of one of his Brixton theatre licences by the London County Council. Under normal circumstances, artistes would have obliged by transferring to another of his halls. When Gibbons proposed such a transfer, to a hall a mere 500 yards away, Gerald and Mountford seized the opportunity to call the companies out on strike, without a proper quorum of the VAF Executive. Gibbons was disliked by the VAF because of his peremptory attitude towards them, and his refusal to change his contracts from turn money and inclusive matinees. By mid-December it seemed as if Gibbons and Payne had capitulated to the artistes and Brixton Trades and Labour Council pickets, when they hosted artistes to a cordial lunch, promising new agreements. These were not forthcoming, and in January 1907 the VAF joined the National Alliance, with the more ebullient and left-wing Amalgamated Musicians Union and National Association of Theatrical Employees.

The VAF consistently adhered to its six-point Charter for reform, which called for: first, no matinees without payment at any hall worked on the two-houses-a-night system; second, no transfer of any artiste without his consent; third, no altering the times of his act without his consent; fourth, no deductions of commission or agent's fees by managers; fifth, barring to be limited (rather than abolished) to appearing at any hall within a mile of the one in which an artiste is engaged, and not to be for more than three months either side of that engagement; and sixth, the establishment of a board of conciliation. Additional demands from the Alliance included minimum wages for musicians and stagehands, and not a closed shop. However, both the Charter and its officials were treated with contempt by the EPA, and a total of 22 halls in London were rapidly affected by the strike for just over three weeks. Eventually, in mid-February, the strike petered out with the establishment of a board of conciliation for all parties. By the summer of 1907 the *Performer* was relievedly proclaiming that 'moderation' had supplanted 'aggression' in the VAF. Gerald was voted out of his secretaryship, moving on to form the Actor's Union in 1908, and Mountford diplomatically disappeared to America until 1911.[56]

More typical of the long-term ideology of the VAF were the aspirations and attitudes aired by its other leaders who came from the Water Rats, wrote in the *Performer* in a very different vein, and gave evidence at the 1907 Arbitration. The voice of moderation in the *Performer* claimed that they were 'not actually to compel but to ask boldly for terms', like a 'big "watchdog"'.

Initially registered as a friendly society, the VAF acquired trade-union status only on the eve of the strike.[57] Ironically, its first chairman, Joe O'Gorman, was adamant that 'theirs was a business to which trade union principles did not apply'.[58] Like many artistes he acted in a semi-managerial capacity himself, running the Grand Order of Water Rats Agency, for which position he eventually had to resign his chair. Although he spoke at National Alliance meetings, his words revealed an entrenched loyalty towards proprietors, underlying the sense of grievance that artistes deserved more gentlemanly treatment. The reluctance of artistes to commit themselves to the union is reflected in the relatively low level of membership. Unlike the IAL, which was only open to acts on £6 or more a week, the VAF only asked for six months' experience; in 1910 it allowed sketch proprietors, actors and actresses to be eligible. But even so, membership fell after the heady, emotional fervour of the strike had dispelled, and remained consistently behind that of the MHARA.

The VAF was at the height of its power in the variety theatre during the years following the strike, their 'emancipation period', as Fred Russell termed it.[59] Yet the VAF remained a rather idiosyncratic body, a 'miscellaneous' union loosely attached to the TUC, and with its aims and achievements firmly rooted in music hall customs.[60] Artistes were not like other occupational groups within the manual working class. The gradations of salaries, from around £3 to over £100 a week, meant that even many less established acts fell within the contemporary lower-middle-class pay bracket; middle-rank acts on £10–£40 a week were possibly within the upper-middle-class income bracket; and stars were on a par with Edwardian barristers and Cabinet ministers.[61] Most of the union's concern, therefore, related to questions of status, contractual and social, rather than salary levels. As Clemart told the Arbitrator in 1907: 'The artiste is of equal importance to a manager as he is to us . . . I object to the word 'employer'. I am a party to a contract.'[62] Indirectly, though, in seeking release from restrictions to their freedom of contract, the VAF leaders were acknowledging that all salaries, however relative, were the way an artist's value and position on the bill were represented, particularly if they relied on exclusives as their income: and they had a keen sense of the way their act could depreciate if they did not tour regularly enough.[63]

The VAF had little bargaining power of its own inside the variety business. It did, however, benefit tremendously from the publicity received by the strike, which was called in the midst of years of wider industrial unrest and labour stoppages. The union owed even more to the consequent appointment of George R. Askwith, who was chosen by the profession to arbitrate in their dispute, even though he knew nothing about the music hall business before the hearings. Askwith's award of 1907 was the first of three such awards before 1920, which moved steadily towards the standardisation of contracts and conditions, bringing variety performers more in line with 'ordinary forms of commercial contract'.[64] There is as yet little evidence to suggest that performers in general were identifying with the labour unrest of the Edwardian era, although several of the VAF activists were clearly try-ing to inculcate the discipline of union democracy among pros in the sum-mer of 1906. However, their ambitious policy of holding weekly provincial meetings, both to disseminate information and gather responses, did not last; neither did the language of brotherhood. By the time of the National Insurance Act, performers were certainly not associated with manual labour, being classified instead as 'high contracting parties'.

It is instructive to compare 'typical' contracts of the 1890s with those of 1907 and after. Clauses relating to safety and discipline inside halls changed little: illness was treated more leniently, but intoxication became cause for dismissal, with the full support of the VAF. The significant concessions sec-ured by the VAF concerned the issues raised in their Charter, and they were moderately successful in securing limitations upon the most unpopular of the innovations imposed by the syndicates. Thus, matinees were to be paid separately; there was a small relaxation in barring clauses; and artistes' con-sent was required in transference cases. Genuine freedom of contract was still only enjoyed by the class of artiste fortunate to have the security of exc-lusive contracts, which were recognised as a 'new "custom"' after 1907, upheld by 'lucrative inducements'. Significantly, when a Standard Contract was finally acceded to in 1919, the VAF's industrial muscle was by then neg-ligible.[65]

Intervention by an independent arbitrator and the trade-union move-ment set a precedent in the music hall business. The VAF appealed to the General Federation of Trade Unions again in 1909, and went to arbitration to prove the principle that agents were 'to represent artistes more than they do managers'. Again, a tolerable victory was secured for 'industrial free-dom', as Clemart saw it, over such issues as commission rates, return engage-ments, and the right to trade both as an agent and as an artiste.[66] On its own, however, the VAF could not enforce the awards, for they did not encompass uniform or obligatory clauses, but carried only a moral and advisory author-ity which was not easily exercised against dishonourable managements. In addition, the VAF was bound over not to strike again, but to refer disputes to quinquennial arbitrations. Consequently, for individual artistes, the most effective source of authority in professional matters remained the law courts. Litigation was the most traditional mode of resolving problems, and one which allowed for a great deal of free publicity when artistes exhibited their extrovert and cheeky behaviour in the dock and the courtroom. Press reports over the years suggest that the public relished the spectacle of the music hall stage personae confronting the law in the flesh, as it were, and both the MHARA and the VAF faced hundreds of applications for legal assistance. On a more serious note, since artistes were not included in legisla-tion for 'Masters' and 'Workmen', the Awards at least offered guidance to judges regarding alleged old and new customs of the stage.[67]

In conclusion, I have suggested that the peculiarly sporadic history of artistes' collective activity owed much to their loyalty to and dependence upon the paternalistic managers with whom they sought to do business as equal contracting parties. As managers became caught up in corporate commercial policies from the 1880s onwards, and progressively moved towards purchasing and possessing their artistes for longer periods, so the professional aspirations coveted by performers could no longer be fulfilled by self-help organisations. By the turn of the century, many of the leading variety artistes entered the profession from middle- or lower-middle-class backgrounds, with more conventional bourgeois expectations of secure status and enviable salaries. As the *Performer* warned in 1907, managers should not 'under-estimate the brains, schooling, general information or business capacity of performers'.[68] Their eventual politicisation bears resemblance to the industrial action of contemporary white-collar associations; for instance in their search for conciliatory relations with employers, their concern for their social and occupational status, and the adoption of trade unionism as a belated reaction to bureaucratisation or career blocks in the work-place. Variety artistes only resorted to moderate unionism when the TUC had gained respectability itself. Moreover, when they did so, it was to protect their traditional aspirations for self-employed status and freedom of contract.

Notes

(Place of publication is London unless stated otherwise.)

1. The quotation is taken from *Performer*, 21 February 1907. Much of this paper is based upon detailed reading of the music hall press and other primary sources in libraries or in private possession. The diffuse and numerous nature of these sources makes total referencing impractical, although I have tried to acknowledge as many as possible. Many people helped and encouraged me in this research, and I owe a particular debt to Gill Sutherland for her supervisory support.
2. *Stage*, 14 December 1905.
3. *Minutes of Proceedings of an Arbitration in regard to the Music Hall Dispute 1907* (hereafter *Arb. 1907*) pp. 397, 366, Counsel for the VAF speaking. I am deeply grateful to Peter Honri for sharing source material, and for discussions about the growth of the early VAF.
4. For this interpretation see P. Summerfield, 'The Effingham Arms and the Empire: Working Class Culture and the Evolution of Music Hall' in S. and E. Yeo, *Popular Culture and Class Conflict 1590–1914*, Hassocks, 1981, p. 226; M. Chanan, *The Dream That Kicks: The Prehistory and Early Years of Cinema in Britain*, 1981, pp. 155–70; J. Macleod, *The Actor's Right to Act*, 1981, pp. 91–3.
5. Billy Merson, *Fixing the Stoof Oop*, 1926, p. 93. For occupational sub-cultures and the modern entertainments industry, see D. Hebdige, *Subculture, The Meaning of Style*, 1979, pp. 73–92; T. Burns, 'Leisure in Industrial Society' and S. Parker, 'The Economics of Leisure' in M. A. Smith, S. Parker and C. S. Smith (eds), *Leisure and Society in Britain*, 1973, pp. 40–55, 189–98; S. Frith, *Sound Effects*, 1983, pp. 61–88.
6. C. D. Stuart and A. J. Park, *The Variety Stage*, 1895, p. 155.
7. *Performer*, 9 August 1906.

8. Sources include J. Parker (ed.), *Who's Who in Variety*, 1916; *Music Hall Magazine*, 1978–; *Era* obituaries and artistes' autobiographies; and R. Busby, *Who's Who in British Music Hall*, 1976.

9. *St James Gazette*, 21 April 1892.

10. See, for example, Tozer's evidence to the Joint Select Committee on Stage Plays (Censorship), *Parliamantary Papers*, 1909 (303) VIII, qq. 4881, 4940.

11. D. Hole, *The Church and the Stage, the Early History of the Actor's Church Union*, 1934, p. 96; Stoll to S. C. Stage Plays, q. 4985.

12. I am indebted to Mr J. Neptune of the North Eastern Music Hall Society for sharing his copies of *Magic* and experience as a society entertainer, also to Joe Ging and Brenda Bagnall for all their help.

13. *Entr'acte*, 12 December 1885.

14. *Music Hall and Theatre Review* (*MHTR*), 11 October 1901; *Era*, 12 October 1901; H. Blake, 'The Birth of the MHARA', *Trap*, 1939, in Grand Order of Water Rats (GOWR) Museum. My thanks to Mr A. Crooks for allowing me to use the collection at the Eccentric Club.

15. *MHTR*, 20 February 1897.

16. *Performer*, 25 September 1919. For information on salaries, I am indebted to the *Salaries and Takings Book* of the London Music Hall, Shoreditch, held at the GOWR Museum, and to *Arb. 1907* comments.

17. G. Gray, *Vagaries of a Vagabond*, 1930. On Gerald, I am very grateful to Mrs B. Walsh of Oxford for details of her father's career: *Performer*, 5 January 1911.

18. See P. Bailey, Chapter 2, this volume.

19. W. J. Goode, 'The Theoretical Limits of Professionalisation' in A. Etzioni (ed.), *The Semi-Professions and Their Organisations: Teachers Nurses and Social Workers*, New York, 1969, pp. 226–7.

20. See letters in *Era*, 24 March – 7 April 1867; T. E. Dunville, *Autobiography of an Eccentric Comedian*, 1912, p. 62; and *Performer*, 1 May 1919, on the evils of 'prossing' and 'tipping' over the decades; and Harry Randall, *Old Time Comedian*, 1931, p. 160; G. Mozart, *Mary Ann*, 1920, p. 161; and Dunville, *Autobiography*, p. 34, on forms of casual begging.

21. E. Friedson, *The Profession of Medicine, A Study of the Sociology of Applied Knowledge*, New York, 1970, p. 76.

22. *Era*, 26 August 1866.

23. M. Baker, *The Rise of the Victorian Actor*, 1978; M. Sanderson, *From Irving to Olivier, A Social History of the Acting Profession in England 1880–1983*, 1984, Chapters 1–7.

24. P. S. Atiyah, *The Rise and Fall of Freedom of Contract*, Oxford, 1979, p. 263.

25. *Era*, 1 September 1872, Harry Hemphrey is accused of working for £7 instead of £7.10s.

26. *Era Almanack Advertisers* 1866, 1868; *Era*, 25 August, 27 October 1872; 16 July 1871; 26 March 1876.

27. G. Crossick, *An Artisan Elite in Victorian Society, Kentish London 1840–80*, 1978, pp. 134–64; *Era*, 24 March 1867.

28. *Era*, 26 September 1885, 29 October 1898.

29. *Performer*, 6 September, 15 November 1906.

30. P. Bailey, 'Custom, Capital and Culture in the Victorian Music Hall' in R. Storch (ed.), *Popular Culture and Custom in Nineteenth Century England*, 1982, p. 190; *Era*, 25 August, 1 September 1872.

31. See PRO, HO45/9575/80993; *Era*, 26 January, 23 March–27 April 1879; *Entr'acte*, 1 February, 15 February–26 April 1879.

32. *Entr'acte*, 29 March 1879; 22 September 1883.

33. *Era*, 7 October 1877, 13 April 1879.

34. *Entr'acte*, 2 and 23 January 1886, on Riley of the Cambridge. See also Bailey, Chapter 2, this volume.

35. *Era*, 29 July 1882.

36. *Entr'acte*, 11 July, 5 September 1885; *Era*, 12 September–17 October 1885; Charles Coborn, *The Man Who Broke the Bank at Monte Carlo*, 1928, pp. 119–20.

37. Fred Russell, *The History of the Grand Order of Water Rats*, privately published, 1947; Bud Flanagan, *My Crazy Life*, 1961, pp. 133–4; see also Gray, *Vagaries*, p. 163, where he disapproves of such behaviour on Sundays amongst these 'rough diamonds'.

38. Hole, *Actor's Church Union*, pp. 94–5.

39. *MHTR*, 20 February 1897; Blake, 'Birth of the MHARA'.

40. G. Crossick (ed.), *The Emergence of the Lower Middle Class 1870–1914*, 1977; D. Lockwood, *The Blackcoated Worker, a Study in Class Consciousness*, 1958; H. A. Clegg, A. Fox, A. F. Thompson, *History of British Trade Unionism, Vol. 1, 1889–1910*, Oxford, 1964, pp. 223–9.

41. H. G. Hibbert, *Fifty Years of a Londoner's Life*, 1916, p. 40; *Stage Year Book*, 1918, p. 46.

42. *Arb. 1907*, p. 929.

43. Ibid., p. 615, Walter Payne, Counsel for EPA.

44. Ibid., pp. 749, 786, Henry Tozer speaking.

45. 'We Can Do Our Own Arithmetic', *Performer*, 19 September 1907; *Arb. 1907*, pp. 790–804, Payne's evidence.

46. *Arb. 1907*, p. 723.

47. Ibid., p. 639. Others agree — see Tozer, p. 783, Gros, p. 825; on Stoll's contracts, see p. 623.

48. For Pink on artistes' gratitude to Stoll, see ibid., p. 578; but see J. Crump, Chapter 3, this volume, for a later professional dispute with Stoll.

49. G. R. Askwith, *Industrial Problems and Disputes*, 1920, p. 104.

50. *Era*, 26 September 1903.

51. *Performer*, 5 April 1906; *Stage*, 15 March 1906.

52. On Gerald's initiative and rejection, see *Era*, 26 September, 31 October, 21 November 1903; on Gray's Scheme, see Gray, *Vagaries*, p. 196, and *Era*, 17 March 1906; on Coborn's scheme, see *Era*, 31 October 1903, in *Performer*, 24 and 31 May 1906, he is rejected.

53. Russell, *History of the GOWR*; 'The VAF 1906–27', *Performer*, 16 February 1927.

54. Summerfield, 'Effingham Arms', pp. 225–6; Chanan, *Dream*, pp. 169–70.

55. Sanderson, *From Irving to Olivier*, pp. 100–6, on socialist actors.

56. *Performer*, 4 July 1907; Macleod, *Actor's Right*, p. 93; *Era*, 29 July 1911.

57. *Performer*, 19 April, 20 June 1907; *Performer Annual*, 1907, pp. 18–19.

58. *Times*, 11 January 1909.

59. Russell, *History of GOWR*.

60. The VAF disaffiliated from the GFTU in 1910; see *Performer*, 12 September 1907, for VAF's view of TUC, and implied inferiority of dialect-speaking workers there.

61. 'Family Budgets', *Cornhill Magazine*, January–June 1901; 'Why Dividends Are Falling', *Daily Mail*, 23 January 1907.

62. *Arb. 1907*, q. 4478, Clemart speaking.

63. Ibid., p. 585, Pink says that the salary is the 'only thing'; Ted Ray, *Raising The*

Laughs, 1952, p. 89; on depreciation through unfamiliarity, see *Arb. 1907*, pp. 404, 514.

64. Russell, *Performer Handbook*, 1921, p . 43.

65. *Select Committee on Theatres and Places of Entertainment*, HC 1892 (240) XVIII, app. 4; 'What Did We Get?' *Performer*, 20 June 1907; on the 1913 award see *Performer*, 29 May 1913 and 29 January 1914; on the Standard Contract, which defined 'exclusive' as the manager barring for a 10-mile radius in return for 20 weeks work a year, at a minimum salary of £40 a week, see *Performer Handbook*, 1921, p. 43.

66. On the agent's dispute, see *Performer*, 5 April, 28 June and 30 August 1906; *Times*, 11 January 1909; *Stage Year Book*, 1910, pp. 33–4; *Performer*, 20 January 1910.

67. Askwith, *Industrial Problems*, p. 104; S. G. Isaacs, *The Law Relating to Theatres, Music Halls, and other Places of Public Entertainment and to the Performers therein*, 1927.

68. *Performer*, 21 February 1907.

Appendix 5.1. 'Professional' societies in the music hall business 1860–1910.

Political Associations — Managers	Managers & Artistes	Artistes	Sociable and Charitable Associations — Managers and Artistes	Artistes
1860 Music Hall Protection Society	1861 Proprietors and Professionals Mutual Anti-Agency Society			
	1866 Music Hall Sick Fund and Provident Society			
	1871 Music Hall Defence Fund			1872 Music Hall Artistes Cricket and Recreation Club
	1872 Music Hall Artistes Protection Society (London) and Music Hall Cooperative and Anti-Agency Society (Provinces)			
1879 Music Hall Protection Association renamed Entertainments Protection Association				
		1885 Music Hall Artistes Association	1888 Music Hall Benevolent Fund	1889 Grand Order of Water Rats and Terriers Association
		1889 Sketch Artistes Association		
		1896 Music Hall Artistes Railway Rates Association		
		1901 International Artistes Lodge		
		1906 Variety Artistes Federation		1906 Music Hall Ladies Guild
1906–7 Variety Agents Association				1907 Variety Artistes Benevolent Fund

Appendix 5.2. Composition of the music hall and variety profession 1868–99

Comedy acts	1868	1878	1899
Comic singers/comedians	170 (20%)	328 (17%)	303 (20%)
Serio comics/comediennes	117	384	267
Negro delineators	100	143	13
Comic duos	75	232	93
Pantomimists	23	39	13
Irish comics	12	43	(not specified)
Comic trios	8	51	20
Sketch troupes	–	–	50
Grotesques/eccentrics	–	–	35
Male impersonators	–	–	7
Entertainer/concert party	–	–	5
Female impersonators	–	–	2
	505 (59%)	1220 (64%)	808 (54%)
Vocal and musical acts			
Sentimental singers	170 (20%)	251 (13%)	–
Duettists	–	–	51
Instrumentalists	–	–	44
Vocalists — female	–	–	44
Vocalists male/mixed	–	–	30 (8% exc. instrumentalists)
Specialitys'/miscellaneous acts			
Wizards/ventriloquists	16	52	–
Ventriloquists	–	–	20
Jugglers	14	38	33
Dog and monkey acts	6	17	–
'Speciality/miscellaneous	–	30	146
Velocipedista/skaters	–	36	–
Animal acts	–	–	36
Continental acts	–	–	28
Child acts	–	–	14
Illusionists	–	–	11
Marionettes	–	–	5
Pictures/cinematograph	–	–	5
Quick change	– (4%)	– (9%)	4 (20%)
Acrobatic acts			
Gymnasts	108	147	123
Dancers	43	105	38
Cyclists	–	–	19
Comic acrobats	–	–	18
Strong/boxing acts	–	–	9
	862	1896	1486

Sources: Era Almanack 1868–78, and A. Voyce (ed.), *Music Hall Directory and Variety ABC,* 1899 (the lists are of acts not individuals).

Appendix 5.3. Music hall and variety artistes with shares in variety theatre

1864 Oxford and Canterbury
Arthur Lloyd   6 shares @ £15

1887 Metropolitan
F. W. Curtis   10 shares @ £5

1887 Canterbury and Paragon
G. H. Chirgwin   10 shares @ £5

Canterbury and Paragon
Michael Nolan   5 shares @ £5

1893 Olympic
Charles Coburn   20 shares @ £1
  + 1 founder share   @ £20
Harry Liston   20 shares @ £1

1893 South London Palace
Harry Freeman   200 shares @ £1
Harry Randall   150   ”   ”
Albert Chevalier   100   ”   ”

1895 Cardiff Newport and Swansea Empire Palaces Ltd.
Arthur Roberts   40 shares @ £5

1896 Croydon National Palace of Varieties
Daniel Leno   567 shares @ £1
Harry Randall   566   ”   ”
Herbert Campbell   500   ”   ”
F. William   332   ”   ”
Harry Bawn   110   ”   ”
E. J. Brown   90   ”   ”
Paul Cinquevelli   50   ”   ”
Billie Barlow   50   ”   ”

1896 Croydon Palace cont.
F. W. Millis   25 shares @ £1
F. Fordham   15   ”   ”
J. Graham   15   ”   ”
Walter Cole   10   ”   ”
George Newham   5   ”   ”
Fred Latimer   5   ”   ”
(This company was atypical in that Leno, Randall and Campbell were directors and managers, too)

1896 Grand Theatre, Islington
Harry Randall   500 shares @ £1

1897 Metropolitan Syndicate
Paul Martinetti   40 shares @ £5

1902 Coliseum Ltd.
George Lashwood   400 shares @ £5
Arthur Lennard   200   ”   ”
Marie Loftus   120   ”   ”
Fred Karno   100   ”   ”
Arthur Roberts   100   ”   ”
Ernest A. Elen   50   ”   ”
Eugene Stratton   50   ”   ”
Ernest Shand   20   ”   ”

1903 Cambridge Variety Theatre
G. H. Chirgwin   110 shares @ £1

Source: Public Records Office, Board of Trade files, BT31. Virtually all these artistes were 'comedians' or 'comic artists' or ventriloquists.

6 'It was not what she said but the way in which she said it': The London County Council and the Music Halls[1]

SUSAN PENNYBACKER*

In 1902, George Sims enumerated the successes of the London County Council's music hall policy:

> Who has brought that family public to the music hall? The County Council. What is it that attracted the father, mother, cousin, sister, and aunt? It is because we have said music halls and theatres should be so decently-conducted, and that they should be so proper for the public, profitable for the employer, because we dare to be Daniels, we dare to repress vulgarity — and to check indecency, and will not allow the music hall to resemble the ante-chamber to a brothel, or the annexe to a vulgar public-house.[2]

By the time that the LCC assumed control of the administrative county of London under the 1888 Local Government Act, the London music hall had become the foremost institution of popular culture in the metropolis; there were 14 million annual visits paid to 35 of the halls alone in the early 1890s.[3] Sims attributed the growth of the London audience to the work of the LCC, suggesting that an improved moral tone added to the prestige and respectability of the halls. This essay investigates the practical workings of LCC policy and considers the purposes and motivations lying behind that policy.

We can gain greater clarity with regard to the history of the halls in London if that history is linked to the aims and practices of the London Progressives who controlled the LCC until the victory of the conservative Municipal Reform Party in 1907.[4] The Progressives were a group of councillors

* I wish to acknowledge the support of the National Endowment of the Humanities Summer Stipend Program, 1985, and of Naomi Amos and Borden Painter of Trinity College, Hartford. I thank Peter Bailey, McKim Steele and Martha Kelly for their assistance in the preparation of this piece. All LCC archival sources are held in the Greater London Record Office.

representing Gladstonian, New Liberal, Fabian, and trade-union interests; their cultural policies in part reflected the attitude toward music hall taken by politicians who were branded with the label 'municipal socialist'. This was a regime committed to a grand political strategy of municipalisation, taken up in the name of the people of London as a whole. It attempted to purify and restrain the tone of music hall performance as well as to regulate and govern the erection of new hall structures and the repair of the older halls.

Though the Conservatives were to continue many policies begun by the Progessive administrations, the history of the reform of London music halls properly belongs to the halcyon days of Progressive rule when many thought that a form of socialism would evolve through successive Progressive electoral victories at the municipal level and the affirmation of collectivist strategies at a parliamentary level. Socialists and Labourites like John Benn, John Burns, Sidney Webb, Susan Lawrence, and Ben Tillett all contributed to the common Progressive platform. But their Liberal colleagues made up the bulk of the Progressive Party leadership and membership in the Council; they resented the label of 'municipal socialist', most often thrust upon the LCC by its opponents.

The Liberal influence within Progressivism frequently combined with the Labour and socialist members' willingness to contemplate a gradual evolutionary transition to a socialised economy to result in a policy of wooing the 'responsible capitalist property-owner' to the Progressive party. This policy was evident in the LCC strategy for the music halls. Guided by the civic vision of a metropolis whose government would be free from the corruption and class legislation of the nineteenth century, the Progressive LCC sought to utilise the music halls in their endeavours. They wished to neutralise some sections of capital, win a larger electoral following, and begin to create a municipal sector of the economy, through direct and indirect control of London's property markets and her social institutions. This is the setting in which the elaboration of LCC music hall policy occurred.

Historians Edward Bristow and Penny Summerfield closely examined some aspects of LCC policy toward the London halls.[5] Bristow concluded that 'anti-obscenity forces gained strength before the war' while noting that LCC hall licences 'were virtually never revoked for indecency'.[6] Instead, he argued, the Council pressured the proprietors to effect self-censorship.[7] Summerfield asserted that the state selected 'from the cultural stock generated by the working class',[8] forcing an outcome in which 'the theatres of variety allowed little scope for alternative views to the Establishment conservative one'.

Alongside this notion of the triumph of a conservative and moralistic tone in the music hall exists the imagery of the halls inspired by the work of Gareth Stedman Jones and Peter Bailey.[9] Stedman Jones sought to explain a London working-class 'culture of consolation' with reference to the subjective concerns of music hall lyrics and the structural constraints imposed upon popular culture by London's workaday world.[10] He has explicitly rejected the assumption of the historic 'diversion of subversive or disruptive aims by ideological-cum-economistic means' guiding studies of the social control of leisure.[11] Bailey cautioned: 'for much of the Victorian period, consumer power in the halls was assertive and effective, and greatly complicated strategies of proprietorial control and artistic embourgeoisement'.[12]

There exists a marked tension in the literature between a tendency to assert the definitive power of the local state, in this case, the LCC, and the proprietors in regulating and reconstructing the life of the halls *and* a desire to maintain a theoretical posture allowing for working-class independence, for the existence of a cultural form which the state did not find to be entirely penetrable. An examination of what the LCC policy on the halls was and how it worked in practice can assist in identifying the origins of the various interpretations offered by historians, allowing us to bring a political perspective – the perspective offered by late Victorian and Edwardian Progressivism – to the more common social-historical portrayal of the halls.

The election of a Progressive majority to the leadership of the newly-founded Council heralded a period of great experimentation in municipal ownership and intervention in London. The LCC was the largest municipal authority in the world for its time and the Progressive party campaigned for the public control of various London utilities. The tramways, Thames steamboats, housing estates, the parks and open spaces, the asylums, the Fire Brigade and eventually even the School Board were in LCC hands. Debate over the extent of municipalisation and the degree to which the LCC ought to confront propertied interests created a profound tension among the local politicians and aspiring parliamentarians in the diverse Progressive camp. When the LCC began to operate its own construction department in London's building industry, for example (the LCC Works Department), a complicated political battle over this assault on propertied interests in the London building industry ensued. Some LCC councillors, conservatives and Progressives alike, could only support such an effort if it was able to remain 'profitable', judged by the standards of the largest private building firms. This large 'direct labour' enterprise helped to shove small jerrybuilders out of the industry, while the larger firms remained competitive especially since they paid trade-union wages, as did the LCC Works Department.[13]

In challenging the small and more vulnerable builder, while failing to municipalise the building industry as a whole, the Progressive policy had the effect of forging a kind of *rapprochement* with the most benevolent capitalist employers, those able to pay higher wages in part because of the fact that they benefited from economies of scale. Such a policy was pursued with regard to the music halls in so far as the LCC brought the larger proprietors into a new mode of licensing and regulation. But not all Progressive politicians wished to forge a middle course. Those who suggested a more militant intervention in the London economy were a minority and a source of great friction for the coalition; most Progressives were wary of any tampering with the private sector in areas not clearly linked with public utilities. Projects like the Works Department had no support amongst Council conservatives; when the Municipal Reform party came to power in 1907, they closed down the Works Department, eliminating several thousand jobs for contracted building workers.

Each successive pillar of Progressive policy, the music hall policy included, necessitated a delicate balancing of interests. In the case of the halls, proprietors, electors as members of the hall audiences, performers (who were themselves unionising), the leaders of the Conservative opposition and the Liberal party parliamentary majority all had to be reckoned with. Far from establishing the cultural hegemony of the local state, Progressivism failed its own political test — most pointedly in the disastrous electoral defeat of 1907. After 16 stormy years in office, Progressivism was voted down in the largest poll in London municipal history prior to the post-1945 period. It was not simply the victim of a reinvigorated Conservative electoral machine. Progressivism had attempted to reconcile forms of liberalism with forms of socialism — each articulated in a rhetoric and language that overlapped with the others. London socialists and Liberals sought an alliance in the midst of the pre-war inflation, deteriorating conditions of life for many of London's working-class communities, and the enormous growth of the Edwardian lower middle-class. Taking these political realities into account, the first section of this essay investigates LCC policy aspirations for the period 1889–1914. The second examines the practices of the LCC Theatres and Music Hall Committee, the central licensing authority for the halls.

LCC Attempts to Control the Halls through Legislation and Policy

Under the Local Government Act of 1888 powers previously held by the justices were transferred to the LCC. While the Lord Chamberlain continued to control most of London's theatres and to act as censor of her plays, the task of watching over other forms of entertainment now fell to the LCC.[14] Exhibition halls, sporting facilities, the mass of buildings used by voluntary and religious societies and the music halls were issued annual licences or licences for specific performances. During the early 1890s, the Progressives attempted to widen their powers in order to control fully the licensing of all London entertainment, challenging the office of the Lord Chamberlain in order to acquire similar privileges to the law courts in relation to persons committing offences.[15] From the Municipal Corporations Act of 1882 until the Act of 1888, regulation of the halls focused on new additions to previously existing structures, emphasising safety and the well-being of the public. The Progressives vowed to subject the halls to greater moral scrutiny. They were determined to rid the halls of impropriety, of the ill effects of readily-available alcohol and to free the public from the pernicious influence of lascivious and vulgar performances. As Sims suggested, the halls were to become centres of family entertainment, a policy in harmony with the civic-minded populism that characterised Progressivism generally. The music hall campaign on the part of the LCC received constant attention from press and public. The Council's sheer size, its prominence as the largest licensing body in the country and its political and geographic proximity to national government all contributed to the interest that the music hall policy spawned.

Among those paying close attention to Council manoeuvres were the proponents of free trade in amusements, who championed the right to the unobstructed growth and development of the halls without state interference. London's West End theatre community did not wish to see the Lord Chamberlain replaced by the LCC, and was critical of the Council.[16] The Nonconformist, 'municipal puritan' reputation of the Council suggested to the West End playwrights and performers that the aristocratic indifference of the Lord Chamberlain's office would more readily allow the continued existence of a relatively less-restricted London theatre. Conversely, the membership and supporters of organisations like the National Vigilance Association, some of whose members held posts on the Theatres and Music Halls Committee, depended on the LCC to uphold decency and sobriety.[17] A divided community awaited the onset of new policy.

The most important aspect of LCC policy was the establishment of criteria and procedures for licensing the individual hall. This decision was made by a vote of the entire Council on the recommendation of the Theatres and Music Halls Committee, the body responsible for overseeing inspection, coordinating the visits of Council officials, and for running the licensing sessions that preceded the vote on a particular application in the full Council. This body, like all LCC committees, included representatives of all of the municipal political parties on the Council. Though the Progressives were in power until 1907, the Theatres and Music Hall Committee always included leading Conservatives amongst its members. This helps explain the basic continuities in policy throughout the pre-war period.

Committee members included Sir Thomas George Fardell, MP for South Paddington from 1895 to 1910 and LCC councillor. He chaired the Committee for six years and had been active in municipal affairs in London since the 1870s. Fardell was influential in the calling of the Royal Commission to investigate the Metropolitan Board of Works in 1888, an investigation which led to the passage of the Public Bodies (Corrupt Practices) Act in 1889 and to the creation of the LCC as the successor body to the Board. The hope that the LCC would herald a new age of municipal respectability would have been uppermost in the mind of a conservative reformer like Fardell. He also served as Chairman of the National Union of Conservative Associations, signifying his commitment to the revival of the Conservative electoral machine in the municipal arena.

Spencer Charrington, brewer and Conservative MP for Mile End and Tower Hamlets, also occupied a place on the Committee. Charrington was one of the last remaining "local magnates" of London politics and, like his cousin Frederick, was an outspoken convert to the movement against vice.[18] The Committee could hardly have included a more notable moral zealot or a more powerful representative of London industry.

Liberals like G. W. E. Russell, chairman of the Churchmens' Liberation League and National Vigilance Society, members like George Lidgett and John McDougall (Lidgett's son-in-law) also served. McDougall and Lidgett were prominent opponents of vice in London, associated with the 1889 'social purity' campaign. Edward Bristow's study of that movement notes that Lidgett's sister, Mary Bunting, was also a leading member.[19] Hubert John Greenwood, a solicitor like many members of the Committee, was its chairman for a time and LCC Councillor for St George's Hanover Square from 1901. During the Great War, Greenwood directed the Government Food Committee for London. Like many of his colleagues, he was active in the Territorials and a patron of St George's Hospital, a major social institution of his borough.

The organisational and political commitments of its members marked the Theatres and Music Halls Committee as a pillar of London municipal and social reform — the zeal of a Conservative who had fought the corruption of the MBW was joined with the Nonconformist, teetotal and anti-prostitution forces of the Committee members in the National Vigilance Society. There were disagreements in the Committee and occasions upon which the Council overturned Committee recommendations, but the general tone of the Committee's approach in the early 1890s and the outcome of votes in the Council was most notably influenced by the Progressive vision. While a consensus around the need for reform of the halls existed in both parties, the extent of municipal intervention, not the necessity of it in principle, provided the grounds for greatest 'party-political' friction.

For a hall to receive a favourable Committee recommendation, it had to receive certification from the LCC Architect's Department. A structural inspection by the Department of the Chief Engineer was incorporated into the licensing procedure and licences were renewed only after inspections by the architect's staff twice yearly and intermittent inspections by the engineer's office.[20] Often a group of Committee members visited a building in order to certify that changes required for licensing had been carried out to their satisfaction. Such a meeting involved the owner, lessee or proprietor, the builder, the hall's architect and various Council bureaucrats.[21] The Committee then took testimony from the applicant for a licence at a sessions house hearing. The applicant was permitted to call witnesses on his behalf and to cross-examine witnesses who petitioned to appear against him. Before such a hearing, the Committee deliberated over the application and issued a public recommendation for or against the issuance or renewal of a licence. A second hearing might occur in the LCC chambers at Spring Gardens, if the applicant or his witnesses requested an appearance two weeks before the vote. As of 1891, the LCC only allowed voting rights to those councillors who had been present for the entire hearing of a case, indicative of the amount of controversy and pleading that often occurred before a final decision was made.[22] LCC councillors themselves could speak out in the Council for or against a licence and were often active in championing a particular applicant.

How was it proposed that 'morals' be regulated by these procedures? Two practices seem to have enabled the Committee members and the Council to arrive at a judgement about the 'atmosphere' of a given hall. The police could testify on behalf of an applicant, or offer evidence of misconduct in a hall. They were invited to do so at licensing sessions, and they also volunteered the names of halls in which unlicensed performances were occurring to the Committee. A second mode of investigation of performances initiated by the Committee and widely practised in the 1890s involved the use of a hired inspectorate, engaged solely for the purpose of filing reports on the halls.

At the outset of the Progressive period, the underlying goal of the LCC with regard to theatres and music halls was to control all entertainment licensing in London, and further, to exact revenues from those property-owners who had a hand in the halls and theatres industry.[23] An even wider vision of municipal and state ownership of opera and theatre, of dance halls and concert halls, had a growing constituency in London, inspired by Continental experiments in state ownership.[24] The London Trades Council, representing most of London's trade unions, called repeatedly for the LCC to open a municipal theatre.[25] But as Chris Waters's work (Chapter 7, this volume) demonstrates, state control was a slippery concept. Those supporting it were often politically divided. The consensus on the early LCC was around the move to gain further powers to dignify entertainment, to prevent calamity, and to suppress the rapacious spirit of the propertied. The LCC did not have the political clout necessary to accomplish all of these ends and Parliament proved unwilling to extend LCC powers.

The LCC drafted three parliamentary bills in the period 1890–1, the first 'To Make Better Provision for the Regulation of Theatres in London' and the remaining two to 'Amend and Extend the Law Relating to Theatres, Music Halls, and Places of Public Entertainment or Resort in the Administrative County of London'.[26] But the Parliamentary Select Committee of 1892 saw no reason to transfer the Lord Chamberlain's theatre powers to the Council.[27] The West End theatre community preferred the 'aristocratic embrace' to being at the mercy of those whom they saw as a prudish, prissy collection of local politicians and parliamentary hopefuls on the LCC. Progressive ties to the temperance lobby and the moral purity campaigners suggested to the West End that the Council would limit the few existing theatrical freedoms and that LCC supervision would lower the standards of performance — the Progressives were perceived as intrusive and culturally philistine. As the critic Herbert Tree put it, 'if we have not the advantage of state aid, let us at least be exempt from state suppression'. And with reference to the Progressive intention to ban alcohol in the halls, he added 'The County Council may have reckoned with its publicans, but without its public'. Performers were appalled at the thought of LCC censorship. One proposal called for the Council to license individual persons on the stage, rather than the hall, prompting singer Charles Coburn to condemn what he termed a 'Literary Contagious Diseases Act'.[28]

Many zealots within the Progressive camp wished to ban alcohol entirely from the halls, though they soon discovered that such a step would have been illegal. Licences could not officially be refused on grounds of alcohol consumption alone if the hall had opened before falling under LCC jurisdiction. But legal loopholes did exist. In 1894, the Council ruled that no *new* licences would be issued allowing a proprietor to serve alcohol, a policy to which the largest proprietors and the grandest halls were best able to adapt.[29]They could offer the most elaborate performances at an admission fee that readily compensated for the loss of revenue from alcohol sales.

This decision helped to further a *rapprochement* between the LCC and the most powerful proprietors, as did a new set of rules allowing for sketch performances in the halls.[30] Always implacably hostile to Council initiatives, the largest syndicate tycoons nevertheless easily complied with the alcohol policy at the expense of their lesser colleagues. After effectively banning alcohol in new halls, the LCC again attempted to widen its powers, motivating the proposed legislation with the rhetoric of the broadly-based Liberal–Progressive campaign of the period for the taxation of ground values. The transcript of a special conference held between Asquith, then Secretary of State, and members of the Theatres and Music Hall Committee, in 1894, illustrates the unwillingness of the government to sanction any of the Council's moves.[31] Even more importantly, the Asquith interview shows that, public outcry and resolutions to the contrary, the Committee had failed to utilise the moral censure of performance as a condition for shutting down halls. Instead, the Committee concentrated on the problem of structural alterations. Yet this preoccupation with public safety cloaked the Committee's real intention, as revealed to Asquith, of orchestrating an attack upon London's ground landlords. As they told Asquith, 'the great bone of contention is the structural alterations. What the proprietors resent is the spending of money.'[32] So the councillors had come up with the option of a 'terminable annuity', something which would take the pressure off those proprietors whose liquid assets were regularly threatened by the cost of structural repair. The ground owners, or reversioners, would be required to pay certain costs toward repairs ordered by the Council.[33] Asquith scoffed at the notion — why, he asked, should reversioners or owners take any interest in rehabilitating structures on their properties if a lease was about to end, of if they did not view the existence of a music hall or palace of variety as a particularly sound, or potentially lucrative investment?[34]

The LCC could not put forward another parliamentary bill in the face of Liberal opposition; its withdrawal points to the discrepancy between municipal policy and national government policy. House Liberals clearly resisted undertaking special pleading for legislation meant to antagonise the landlords. (As Avner Offer's work suggests, their venom was reserved for grander efforts like the People's Budget of the next decade.)[35] And, mutually hostile interest groups at both the parliamentary and municipal levels never did come to a coherent strategy of attack on the propertied interest in the capital. In summary, the Council failed to *extend* its control over regulation.

The councillors' naivety was indicative of a more generalised and unwarranted optimism about the possibilities of redistributive mechanisms being instituted by national government. The LCC was left to pursue a moral agenda which had made the Council unpopular in many quarters. This agenda was now bereft of any real connection to a wider political strategy of social change. There was little point in the Council's pushing its critics further, or in antagonising proprietors who were willing to come to terms with a regularised and predictable mode of inspection and licensing. Divested of any ultimate reward at the parliamentary level, the LCC still had to attempt to uphold its commitment to order and decorum in the halls. After all, the Progressives had harnessed their electoral campaigns to such promises.

Inspection and Licensing in Practice

Despite LCC legislative goals the early inspection practices of the Council certainly *appeared* to underline a commitment to moral propriety. The first task of the newly-constituted Theatres and Music Halls Committee was that of reviewing the status of licensing in London generally, in order to close down obviously defective structures, making it difficult for pubs that had surreptitiously slipped into becoming halls to continue to function. In 1890 the Committee was authorised to employ a select group of inspectors; these posts were never advertised since coverage in the press elicited a rash of voluntary applicants. From this pool the Committee drew its original team, whose function seems to have been rapidly superseded by the annual or semi-annual inspections of the Architect's or Engineer's Departments. But at the outset of the Progressive period, this first group of inspectors attracted public attention. The group were occupationally diverse, though all were minimally of lower-middle-class standing — a travelling engineer, a draughtsman from the LCC architect's department, an architect's surveyor, the manager of a stationer's, and several clerks. Some had been in the military, some had worked in public service.[36]

LCC music hall inspectors inhabited a furtive, twilight world. Amidst the gaiety of the halls, they darted from section to section, checking seating provisions, watching suspected prostitutes, scribbling down remarks on lyrics and performers' styles, even contributing drawings to the Committee on their inspection forms. They were asked to go to specifically assigned halls, to sit with a good vantage point on the seating arrangments in the auditorium, to evaluate the management's security measures, the performance and the audience, and never to identify themselves as sent by the LCC. Copies of programmes were submitted to the Committee, along with a completed form recording the inspector's views of the structure, the class composition of the audience, and the nature and tone of the proceedings. Despite their later disclaimer to Asquith, in mid-1890, the sub-committee on inspection had resolved that:

the Inspectors should be instructed to devote their attention chiefly to the nature of the performance, and to the character and conduct of the audience, especially the female portion thereof, rather than to the structured condition and exits of the building; and to frame their reports for the committee accordingly.[37]

This emphasis on observing women was pervasive in the rhetoric of LCC intervention in the halls. Women were the object of attention as prostitutes, as performers, and as the ideal symbols of the new family-centred style being promoted by the Council, but this did not divert the inspectorate from paying close attention to overcrowding and the condition of the halls' structures and facilities.

The initial results of assiduous Committee supervision were predictable: the cost of repairs caused many small houses to relinquish their licences. Singers performed on premises unlicenced for singing; dancing was popular in establishments with 'music only' licences; pubs served as music halls. The Committee directed the proprietors of the new halls to proceed in applying for licences only if the proposals contained the structural features desired by the Committee. The Committee, for example, failed to approve the bars included in the architectural designs of the Metropole. A system of threats and rewards emerged — the proprietors understood what was expected and anticipated these expectations. The alcohol policy of 1894 assisted in institutionalising this system.

Halls were also chosen for inspection on the basis of previously-existing complaints. This strategy became official policy after 1893.[38] In this sense, those Committee members who told Asquith that moral censure had been practiced very little were being truthful. Little attempt was made to patrol those halls for which complaints had not been received, but particularly troublesome or popular halls were still identified by the Committee. And many halls were undoubtedly visited by the police. Eventually, the various organisations, clubs, trade and performers' societies and municipally-minded citizenry formed an alert system for Council inspection and the outward signs of Council vigilance meant that the 'municipal puritan' reputation of the Council was never lived down. Critics of the puritanical tendency, like clergyman and East End councillor Stewart Headlam, emerged within the ranks of Progressivism itself.[39] For these critics, music hall inspection was linked to other LCC social legislation — the Council inspected midwives, regulated behaviour in the parks, stipulated shop hours, licensed employment agencies, and dictated the weights and measures of what Londoners bought and sold.[40] The internal contradictions of LCC policies, the inconsistencies in practice that existed relative to public assumptions about the harshness and censoriousness of judgement, or about the degree of commitment to moral fervour motivating any individual inspector, often remained obscured.

A typical early inspector's report commented on the absence of vice, attributing it to the social origin of the hall's audience. Here are excerpts from the report on Gatti's Palace of Varieties in Charing Cross in 1891:

> I saw no drunkeness . . . in fact most of the drinking was done at the 'bars' (not at the tables and benches). The audience was respectable — there were 'prostitutes' in the hall, but there were none 'soliciting'. In my opinion, this hall is not 'a house of call' or 'place of meeting' for prostitutes and their confederates.[41]

The inspector added, however, that 'in the event of an accident — fire or a panic — this hall would be nothing more or less than a "Death Trap". The audience could not get out and in my opinion, the consequences would be something appalling.'[42] When the proprietors of the hall were told by the Council of complaints about lyrics made by a member of the audience (who felt that the lyrics alluded to sodomy and extra-marital sex), they immediately and predictably removed the offending pieces from the roster. But, by 1908, this hall had been converted for use in cinematography; its structural defects due to its location under one of the arches of Charing Cross station, necessitated the abandonment of live performances.[43]

Unsafe structures and inadequate facilities for performers were the cause of the most habitual complaints of the inspectorate. Conscious of the horrific history of theatre and hall disasters and sensitive to pressure from the increasingly organised trade opposition to poor working conditions in the industry, the Committee found its work dominated by these concerns.[44] Grounds for complaint included inadequate lavatory accommodation, improper attention to external lighting or ventilation, inadequate seating provisions, blockage of exits, and flammable lighting or scenery.[45] But aside from pursuing 'structural considerations' the work of the Committee in the early 1890s did include paying special attention to establishments of particular notoriety. These cases undoubtedly helped to sustain the zealous image of the Progressive Council.

In 1890, for example, the Committee required the continual inspection of the Rose and Crown in St George Street near the Tower. This was a small house with a shady reputation. The inspector noted that Tower Hamlets was one of the poorest districts of East London; there were sailors' lodging houses near the bar. The entertainment of the evening consisted of a 'rough and ready band' of street musicians.[46] There were dancing and drinks for an audience consisting of a majority of foreign sailors and women of ill-repute, all of whom were smoking. He himself was approached by a woman and observed an elderly woman reproaching younger women for arriving unaccompanied, as if to suggest that they ought to engage in more soliciting. Not surprisingly, in this early case involving what was really a glorified pub, the licence was refused. Spencer Charrington, president of the Tower Hamlets Federation for the Suppression of the Drink Traffic, lobbied against the licence.[47]

The association of vice with the poorer districts of London had it counterpart in the inspectorate's praise for halls whose clientele was judged more respectable, or 'mixed' in class terms. The Collins in Islington Green merited

this evaluation in 1890: 'With one or two exceptions, this is a place of entertainment that I would not hesitate to take my wife and family to.'[48] The
inspector's complaints included the fact that toilets were visible and ought to
be more privately located; he suggested that superintendents in all London
halls might require women to be seated at all times in order to improve the
character of the halls. By 1900, an inspector noted of the Collins that with
newly-undertaken construction, 'It is frequented by a better class of people
than most outlying halls'.[49] By 1907, the Islington Trades Council and ILP
were writing to the LCC for permission to use the halls for a programme
including labour hymns sung by a 50-voice Clarion choir. Thus, some halls
cultivated a constituency in the neighbourhoods, allowing societies and trade
organisations to make use of their facilities, a practice stressed in Peter
Bailey's work.[50]

In 1891, the inspectorate commented upon the Canterbury audience's
social composition, in a typical report:

> The audience seemed to consist principally of mechanics and was generally
> rather rough and noisy, whistling, shouting, hissing, and joining in the songs.
> There was, however, no quarrelling or drunkenness. The women were not
> numerous and were of the same class as the men. I saw none that I should con-
> sider to be prostitutes. There were policemen and attendants in every part of
> the house . . . the audience were principally trades people, and their wives,
> working men, lads and girls, and considering the neighbourhood, well-
> behaved. I saw no disorder, and I did not observe any persons whose *behaviour*
> (his emphasis) would mark them as prostitutes, though doubtless among such
> a large audience, there were many loose characters. I went in the fauteuils,
> stalls, pit, promenade, and balcony.[51]

This issue of the class composition of the audience paralleled the preoccupation of both Committee and inspectorate with the content of lyrics and performances. While they did not directly censor lyrics, they could call upon the
management to restrict certain pieces from their programmes; the proprietors increasingly claimed that they were enforcing the Council's standards
themselves. Some halls forbade 'coarse jests and rough language'; these were
'to be particularly avoided'.[52] Others, like the Foresters Hall, specified: 'Any
artiste giving expression to any vulgarity, or words having a double meaning,
when on the stage, will be subject to instant dismissal',[53] forfeiting that week's
salary. The Royal Albert in Victoria Dock Road forbade direct reference to
'political, religious, or local matters'.[54] Many halls refused performers the
right to mention officials of the LCC in satirical asides.

The Canterbury, at one time cited for an instance of prostitution in a
theatre box which had never been proven, drew complaint for songs like
'The Bewitched Curate', in which a woman passed out on stage after her leg
had been stroked by the cleric in question.[55] Another song was deemed
objectionable by a member of the audience 'an old frequenter of twenty-five
years' standing'[56]who wrote to say that he disliked Peggy Prior's song
describing a couple's wedding breakfast; his objections were more serious

than those of the inspector. The programme of the hall included a typical management statement, devised in order to satisfy complaints made about lyrics:

> It is the desire of the management that the entertainments offered at this establishment shall be at all times absolutely free from objectionable features; they invite the cooperation of the public to this end, and will be obliged to anyone who will inform them of anything offensive upon the stage that may have escaped the notice of the management.[57]

In fact, the inspectorate occasionally demonstrated a remarkable preference for aesthetic concerns over suppression of vice. When in 1893 an inspector visited the Palace Theatre of Varieties, he noted that it offered entertainment of 'the customary kind, singers, skirt dancers, eccentric comedians, ballet, etc., which involved the usual display of limbs encased in tights'.[58] He wrote of them as

> skilful and artistic living representations of well-known paintings and sculptures. Some people, however, would simply object to such public and complete display of the female form, by living women . . . It is a matter of difficulty to fix the exact point where propriety ends and impropriety begin. The borderline which divides the legitimate from the objectionable is not well-defined. I have endeavoured to report the facts as impartially as I can, and it is not for me, but for the Committee, to approve or condemn.[59]

A second inspector wrote, in 1894, of the Palace tableau vivants, 'the whole is very beautifully and artistically produced'.[60] A letter from a member of the public then arrived, informing the committee of posters outside the Palace which he found 'suggestive . . . demoralizing the crowds of young men and boys who linger about the place'.[61] The writer added that the young girls participating in the performance were degraded by it. He made specific reference to the similarities between the Palace posters and those at the Empire — fearing that a blight of such advertising would engulf all the London halls. But the inspectorate thought that increased draping of parts of the body was improving the Palace performance, arguing that the fourth series of tableaux which included the 'daring Moorish bath' scene still had nothing objectionable about it, noting that 'it was vigorously applauded'.[62] Another inspector did record an objection. Finally an MP wrote to the Committee: his plea illustrates the pressure flowing from Parliament to the Council and replicated in many of its operations: 'I have received several complaints since writing to you as to the tableaux vivants. I would suggest if you wish to conciliate public opinion, which I believe is becoming increasingly hostile to these representations, that *prompt* action on your part is desirable'.[63] The same day, the manager of the Palace withdrew the 'Moorish bath' scene.

But drawing a line, both with reference to the tableaux vivants and lyrical intent, was difficult to do. As the case of the Oxford hall licence hearing demonstrates, the Council's representatives could play the role of inter-mediaries. These proceedings, held in October 1896, included complaints from a witness with regard to two pieces, the first sung by Marie Lloyd, and entitled, 'I asked Johnny Jones, so I know now'.[64] Lloyd, dressed as a school-girl, precociously inquired in several encounters with her parents and a schoolboy, 'what's that for, eh?'[65] with obvious sexual implication. A second skit involved Lady Mansel, singing about a dancing girl whose tights burst while on the stage with the rejoinder, 'and what I saw I mustn't tell you now'.[66] These were felt to be 'improper for mixed audiences'.[67] But the wit-ness against the licensee was pursued by a Committee member: 'Are not such innuendos suggested in the theatres?'[68]

Much of the rest of the session involved testimony from representatives of the social purity wing of the British Women's Temperance Association, well-known in London for its ardent crusade against prostitution, an issue bound up with the halls and made explicit in the case of the Empire promenades. Again the presiding councillors appeared sceptical of the witnesses rather than encouraging. The proprietors' representatives were permitted to engage in hostile questioning. Carina T. Reed, secretary of the social purity section of the association, recounted various songs and skits which she and her colleagues had found especially objectionable: 'The thing that called down the most applause was when Ally Sloper gave an account of his court-ing a girl at Epping Forest'.[69] Under questioning, Reed admitted that she had never attended a performance before doing so for the cause, and that she favoured halls like the Metropolitan, Middlesex and Collins.

Mr Charles Cory Reed, buyer for a City firm by day and temperance move-ment member by night, spoke of his attendance at an obscene performance and of his encounters with women at the Oxford. He was then cross-examined by a representative of the applicant:

When I say I was accosted — a girl spoke to me in what I may call the usual way, 'Well', and I turned away. Soon after another girl asked me if this was the last item in the programme. It was not what she said, but the way in which she said it; and immediately after that another girl came and looked over my prog-ramme very closely. I do not say that this is accosting. I tell you what happened.
Q. Have you much time to spare?
A. No.
Q. But you are able to devote a considerable part of your time to looking after the morals of other people.[70]

After tough questioning, the Committee members admonished that lyrics and objective plots were not at issue, but tone, innuendo and gesture were the modes in which immorality thrived. An example cited were the words, 'Meet me by moonlight alone . . . It would depend on how it was sung and who sung it'.[71] In defence of the Hall, the representative of the proprietor bemoaned the fact that they could not prosecute the witnesses who were tes-tifying against them: 'Gratifying it must be to these people who live at Crouch End and Hornsey to look at the rest of the world from that point of view.'[72] He explained that the Oxford did not allow soliciting, and stated that the manager approved all songs sung, an important feature of the sort of self-censoring by then common in London halls. But the defence closed with a reminder to the Committee, as if to excuse the management from full control of the halls: 'I suppose it would be absolutely impossible in any form of entertainment — whether it is at a music-hall or at a theatre — to prevent some construction being put upon things that are said.'[73] The Committee rested on behalf of the hall and granted the licence, asking for greater care in song selection. This illustrates the most common, subtler form of negotiation characteristic of the licensing sessions involving the more established halls.

Opposition to the consumption of alcohol in the halls unified Council policy and practice — it was easier to clamp down on the use of drink than it was to ferret out the offensive gesture or the suggestive lyric. When the Committee recommended the renewal of the Jolly Tanners Music Hall licence in 1892, it did so with the proviso that no bar ever be opened inside and that there be no sale or consumption of alcohol in the auditorium. This decision anticipated the further steps taken in 1894. Even though it was asserted in the licensing session that the entire neighbourhood surrounding the hall opposed its existence, because it was located at the crossroads of two narrow streets in a heavily populated area, the licence was renewed. The committee questioned the spokesman for the opposition as to why there had been no petition, the chief weapon of factions and communities *vis-à-vis* the Committee, the licensing hearing and the Council in general — a hallmark of its *modus operandi* within the London boroughs. Those opposing stated that the neighbourhood was too poor to have got a petition together, as it was full of 'working tanners and costermongers'.[74] Herein lies a key to policy in practice — those with a greater voice in protest began to be viewed as speaking for London. This was never more the case than in the dispute surrounding the Empire.

The opposition in the Empire case has been immortalised; there were temperance advocates, led by Mrs Ormiston Chant, and those who specifically opposed the presence of prostitutes on the promenades. The sharp reaction on the part of the Council, the quick surge of defensive public opinion, from advocates of 'free trade in amusements' to younger members of the aristocracy, are legendary and tend to obscure other kinds of expression of popular sentiment, emanating from distinct and vocal minorities at the time of the Empire case.

For example, the London Patriotic Club of Clerkenwell, established in 1871 with the object of pursuing 'the furtherance of Democratic Principles to assist in all Progressive Movements', resolved:

1. That the People have a right to be amused in the manner which best suits them, and that they are the proper authorities of the same.
2. That there has been no complaint from the Public against the exhibition shown at the Empire Theatre. We therefore ask the LCC to

disregard the recommendations of the Licensing Committee and the action of a narrow-minded and bigoted faction against the well-conducted plan of amusement.[75]

The Cane and Bamboo Workers similarly protested:

> That the Union while deploying the existence of prostitution and vice, protest against the ridiculous and Puritanical attitude of the Licensing Committe of the LCC believing that the cause of this vice lies deeper than that Committee seem to comprehend and can only be extinguished by the removal of that cause and not by throwing more women out of work to starvation or the streets.[76]

These must be seen against resolutions like that of the United Methodist Free Church where a large public meeting resolved in favour of removing the lounge at the Empire, expressing gratitude to the Council for 'endeavouring to purify the public places of amusement'.[77]

By October 1895, the Inspection Sub-committee of the Theatres and Music Hall Committee had accumulated petitions from thousands of Londoners. These dealt especially with the issue of unrestricted licences, many favouring bans on alcohol sale and consumption; they usually made specific mention of the Empire or the Palace. The petitions with the greatest number of signatures sanctioning Council restrictions policy on alcohol included inhabitants of Holloway (243), worshippers at Fulham Congregational Church, the Queens Road, Battersea (150), the Gospel Temperance Society (170), the East London Women's Christian Temperance Union for Poplar and Limehouse (131), the Gresham Baptist Church (137), and inhabitants of Plumstead (261). Those supporting the recommendations which would have lightened restrictions, notably put forward by the Committee itself, but which were overturned in the Council as a whole, included: inhabitants of many districts of London listed as such, typically, inhabitants of West Newington (135), or inhabitants of Hackney (62), the ratepayers of South Hackney, and the Clapham Reform Club.[78]

The Empire thus represents a case that embodied the *contradictory* forces in the music hall debate in London. There was no clear 'Establishment'. It was the political 'centre to left' that sought the purification and transformation of the halls most aggressively. As Judith Walkowitz has recently pointed out, working-class men and women were not simply passive targets of social purity drives. In cases like the Empire, vocal factions from across the metropolis expressed their positions.[79] Rather than simply presenting the opposition to LCC policy at the Empire as exemplified by the young Winston Churchill, the records of the campaigns reveal two other related phenomena: the existence of an articulated anti-moralist, anti-purification position best termed 'libertarian', *and* of groups championing the Council.[80] These were distinct minorities not necessarily representative of those attending music hall, but of those whose political and religious commitments led them to take a public stance on the music hall issue.

Even after their 1907 defeat, the Progressives claimed that their policy remained that of the Council, despite certain lapses on the part of the new administration. Progressive leader John Benn warned in 1910 that 'three attempts have been made to break down . . . that temperance license policy . . . Our present municipal Masters are too much allied with "the trade" to have a free hand in this important matter.'[81] Eventually promenades returned to the Empire and liquor licenses were sometimes granted despite ardent opposition from LCC councillors like Labour member, Harry Gosling. But in the licensing sessions, in which owners of the larger syndicates, like Oswald Stoll, played a greater and greater role, the desire on the part of the Council to continue to exert certain controls on the proprietors did persist.

From the point of view of the Stoll machine, there were four types of opposition which anyone seeking a licence had to confront and overcome. Each came to light in the disputes surrounding the application of the Fulham Empire in the years just before the war. The first of these was the 'trade opposition', represented by other music halls in the neighbourhood (in this case the Granville Hall, which sold alcohol) and those seeking cinematography licences. Stoll approached the Committee with the object of forfeiting the right to sell liquor, attempting to entice councillors into letting him operate a non-alcoholic hall as an alternative to those owned by his competitors. There was the 'clerical opposition' — those who claimed that the halls were demoralising. To this charge. Stoll's representative presented their operation as 'an entertainment to which a family can be taken, to which a man can bring his wife and his sisters and daughters and young people'. The 'educational opposition' claimed the hall would draw away from evening classes now offered by the LCC and other public bodies. Finally, the syndicate feared a 'property opposition', of the sort that in Fulham worried about damage to a Wesleyan chapel located near the proposed hall site. It is acknowledged in these hearings that by this time there existed 'a new music hall public and an old';[82] the contention of the Stoll camp was that they would attract some of both, that existing halls could not hope to accommodate all with interest in attending the performances.

But, by 1913, those, like the smaller proprietors, who opposed the syndicates spoke before Council of the 'over-production' of halls[83] and of the need to be more 'sensational' in order to attract audiences to pay the bills.[84] This testimony included a record of receipts of theatres owned by Variety Theatres Consolidated, one of the large conglomerates in the industry, revealing a decline in net profits over the period 1908–12, information collected by the owners of the Chelsea, Euston, South London and Walthamstow Palace Theatres.

A representative for the small proprietor opposing Stoll addressed the Committee:

> You have forced us to spend thousands of pounds on our undertaking, we have got to comply with your restrictions in every particular, we have sunk our capital in it, and we have endeavoured to comply, not only with the letter but with

the spirit of what you wanted us to do. We have brought our entertainment up to the high standard it is, and here you have this mammoth monopolist, Mr Stoll, to kill us . . . you will put both him and us to the risk, in order to make profits . . . there are a great many things which it is difficult for a Committee or a Council to get hold of — the suggestive attitude for instance. There are songs which to look at in print absolutely mean nothing; but the suggestive attitude, or even the wink or look put into them, can make them most indecent; and I do, therefore, in the interest of the high class of music hall entertainment that you have hitherto insisted on in London, ask you not to put too great a strain on the resources of the people whom I represent.[85]

He further explained that increasing expenditures did mean increasing salaries for the performers and more trouble for the lesser owners in the industry. After several attempts at gaining a licence for Fulham, Stoll was refused, as he would be during the War.

Stoll had been granted many other London licences. In this instance, perhaps it was felt that he had reached too far. Perhaps the Council was feeling the heat from the trade unions in the industry who were mounting concerted protests against Stoll's wages policy. One resolution against LCC complicity with Stoll put forward to the London Trades Council during the War asserted that the smaller proprietors were more willing to pay higher wages and were now being squeezed out of existence by Stoll and his henchmen.[86] As far as the LCC was concerned, Stoll was hardly an outcast, he was simply being asked not to step too far afield of the accepted norms of conduct. The Progressive vision for London never came to fruition but the code of etiquette forged with the proprietors and the semblance of moral uplift associated with the Progressive reign had been assimilated into the Council's practice and its reputation.

Conclusion

The legacy of the Progressive period was preserved in the successful institution of licensing and inspection procedures that forced the Council and the proprietors to meet, to operate within a set of rules deemed acceptable by both sides and to secure the continued existence of the industry at the expense of the smaller, less competitive halls. Ironically, it was not the syndicates, nor the Theatres and Music Halls Committee, nor the vigilance and moral purity crusaders who had disappeared by the 1920s; it was Progressivism itself that had almost entirely vanished.

In order for the Progressives to continue to win elections and to achieve the goal of a unified London government administering ambitious reforms through an aggressive tax on wealth, the Party needed a stronger working-class vote, especially given the franchise restrictions faced by London's working class. The Progressives could certainly have benefitted from the growth of London's lower middle class, had that stratum not been so divided politically. Instead of becoming more united, Progressivism encountered increasing division in its ranks. Music hall policy might have helped to unite the Party's supporters — instead, it proved highly controversial. The failure to secure greater control of leisure from Parliament disappointed the proponents of a wider municipalism. The unwillingness of the party to force the issue of trade-union wages on the proprietors inflamed the labour organisations in the entertainment industry. These goals could have been realised only with more interference on the part of the LCC, yet the political consensus necessary for the LCC to intervene was lacking. The early Liberal–Progressive focus on ground landlords took precedence over Council attacks on the larger proprietors. The latter proved useful in effecting self-censorship and in conveying, at least at a rhetorical level, the Progressive ethos of a family-centred form of entertainment. Because it had placed ill-considered hopes in the eventual extension of LCC powers, the Council was left with the option of rewarding those proprietors who would accept the new constraints imposed on the industry, constraints that could be upheld without extended parliamentary mandate.

This essay calls attention at its outset to two tendencies within music hall historiography. The first, the assertion of the increasing role of the state in attempting to mould a music hall culture of a new type, is corroborated by the account of LCC policy-making above. But the second tendency, what I have termed the persistence of working-class independence, requires further comment and attention in research extending beyond the confines of this piece. Some preliminary speculation is, however, possible.

Those millions who attended music hall may well have wanted cleaner, larger, safer facilities. The elimination of alcohol from some of the halls and the curbing of prostitution, if only of limited success, were, arguably, of little consequence to those who frequented the halls principally in order to view the performance. Whatever objections many may have had to the most 'vulgar' aspects of song or programme, the pervasive sexual repartee, the celebration of gender difference and the seductive tease that thrived in the halls were clearly preserved.

It has not been proved that moral regulation or supervision was wholly successful. Nor has it been proved that these attracted an increasing audience to the halls. Demographic and economic factors were arguably more determinant in the growth of audiences. The rapid increases in white-collar employment and the concomitant growth of suburban housing, the increased migration to London and rising incomes in some sectors of the population may have been far more causal than a change in programme or performance. We do not know if the audiences might have grown even more rapidly if the industry had been less restricted. Perhaps, then, the most salient fact about audience participation was the persistent display of sympathy for allusions to sexual impropriety and the satirical portrayal of public and private life in performance.

We do know that music hall policy, along with many other facets of the Progressive programme were not popular enough to gain a public following for the Council. Those most enthusiastic about the attempts to purify the halls were not themselves entirely satisfied with the outcome; the organisations and individuals who fully supported temperance, social purity, the quelling of prostitution, the removal of song and sketch, continued to harrass the Committee, *despite* its efforts. And, however vocal, these were a pitiful handful as compared with the audience in the halls, many of whom were likely to have voted *against* the Progressives in 1907, *if* they voted at all.

Does the notion of 'social control' appropriately characterise the theory and practice of the LCC? It would seem that the inspectorate functioned as a discriminating but nominal body in the process of making a licensing decision. The proprietors' self-regulation was more important than direct action by the Licensing Committee. The tone of Committee discussion and decision ran clearly in favour of disavowing especially vulgar pieces or performances, but Committee members often acted as moderates compared with some of the vigilant crusaders so vocal within the wider London community.

Masses of people do seem to have been subjected to a general moderation of certain kinds of lyrics, nudity and outright suggestiveness on stage, at least when someone in authority was looking. The entertainment, however, seems to have remained in many ways similar in thrust to what it 'traditionally' had been, but with a greater reliance on gesture or style of speech — insinuation rather than the words themselves.[87] But perhaps the intent of less respectable audiences had never been that of relishing the lascivious *per se*. As Smyth Piggott, examiner of plays, told the Select Commission of 1892:

> I have always found this, that the equivocal, the risky, the immoral and the indecent plays are intended for West End audiences, certainly not for the East End. The further east you go the more moral your audience is; you may get a gallery full of roughs in which every other boy is a pickpocket and yet their collective sympathy is in favour of self-sacrifice; collectively they have a horror of vice and a ferocious love of virtue.[88]

The attempt at purification of the halls is most important as a feature of the *failure* of a wider Progressivism at the century's close; the eradication of certain abuses and the successful incursion into the domain of the smaller, less visible forms of music hall is, in and of itself, less significant. While the failure of Progressivism may indicate the apoliticism of the masses of London voters and onlookers, or even their recruitment in substantial numbers to a form of popular conservatism, it must equally be seen as a firm rejection of the attempt to control precious leisure hours and beguiling traditions of performance, so dear to the hearts of the most typical inhabitants of the metropolis. Perhaps George Sims had judged too hastily. As the beleaguered manager of the Middlesex informed the Select Committee of 1892: 'We have found cases where boys in the street have altered the text somewhat. They have applied other words to the same melodies, but you cannot attribute that to the music hall or the artiste.'[89]

Notes

(Place of publication is London unless stated otherwise.)

1. From testimony of Chas Cory Reed, Proceedings of the Licensing Committee (LC) of the London County Council (LCC) October 1896, Oxford Music Hall, p. 17.
2. Theatres and Music Halls Committee of the LCC (THMC) Palace Theatre of Varieties, 1888–1903, attached to report of licensing discussion, 28 November 1902.
3. *Parliamentary Papers*, Select Committee on Theatres and Places of Entertainment, HC 1892 (240) XVIII, cols 3004–6.
4. For histories of the LCC and related topics, see Sir Gwilyn Gibbon and Reginald W. Bell, *History of the London County Council*, 1939; Paul Thompson, *Socialists, Liberals and Labour: the Struggle for London; 1885–1914*, 1981, Part IV; John M. Davis, 'The Problem of London Local Government Reform, 1880–1900', unpublished D.Phil. thesis, Oxford University, 1983; S. D. Pennybacker, 'The "Labour Question" and the London County Council, 1889–1919', unpublished Ph.D. thesis, Cambridge University, 1985.
5. Edward J. Bristow, *Vice and Vigilance: Purity Movements in Britain since 1700*, Dublin, 1977; and Penelope Summerfield, 'The Effingham Arms and the Empire: Deliberate Selection in the Evolution of Music Hall in London' in Eileen and Stephen Yeo (eds.), *Popular Culture and Class Conflict*, Hassocks, 1981.
6. Bristow, *Vice and Vigilance*, pp. 214, 211.
7. Ibid., see pp. 209–215.
8. Summerfield, 'Effingham Arms', p. 237.
9. See Gareth Stedman Jones, 'Working-Class Culture and Working-Class Politics in London, 1870–1900: Notes on the Remaking of a Working Class' and 'Class Expression Versus Social Control? A Critique of Recent Trends in the Social History of "Leisure"', in *Languages of Class*, 1983. See Peter Bailey, *Leisure and Class in Victorian England*, 1978, and 'Custom, Capital and Culture' in R. Storch (ed.), *Popular Culture and Custom in Nineteenth-Century England*, Cambridge, 1982.
10. See Stedman Jones, 'Working-Class Culture'.
11. See Stedman Jones, *Languages of Class*, p. 16.
12. Bailey, 'Custom, Capital and Culture', p. 204.
13. See Pennybacker, 'The "Labour Question"', *passim*.
14. See John Palmer, *The Censor and the Theatres*, New York, 1913; Archibald Haddon, *The Story of the Music Hall*, 1935; LCC, *Annual Report*, 1889–1890; TMHC, *Proposed Legislation*,1887–1905; D. Howard, *London Theatre and Music Halls, 1850–1950*, 1970, pp. xi, 269.
15. TMHC, Minutes of the Inspection Sub-committee, 16 October 1893.
16. See the *Daily Telegraph* summary of letters of opinion received on these questions, 12 March 1891.
17. See Bristow, *Vice and Vigilance*, pp. 209–211.
18. Thompson, *Socialists, Liberals and Labour*, pp. 73–74.
19. See Bristow, *Vice and Vigilance*, pp. 209–211.
20. See TMHC, *Register of Inspections*, 1905–9.

21. See, for example, TMHC *Minutes*, 11 January 1893, concerning the Committee visit to the Oxford Music Hall.
22. See description of established procedures contained in TMHC, 'Report', 12 November, 1909, *Printed Papers of Sessions*, 1909–1911.
23. See TMHC, Minutes of the Inspection Sub-committee, 16 October 1893.
24. See the arguments put forward in Stewart D. Headlam, 'On the Danger of Municipal Puritanism', n.d. For a larger perspective, see 'Subsidized Shakespeare: A Municipal Innovation by the LCC', *Municipal Journal*, 30 May 1919; 'Municipal Amusements: A Renewed Crusade for a Rate-Aided Opera', *Municipal Journal*, 8 August 1919.
25. See, for example, London Trades Council, *Minutes*, 10 October 1901, calling for the LCC to receive a deputation for the purpose of discussing the creation of a municipal theatre like those on the Continent.
26. Howard, *London Theatre*, p. 270 and LCC, *Annual Reports*, 1890–3.
27. *Parliamentary Papers*, Select Committee on Theatres and Places of Entertainment, HC 1892 (240) XVIII.
28. Ibid.
29. See TMHC, Minutes of the Inspection Sub-committee, 28 February 1894.
30. See letter from the London Entertainments Proprietors Association to Mr Yeats, 14 February 1905, in TMHC, *Proposed Legislation*, 1887–1905; LCC, *Annual Report*, 1892–3.
31. See report on the meeting with Asquith and transcript, 17 April 1894, in TMHC, *Proposed Legislation*, 1887–1905.
32. Ibid., see comments by Russell, p. 12; exchange between Russell and McDougall, p. 13, in which, for example, Russell states: 'But I mean that you have not relied upon questions of decency or quality of performance such as the Lord Chamberlain might take into account.'
33. Ibid., p. 12; for the 'terminable annuity', see pp. 19–20, referring to theatres (London) (no. 2), p. 16, clauses 32, 33. This would have stipulated that if an owner neglected to carry out repairs, the occupier could do so and the Council would certify completion; the 'amount certified shall be repayable through a yearly annuity charged on the premises'.
34. Ibid., see p. 21, 22–6.
35. A. Offer, *Property and Politics*, 1981, part V.
36. TMHC, *Minutes*, 22 October 1890.
37. Ibid., 31 July 1890.
38. Ibid., 11 January 1893.
39. See Headlam, 'Municipal Puritanism' and Pennybacker, 'The "Labour Question"', Chapter 3 and Epilogue.
40. See Pennybacker, 'Labour Question', Chapter 3, Epilogue.
41. TMHC, *Presented Papers*, Charing Cross Hall, 1889–1908, 20 August 1890.
42. Ibid.
43. Ibid., 22 July 1908.
44. See LCC, *Annual Reports*, 1890–1, 1906–7, 1907–8.
45. See, for example, TMHC, *Presented Papers*, Britannia Theatre, Hoxton, 1888–1909, 24 January 1890; report from Public Health Department, 6 September 1899, 10 April 1905; closure, 30 April 1909.
46. TMHC, *Presented Papers*, Rose and Crown, 1889–96, 30 December 1890.
47. Ibid.
48. TMHC, *Presented Papers*, Collins Music Hall, Islington Green, 1889–1909, 25 August 1890.

49. Ibid., 9 August 1900.
50. Ibid., 3 October 1907 and Bailey, Chapter 2, this volume.
51. TMHC, *Presented Papers*, Canterbury Music Hall, 1888–1904, 23 February 1891, 9 August 1891.
52. *Parliamentary Papers*, Select Committee on Theatres and Places of Entertainment, HC 1892 (240) XVIII, p. 440. This was by order of English's New Sebright Wholesome Amusement Temple.
53. Ibid.
54. Ibid., pp. 441–2.
55. TMHC, *Presented Papers*, Canterbury Music Hall, 1888–1904, 28 August 1897.
56. Ibid.
57. Ibid.
58. TMHC, *Presented Papers*, Palace Theatre of Varieties, 1888–1904, 28 August 1897.
59. Ibid.
60. Ibid., 27 February 1894.
61. Ibid., 7 March 1894, letter from Edward Webb.
62. Ibid., 10 August 1892.
63. Ibid., 23 August 1894, letter from MP (signature unclear) to J.S. Fleming, Chairman of THMC.
64. LCC, Proceedings before the LC, Oxford Music Hall, October 1896, p. 2.
65. Ibid.
66. Ibid., p. 3.
67. Ibid.
68. Ibid.
69. Ibid., pp. 11, 13.
70. Ibid., p. 17.
71. Ibid.
72. Ibid., p. 35.
73. Ibid., p. 36.
74. LCC, Proceedings before the LC, The Jolly Tanners Music Hall, 5 October 1892.
75. TMHC, *Presented Papers*, Empire Music Hall, 10 October 1894.
76. Ibid., 25 October 1894.
77. Ibid.
78. TMHC, Minutes of the Inspection Sub-committee, 23 October 1895.
79. 'Male Vice and Feminist Virtue: Feminism and the Politics of Prostitution in Nineteenth-Century Britain', *History Workshop*, no. 13, Spring 1982.
80. See Winston Churchill, *My Early Life*, 1930, p. 71.
81. 'Progressive–Socialist Manifesto', *London Municipal Notes*, July 1909, p. 124.
82. LCC, Proceedings before the LC, Fulham Empire, 14 and 15 November 1912, p. 25.
83. LCC, Proceedings before the LC, Fulham Empire, 1913, p. 74.
84. Ibid., p. 75.
85. Ibid., p. 79.
86. London Trades Council, *Minutes*, 9 November 1916.
87. Summerfield suggests this when she observes. 'Vulgarity increasingly became an aspect of the style of performance rather than the content of the song.' ('Effingham Arms', p. 234), though she also links this to a wider analysis of lyrical content.
88. *Parliamentary Papers*, Select Committee on Theatres and Places of Entertainment, HC 1892 (240) XVIII, col. 5197.
89. Ibid., col. 2944.

7 Manchester Morality and London Capital: The Battle over the Palace of Varieties

CHRIS WATERS

In 1851 Charles Morton opened the Canterbury Arms in Lambeth. Historians have considered Morton's venture to be a watershed in music hall history, and they have viewed the Canterbury as the precursor of the massive 'palaces' and 'empires' of the late nineteenth century. Until recently, the history of the halls has been written in a Whiggish manner: First there were the singing saloons and 'free and easies' of the 1830s and 1840s, then the small, purpose-built halls like Morton's, and finally, following the introduction of limited liability in 1862, the large syndicates which, between them, had established a whole new leisure industry by the 1890s. As one observer wrote in 1900, music hall slowly developed from the public house sing-song, where the 'audience provided its own entertainment', to the variety concert, orchestrated by entrepreneurs to attract a large, paying audience.[1] Or, as Peter Bailey has put it: 'The caterer's conversion of the pub sing-song into modern show business can . . . be likened to the shift from domestic to factory production, with the same organizational imperatives to economies of scale, division of labour and the specialisation of plant.'[2]

Despite the emphasis historians have placed on the transformation of popular musical entertainment into one of the corner-stones of the late Victorian leisure industry, the manner by which that transformation took place was complicated. As several pieces in this volume suggest, the music hall 'industry' developed unevenly. In the North, the links that existed between commercially packaged 'mass' entertainment and earlier working-class cultural traditions were rarely severed.[3] Moreover, even in London the success of the large halls was only guaranteed because their owners were able to urge the adoption of a series of new relationships between work, leisure and emerging forms of consumer capitalism within the context of traditional assumptions about the content and uses of leisure.

Manchester was not immune from this process of 'uneven development'.

As early as the 1830s a large number of publican entrepreneurs built concert rooms in their pubs, and these became more numerous in succeeding decades. Their expansion was so rapid that the temperance movement, always strong in Manchester, viewed the process with alarm. Voices were raised against the existence of these concert rooms as early as the 1840s, and by the 1880s they had become much louder, prompting Walter Tomlinson, a journalist for the *Manchester City News*, to study the phenomenon. He concluded that there was no evidence to support the widely held belief that music halls bred crime and immorality, and he suggested that it was only a small number of music hall *habitués* 'who now and again lose their heads and run amuck like mad Malays'.[4] Still, the guardians of Manchester morality were troubled by the existence of 'mad Malays' in their city, and for them the threat of an ever increasing number of music halls conjured up a vision of moral disorder, of even more 'Malays' running amuck. By 1891 licences were held by some 400 of these smaller halls. While other northern towns experienced an influx of capital for the construction of large, purpose-built halls, in Manchester the smaller concerns were still predominant. This is of some importance, for it was the response to these halls that shaped the attitude of Manchester's ruling élite to the initial development of a music hall 'industry' in Manchester in the 1890s and early 1900s.

Despite the prevalence of a number of concert rooms catering for an average audience of a mere 50 spectators, the city could boast a few larger establishments. In the eyes of many middle-class observers they tended to provide more wholesome entertainment and were thus considered more respectable. As early as the 1860s critics contrasted the bulk of the halls, which were primarily concerned with the sale of alcohol, with a few establishments — such as Burton's People's Concert Hall, the Alexandra, the Victoria and the London — each of which sat upwards of 1,500 people and subordinated the sale of alcohol to the provision of entertainment. None the less, by the 1890s the pattern of music hall development in Manchester was threatened not by these local concerns but by the new Palace of Varieties. From the beginning the Palace was to be larger, grander and more respectable than either the smaller halls that dotted the urban landscape in and around the centre of the city or the few larger halls that were still in existence. George Scott, the manager of the Palace, declared with confidence: 'This is not to be a music hall, but an entirely different thing. It is to be a theatre of varieties.'[5] Designed for the 'purpose of an English variety theatre of an advanced type', the Palace was located on the corner of Oxford Road and Whitworth Street. Opened in 1891 at a cost of £40,000, the building contained a winter garden, a café and an auditorium that could accommodate an audience of 3,000 people with ease.[6]

The proprietors of the Palace were eager to convince their critics that the new venture had nothing in common with the smaller halls. While critics attacked the old concert rooms for offering what they believed to be third-rate amusements, the Palace hoped to counter this criticism by claiming that it would guarantee the moral and artistic integrity of the entertainment it offered. And while critics thought that the smaller halls attracted disreputable individuals, the Palace argued that it would carefully supervise the behaviour of its own, more respectable audience. In 1913, reviewing the history of the Palace, the directors claimed once again that the Palace had played an important role in transforming Manchester's night life:

> Its opening marked a new era in the domain of public entertainment, for up to that time the old-time music hall — with its ill construction, bad accommodation, and . . . objectionable pabulum — held sway. . . . [B]ut, with the advent of the Palace . . . this changed. . . . The Palace proved the triumph of good, clean wholesome vaudeville entertainment over the piffle that previously had been ladled out to music hall patrons.[7]

The management may have convinced itself that its venture was a worthy one, but it failed to convey that message to the city's moral and political guardians. For more than a decade the Palace struggled to acquire the kind of licence that would allow it to realise a profit. And for more than a decade its critics mounted a massive campaign that effectively blocked the Palace from acquiring such a licence. In the debates that took place over the worthiness of the Palace much was revealed about the actors involved. Behind the façade of respectability developed by the Palace were a number of opportunist businessmen, ruthlessly struggling to protect their investment. And behind the moral self-righteousness of the critics were a number of worried teetotallers who attempted to counter the perceived threat posed by the Palace through a series of tired homilies that may have worked against the smaller halls but were wholly inadequate in meeting the challenge they believed was implicit in the entertainment industry of the 1890s. Moreover, the debates about the Palace shed considerable light on the struggle to remake popular culture in the late nineteenth century. Not simply a feud between a music hall and its critics, the battle over the Manchester Palace of Varieties is illustrative of a larger struggle to redefine the relationship between capitalism and morality, leisure and respectability, and also between popular culture and the state.

The Palace and the licence

Before the 1880s, many towns made no provision for the licensing of places of entertainment, while others developed policies that were haphazard at best. But in 1882 the Municipal Corporations Act attempted to standardise licensing procedures. Clauses 25 and 26 of that Act stipulated that music and dancing licences were to be granted by the local corporations, while theatre licences were to be dispensed by the county councils. This form of joint jurisdiction over places of entertainment lasted until the passage of the Local Government Act in 1888. The following year Manchester became a county borough and the theatrical licensing powers that had, in theory at least, been the preserve of the Lancashire County Council were now handed over to the administration in the new county borough. From 1889, the power to license both theatres and music halls resided in the Watch Committee of the local council, the public body most responsible for supervising the moral life of the community. This changed following the passage of the Public Health Acts Amendment Act of 1890, after which date the licensing of theatres remained in the hands of the Watch Committee while the licensing of music halls was delegated to the city justices, who, unlike the council members, held office by appointment and not by election.[8]

The city justices were also responsible for licensing the halls to sell alcoholic beverages. By contrast, legitimate theatres received permission to sell alcohol from the Excise Board. Temperance advocates were generally enthusiastic about the provisions of these Acts. They claimed that since licences were now granted by the local corporation and its delegates, all citizens had the obligation to elect representatives to the council who would use their powers to prevent publicans and brewers from contaminating the city with their 'pollutants'.[9]

Despite the fact that by 1890 procedures for the acquisition of various types of licence seemed clear, there remained the question as to what kind of licence a given place of entertainment was eligible for. Outside London, for example, some establishments held both stage and music hall licences. And in Manchester the Palace tried to use its anomalous position of being neither a serious theatre nor an old-fashioned music hall to its advantage in the licensing battles it found itself embroiled in. The extent to which the newer palaces and empires confused the working of traditional licensing practices was evident in the debates that took place before the Parliamentary Select Committee on Places of Entertainment. In 1892 that committee recommended that there should be at least three licence categories: one for legitimate theatres; one for variety theatres; and one for concert and dancing halls.[10]

At one time or another the Palace applied for every licence it considered itself eligible for. The process began in October 1890 when the directors applied for a music hall entertainment licence. The hearing was brief and the magistrates decided to reject the application on the grounds that the building was still under construction and the Palace's financial arrangements were highly unstable.[11] In February 1891 the Palace filed its second petition for a licence with the justices. This they did under the name of George Edwardes, the London-based music hall entrepreneur and director of the company. By this time the temperance movement was beginning to organise against the Palace and it managed to convince the justices to deny the request by a vote of 20 to six.[12]

A week later the directors met to chart a new course of action. Because critics objected to another music hall in the city, they debated — without reaching a conclusion — whether or not they should apply for a drama, rather than music hall, licence. Moreover, because the temperance movement had drawn public attention to its cause, the Palace decided to mount its own publicity campaign. The city was placarded, magistrates were invited to see the building, approaching completion, and 60,000 signatures were attached to a petition which claimed that the Palace would encourage high-class entertainment in an area of the city well known for its more disreputable pastimes.[13]

As we shall see, the Palace's critics objected to the existence of a music hall in Manchester run by financial interests based in London. Thus, when the directors again decided to apply for a music hall licence in March 1891 they did so under the name of George Scott, the manager of the Palace. For some four years Scott had run the respectable Comedy Theatre in Manchester, and it was hoped that his name would confer a degree of legitimacy on the new undertaking. On this, their third attempt, the directors finally secured a licence. But the vote was won by a narrow margin, prompting Manchester's *Sunday Chronicle* to warn the management that the Palace was now on trial: 'Its own existence depends . . . on its ability to raise the standard of music-hall recreation'.[14] On 15 May the Palace staged its first performance before an invited group of church leaders, temperance crusaders and local dignitaries in an effort to convince them of the respectability of the venture. Three days later the Palace opened its doors to the general public.[15]

As much as the battle to secure an entertainment licence was difficult and costly, it was less complicated than the subsequent battle to secure a licence to sell alcoholic beverages. In August 1891 the directors applied to the justices for a drink licence, which was granted subject to the approval of the entire council. At this point, temperance advocates developed their campaign to the fullest, submitting a resolution to the congregations of local Wesleyan, Primitive Methodist and New Connection chapels urging the council to overturn the decision of the justices. Largely on the basis of that resolution, the council rejected the application by a vote of 40 to 18.[16]

Throughout 1891 the Palace found itself in severe financial difficulties. While the Palace's opening performance managed to convince a few critics that the venture was indeed devoted to the cause of 'wholesome' amusement, it was expensive to produce and box-office receipts alone failed to pay the bills. In April the directors each agreed to lend the company £250. The following year they decided to cut the size of the orchestra and reduce the scope of their advertising. In order to gain the support of the community they also decided to ask several aldermen opposed to the Palace to become honorary members of the board. The plan backfired, merely fuelling the campaign mounted by temperance advocates who could now claim that the drink and entertainment industries were attempting to buy the votes of the council.[17]

While the management claimed it wanted to sell alcohol merely to please its patrons, the truth of the matter was different , for without a drink licence the whole venture was likely to collapse. Thus, in March 1892, the directors decided to change their strategy and apply for a drama licence, knowing that a licence to sell alcohol could be acquired from the Excise once a drama licence had been secured. The Watch Committee provisionally granted the request. This led temperance advocates once more to express their opposition, and in this they were now joined by owners of legitimate theatres who feared competition from the Palace, were it to be licensed as a theatre. Together they succeeded in convincing the council to overturn the decision of the Watch Committee. That summer Scott decided to test the determination of the council to deny the Palace a drama licence by illegally staging a play. The authorities clamped down, fining him five pounds for ignoring the stipulations of his entertainment licence.[18]

In October, Scott again applied for a drama licence, arguing that the success of the play he had staged during the summer had convinced him that the public desired such forms of 'refined' entertainment. The Watch Committee was not convinced and rejected the application. In December the directors submitted another application and were willing to sign a covenant in which they promised not to apply to the Excise for a drink permit. On this occasion, the Palace was finally granted a drama licence by a vote of 14 to four.[19]

In the 1890s such covenants were unusual phenomena. But the Palace was willing to accept it, hoping that its legality could eventually be tested. For the time being, at least, the Palace could perform stage plays, but it could still not sell alcoholic beverages. Each year the Palace requested a renewal of its drama licence, and each year the authorities granted the request, subject to the simultaneous renewal of the covenant. Finally, in 1898, the Palace appealed to the Chancery Court of the County of Lancashire, claiming that the council had not been acting within its statutory powers when it coerced the Palace into accepting the covenant. The Court dismissed the case without a hearing, claiming that it was not in its jurisdiction to decide such matters.[20]

In 1900 the Palace closed for remodelling under the supervision of the major architect of the halls, Frank Matcham. Part of the foyer was turned into a grotto in order to placate those critics who believed that it was being used for purposes of solicitation by prostitutes. On reopening, the Palace operated under its old music hall licence, applying to the magistrates for a drink licence. Temperance leaders were infuriated, and the Bishop of Manchester was quoted as claiming that he 'did not object to a reasonable number of well-conducted theatres or well-conducted public houses, but he did object to the double stimulus to the emotions furnished by the dangerous combination of the two in such a house as this'.[21] Needless to say, the application was rejected. For the next decade the Palace managed to struggle on until it finally closed its doors, shed its music hall past, and was resurrected as the Palace Theatre, a name it retains to this day.

The Palace and the critics

In trying to make sense of this extraordinary battle, we need to begin by stressing the importance of the sale of alcoholic beverages for the success of the halls. In its prospectus to shareholders the Palace claimed it would make £10,000 a year from the sale of drink — an unfortunate claim that its enemies were eager to exploit.[22] Without a drink licence it was difficult for the Palace to pay its bills, let alone show a profit. Although many observers claimed that drink was of declining importance for the profitability of the halls, the financial records of the Palace suggest otherwise. This can be seen by comparing the Palace's balance sheets with those of the Empire in Leicester Square, also directed by George Edwardes. The Empire's financial report for 1892 disclosed costs of £97,000, box-office receipts of £95,900 and earnings of £21,787 from the sale of drink. Thus, more than 18 per cent of the Empire's total income was drink-related. By contrast, for the same period the Palace's income consisted of £37,846 from the sale of tickets, and a mere £1,895 — less than 5 per cent of the total — from the sale of non-alcoholic refreshments. Thus when Edwardes claimed that it was 'in the gate money and not in the drink that we make the profit', he was clearly ignoring the evidence provided by his own variety theatre in London.[23]

For a while the management tried to discourage patrons from bringing alcoholic beverages into the auditorium. It also tried to increase the consumption of teetotal refreshments. But patrons did not take too kindly to these efforts, and many of them slipped out during the performances in search of a thirst-quencher at one of the many public houses in the neighbourhood. Edwardes eventually made sure that some of their coppers lined his pockets when, in 1894, he acquired the lease of the nearby Railway Inn. Prior to this the company was unable to pay its shareholders any dividends. But after acquiring the inn dividends were paid regularly at the rate of 5 per cent.[24] This permitted the Palace to survive financially, but of course it also intensified the opposition of its critics.

The opponents of the licence were nearly all temperance advocates who together exercised an extraordinary influence on local government in the greater Manchester area. Not only did they oppose the Palace, but they also opposed the licensing of other large halls. In 1889, when the New Variety Theatre in Salford applied for a drama licence, its rejection was guaranteed once temperance leaders presented a petition expressing public opposition to the venture. Likewise, when Oswald Stoll applied for a drama licence for his Ardwick Empire Theatre of Varieties in 1904, many of those who had battled the Palace now turned their wrath against Stoll. They managed to convince the council to issue a licence only after Stoll also agreed not to sell alcoholic beverages.[25]

For decades the temperance movement in Manchester had been trying to rid the city of the curse of drink. If it was sometimes successful it was because throughout Yorkshire and Lancashire the movement was more organised than it was elsewhere in the country. As early as 1851 the Manchester and Salford Temperance Society was formed to co-ordinate the efforts of local temperance bodies to combat the high incidence of drunkenness in the area. The evidence seems to substantiate their claim that drink was rampant in the North-West. In 1871, for example, legal proceedings taken against individuals for drink offences ranged from a low of 17 per 10,000 people in the rural southern counties to a high of 154 in Lancashire and Cheshire.[26] Moreover, reformers claimed that such figures were directly related to the excessive number of drink licences held by publicans in Manchester. In 1892,

Burnley's chief constable studied the number of drink and music licences in existence in 23 Lancashire towns. His investigation revealed that there were more licensed victuallers and beerhouse keepers per capita in Manchester than in any other town (Table 7.1). Moreover, while in terms of such places licensed for the performance of musical entertainment Manchester only ranked sixth (Table 7.2), in absolute terms it also had more music licences than any of the other towns he surveyed.[27]

Table 7.1: Licensed Victuallers and Beerhouse Keepers in Lancashire, 1892
(Top ten towns listed in order of licence–population ratio)

Town	Population	Licensed victuallers and beerhouse keepers	Ratio of licences to population
1. MANCHESTER	505,343	3,031	1:167
2. Liverpool	517,961	2,196	1:236
3. Rochdale	71,458	300	1:238
4. Preston	107,000	444	1:241
5. Ashton-u-Lyme	40,494	165	1:245
6. Blackburn	120,064	461	1:260
7. Blackpool	25,000	95	1:263
8. Chorley	23,082	85	1:272
9. Wigan	55,013	200	1:275
10. St Helens	71,288	258	1:276

Table 7.2: Public Houses Licensed for the Performance of Music
(Top ten towns listed in order of licence–population ratio)

Town	Population	Public houses with music licences	Ratio of licences to population
1. Oldham	131,463	268	1: 491
2. Bury	56,418	102	1: 553
3. Clitheroe	10,815	14	1: 773
4. Burnley	90,000	111	1: 811
5. St Helens	71,288	74	1: 963
6. MANCHESTER	505,343	468	1:1,080
7. Liverpool	517,961	400	1:1,295
8. Wigan	55,013	29	1:1,897
9. Salford	201,058	105	1:1,915
10. Rochdale	71,458	35	1:2,042

In the 1890s, the Manchester Palace of Varieties drew the venom of those alarmed by such figures. As many of its critics were eager to point out, the Palace was so large that to grant it a licence would be like granting at least six regular licences. Thus, when the directors prepared for their first hearing in 1891, various temperance agencies — including the General Committee of Citizens, the Blue Ribbon Army, the Manchester, Salford and District Temperance Union, the Friends' Total Abstinence Society, the Lancashire and Cheshire Band of Hope Union, the Sunday School Union, and the Church of England Temperance Society — sensed the danger and joined together to block the application. The thrust of their argument was clear: the Oxford Road area offered too many opportunities for drunkenness, and its working-class inhabitants had proved themselves incapable of resisting the appeal of drink. 'Every increase of temptation', claimed the *Manchester Guardian*, 'means an increase of intemperance.'[28] Small wonder, then, that a prayer was also offered: 'That it may please Thee to keep thy magistrates, giving them grace to execute justice and to maintain truth.'[29]

Even when the directors applied for a drama licence, temperance leaders viewed this as an attempt to gain a drink licence under a new guise. As the *City News* put it: 'Summed up in a sentence, all of the speeches in opposition . . . were in effect, "Disguise it how you will, this theatrical licence means another drink licence; we won't have it at any price."'[30] When the Palace then argued that the critics were ignoring the threat posed by the more dangerous, smaller halls, its opponents argued that a victory over the Palace would initiate a struggle against the other halls: 'We shall not stop with the Palace,' wrote one Sunday school teacher, 'and we shall put all places of entertainment on the same level.'[31]

In the debates that took place in 1891 the *Guardian* published some five letters a day from readers opposed to the licence. Most of them believed that the Palace's desire for a drink licence indicated just how unscrupulous the entertainment industry was in its quest for profit. Arguments like this led the critics into uncharted territory. Not only did they claim that by selling drink the Palace would undermine public morality, but they also believed that Manchester, a moral city, was being invaded by profiteers from the great, immoral metropolis. One writer claimed that the Palace was engaged in 'a flagrant attempt . . . to subject our municipal government to the pecuniary interests of a private company of traders', a company without any roots in local society. As the *Guardian* put it, the choice was between 'the moral sentiment of the community' and 'the desire of a body of London capitalists to add some thousands each year to the[ir] profits'.[32]

Such sentiments were widely shared by those who believed that London was a den of vice and iniquity. George Edwardes, manager of the Gaiety Theatre in London before his involvement with the Empire in Leicester Square and the Palace in Manchester, was criticised on numerous occasions for wanting to turn Oxford Road into another Leicester Square. One opponent of the Palace claimed that at 10 p.m. Leicester Square was 'crowded by fast young men and loose young women who are attracted by these music halls'. To grant a licence to the Palace would be to encourage a similar 'loose-ness of living' in Manchester.[33]

The Palace, then, was equated with the desire for profit, a desire which appeared to be incompatible with the promotion of public morality. But underneath the rhetoric was a vague concern about something very diffe-rent, about a kind of hedonistic behaviour that threatened to subvert more desirable values in working-class uses of leisure. The Bishop of Manchester, for example, opposed the Palace because it seemed to him to represent an 'intensifying of the excitement of public entertainments' which would loosen the bonds of social restraint. By contrast, he yearned for a kind of moral gui-dance over popular entertainment which he believed could not be offered by the Palace. Other critics shared the Bishop's sentiments, but they seemed sin-gularly ill-equipped to express them clearly. Some of them began to realise that the moral homilies espoused by temperance leaders were inadequate weapons in the battle against the Palace, and they attempted to develop their own metaphors through which to capture what they sensed to be a new danger posed by this new form of amusement:

> There exists . . . a sort of Parisian hankering after . . . depraved . . . pleasures, such as did not once exist. Our greatly increased intercourse with the French nation has created a taste and a desire for amusements which have had a great deal to do with the bitter sorrows of that giddy, fickle and licentious nation. . . . Our taste [is] for real, solid, enduring pleasures.[34]

The net was cast wide. Not only was London to blame for the troubles in Manchester, but now Paris had to share the blame as well. Today such utter-ances may appear at best amusing, at worst nonsensical. But while most cri-tics could not understand the way in which the Palace was actively recon-structing popular culture, a few of them attempted to develop reference points for a critique of the new industry. If the older halls were opposed because they encouraged 'loose' living, the Palace was opposed because it encouraged 'fast' living amongst an audience of nameless and faceless stran-gers on a scale unparalleled by the smaller concert rooms. As one critic claimed, the directors of the Palace were 'seeking to provide for a new class of people a new form of entertainment', attracting youths from Rochdale and the surrounding area 'to a new form of fast life'.[35]

The panic that the establishment of the Palace gave rise to in middle-class circles cannot be explained simply in terms of traditional temperance battles, despite the extensive teetotal rhetoric evident at the licensing hearing. Nor can the fear that London capital was encouraging new forms of 'fast' living be understood properly without reference to a more profound crisis in bourgeois ideology. It was this crisis which led the battle over the Palace to assume such gigantic proportions. Indeed, the outbursts occasioned by the existence of the Palace can only be understood within a larger framework suggested by the history of bourgeois self-perception in the city.

Middle-class attempts to create a working class in its own image are well documented and can be traced back at least to the establishment of the

Mechanics' Institute in 1824. While such institutions were a precondition and guarantee of bourgeois legitimacy, it was soon apparent that they were not succeeding in their goals. Merely offering the working class the means of access to the values of their social superiors did not necessarily imply the acceptance of those values. Thus, in the 1830s, Manchester's reforming élite began to develop a new strategy which placed greater emphasis on intervening directly in working-class life. For example, the decade witnessed the creation of the Domestic Mission, an organisation which hoped to encourage the principles of individualism, thrift and self-help in working-class households. It also saw the foundation of the Manchester and Salford District Provident Society, which became one of the most influential philanthropic organisations in the city. As one of its historians has written, the establishment of the Society suggested that 'nothing less than complete transformation of working-class habits became a central feature of bourgeois cultural strategy'.[36]

The strategies developed by such organisations underwent few changes during the course of the century. None the less, middle-class faith in those strategies began to wane as early as the 1860s. In that decade numerous studies of poverty in Manchester revealed that direct intervention in working-class life had failed to effect much lasting change. Moreover, in the last quarter of the century a significant rise in levels of unemployment and underemployment further eroded middle-class confidence in its own reforming efforts. None the less, instead of leading to a wholesale questioning of the methods of reform developed in the 1830s, this merely led the urban élite to devote even more energy to pursuing traditional methods of reform. Thus the 1880s marked an era in which philanthropists and reformers intensified their work in domestic visiting, and in establishing cultural institutions in working-class districts, while slowly coming to believe that such efforts might well be in vain.

In such an environment even the smallest challenge to bourgeois self-confidence could not be tolerated lightly. And of course the Palace posed such a challenge. As John Seed and Janet Wolff have written, 'capitalist entrepreneurs, keen to profit from the new mass market for entertainment, often undermined the attempts of the liberal bourgeoisie to "civilise" the working class and wean it away from drink, sport and "popular culture"'.[37] According to reformers, workers, once locked into new patterns of consumption encouraged by the leisure industry, would be even less likely to adopt the values of thrift and moral sobriety which the middle class was eager to promote. Thus they feared that the Palace, by encouraging working-class hedonism, was counteracting their own reforming efforts. Moreover, despite what the supporters of the Palace might say in its defence, this was no match for the pent-up fears and frustrations of a reforming élite which felt threatened and uncertain amidst the changes taking place in Manchester society.

Against such an outpouring of bourgeois reforming zeal, tinged with genuine fear, the Palace could mount few convincing arguments. None the less, the directors persevered in their attempts to play down the financial troubles faced by the venture and to demonstrate that the Palace would indeed offer wholesome, rational recreation, thereby encouraging forms of behaviour reformers wished to promote. As early as 1890, they recognised that the battle for a licence would be a difficult one. Thus they appointed Ambrose Austin to the board. Austin, a well-known individual in the entertainment world who for 30 years had successfully managed the St James's Hall concerts in London, spoke at the licensing hearings held in February 1891. He claimed that music hall fare 'might be . . . made better for the amusement of the public by engaging good artists and elevating their minds by giving them good things'. The Palace, of course, was to do just that. But when Austin compared the Palace with the Empire and the Alhambra in London, he was roundly attacked. Moreover, he seemed to demonstrate a total ignorance of the financial workings of the Palace, leading the critics to claim — quite correctly — that Austin's appointment to the board was a mere window-dressing, undertaken to improve the Palace's image.[38]

At this point the manager of the Palace, George Scott, stepped in to defend the venture. In particular, he tried to dispel the notion that the provision of entertainment would be subordinated to the sale of drink. The Palace, he claimed, would provide wholesome amusement, and that wholesomeness would be guaranteed by the 'very magnitude of the capitalist stake'. Arguing that the Palace needed to please both customer and critic alike, Scott suggested that too many people had too much money invested in the company for the management to ignore the demands of those who questioned the morality of the whole undertaking.[39] Thus did the music hall industry attempt to promote itself as being in harmony with the aspirations of the city's moral élite, rather than as being subversive of its efforts.

To prove that music hall entertainment could indeed be edifying, the directors considered opening the Palace on Good Friday with a religious concert. While they decided against this, they went to great expense to hire *Cleopatra* — a musical ballet of the 'highest order' — from the Empire in London. If 'wholesome' variety entertainment was supposed to offer the public 'the story in action of manly courage, mutual help, English heroism, and honest endeavour', as one of its supporters claimed,[40] then *Cleopatra* seemed to fit the bill, extolling the virtues of patriotism and honesty while staying clear of any hint of indecency. At least the guardians of Manchester morality might rest assured that the Palace's audience would witness scenes designed to render them fully supportive of Britain's imperial destiny.

In order to dispel the belief that the Palace encouraged rowdyism and immoral conduct, the management also stressed the ease with which its audience could be supervised. Again, this was aimed at bourgeois ideologues who were becoming increasingly worried about the growing physical separation of the classes and hence about the difficulty of penetrating the depths of working-class life. As Penelope Summerfield has suggested, proprietors of the new palaces often policed the halls carefully with the knowledge that if they failed to do so their licences might be placed in jeopardy.[41] The attorney representing the Palace at the March 1891 hearings suggested that the smaller halls were hidden from the influence of public morality, and that the very size of the Palace would be a guarantee of its constant supervision. 'Their property', he claimed, 'would be under the strict supervision of the police, and far more under the public gaze than the bulk of the buildings which now possess licences'.[42]

The Palace also attempted to bolster its image by pointing to the respectability of its audience. While the smaller halls appeared to draw their clientele largely from the neighbourhoods in which they were located, the Palace drew visitors from as far as Rochdale and beyond. Critics may have worried about a mass of 3,000 strangers converging on Oxford Road, but George Scott claimed that such people were serious entertainment lovers who went to the trouble and expense of visiting his theatre for a special evening out.[43] The Palace was not a 'local' which attracted the more disreputable elements of the community night after night, but a well-regulated centre for the edification and entertainment of a self-selecting, respectable audience made up of rational consumers of variety amusement.

If the Palace's audience was a mass audience, dispersed over a wide geographical area, it was also a fairly affluent audience. Admission prices were not cheap: Boxes cost 1gn or 2gns, while tickets for the pit cost 1s. 6d., and those for the gallery 1s. (reduced to 1s. for the pit and 6d. for the gallery for late admissions). By contrast, the price of admission to a football match averaged 3d. or 4d. in the 1880s and 6d. in the 1890s.[44] Although the Palace's prices were comparable with those charged by many variety theatres in London, they were much higher than those charged by the smaller halls in Lancashire. One observer claimed that in such halls the most expensive seats were 1s. or 1s. 6d., while the cheapest seats were a mere 3d. Even the larger halls in Manchester in the 1860s — the Victoria, the London, the Alexandra and Burton's People's Music Hall — charged a maximum of 1s. for their seats.[45] The directors of the Palace noted the difference and claimed that its own high prices, coupled with the distance its patrons travelled for an evening's amusement, guaranteed the respectability of the audience. The *Sunday Chronicle* agreed:

> What the amusement-seeking world of Manchester has to congratulate itself upon is the fact that at last we have a . . . place of entertainment to which we can take our wives and daughters to hear a good song and see an artistic ballet without fear of rubbing shoulders with a preponderance of the shadier elements of society.[46]

As Dagmar Höher suggests in her article on music hall audiences (Chapter 4, this volume), the presence of whole families in the newer halls could be used by the owners to stress the respectability of their ventures. Moreover, the wife was the respectable counterpart of the prostitute, and by emphasising her role in the audience the owners could claim that women were exerting a 'civilising' influence on male behaviour in the halls. None the less, the real guarantee of the Palace's respectability was its admission prices, which did indeed tend to exclude 'the shadier elements of society'. In short, the audience created by the Palace was a new type of audience, and in the cavernous auditorium on Oxford Road new consumers of leisure were flattered with the image of their own social superiority.

Despite the need to convince the critics of its respectability, more important was the need for the Palace to shed its ties — or at least to appear to shed its ties — with the world of London finance. To some extent this was achieved by playing down Edwardes's role in the venture and forcing George Scott, the manager, to represent the interests of the Palace. But despite such superficial changes, most of the major shareholders in the company in its earliest days were Londoners, while meetings of the board were held in the Empire in Leicester Square. Both of these points were seized upon by critics when they denounced the venture as having virtually no roots in the North-West. During the height of the licensing battles in 1891 and 1892 several prominent Manchester men were appointed to the board, including George Essayan, a Greek merchant who held 6,320 shares in the company, John Kershaw, a member of the Royal College of Surgeons, and H. Fecht, another prominent businessman. By April 1892 six of the eight directors resided in the vicinity of Manchester. But these changes were too few and too late, and it was easy for the opponents of the licence to claim that the board had been 'packed' in order to deflect criticism.[47]

In 1892, the Palace claimed that of 320 shareholders in the company, roughly half resided in Manchester. A complete record of shareholders exists for 1895, which attests to the prominence of Lancashire businessmen amongst them. Perhaps the most important of these was Edward Hulton, the proprietor of the *Sunday Chronicle*, who owned 500 shares in the Palace and who used his paper to argue in its favour. Unfortunately, few addresses are listed in the register. None the less, the majority of shareholders — whether Londoners or not — appeared to be small investors. A full 71.5 per cent held less than 150 £1 shares, 47.1 per cent held 50 shares or less, and 11.9 per cent held a mere five or ten shares. This would suggest that the pattern of shareholding in the Palace was similar to that in another branch of the new entertainment industry — the football club. Shareholding in both cases was dominated by a few rich entrepreneurs and a large number of petty-bourgeois investors, although it included a sprinkling of better-paid workers.[48] But for the critics it didn't matter that investment patterns brought members of various classes together, nor did it matter that some of the larger investors were from Manchester; it still appeared to them that the shareholders in general had fallen for a get-rich-quick scheme that had been initiated by a group of London profiteers.

It was of course to the advantage of shareholders that the Palace receive a drink licence. When in 1892 the Watch Committee provisionally granted the Palace a drama licence — and thus increased its chance of securing a drink licence — share prices rose by some 20 per cent.[49] But this merely underscored what its opponents had said all along, namely that the chief concern of the Palace was the accumulation of profit from the sale of drink. Packing the board with Manchester-based directors, or claiming that a number of the smaller shareholders resided in Manchester, was not an adequate response to fears about the relationship between drink, profit and public morality. No matter what the Palace might say in its defence, many opponents would have agreed with Charles Rowley's assessment of it. Founder of the Ancoats Brotherhood, an organisation which offered rational recreation in the slums of the city, Rowley was one of a number of philanthropists and reformers who, in the 1880s, attempted to reinvigorate the strategies of intervention in working-class life that dated from the 1830s. But like his colleagues, Rowley believed that the Palace posed a threat to those efforts at instilling new virtues in the inhabitants of the slums of Ancoats. For him, the directors of the Palace remained 'purveyors of a degraded and vicious art'.[50]

Although opposition to the Palace was widespread, this is not to suggest that the venture was without friends. In 1889, for example, the *Era* claimed that there were 423 music licences in the city, owned by halls offering entertainment known for its 'dreariness and stupidity'. Larger variety halls, the paper claimed, would draw their custom from such places and improve the quality of popular amusement.[51] The *Era*, the leading music hall journal, published in London, lent its support to the new palaces. Moreover, many individuals in Manchester accepted the logic of its argument. For them, the Palace was 'a counter-attraction to those sinks of iniquity' and was thus one of 'our most powerful agencies for good'.[52]

The socialist movement in Manchester tended to adopt this position. While some socialists and labour leaders, like John Burns, believed that in the halls 'the best interests of the profession are subordinated to dividends',[53] others were less sceptical. A. M. Thompson, for example, drama critic for Robert Blatchford's socialist weekly, the *Clarion*, claimed that while many philanthropists aimed at 'elevating' the working class by providing rational recreation, the 'hooligan' merely scoffed at their efforts on the way to the music hall. He thus suggested that halls offering wholesome amusement — like the Palace — should be encouraged.[54] This particular position was shared by a number of socialists who flatly rejected those elements of bourgeois ideology — 'debased Calvinistic morality', as William Morris and Ernest Belfort Bax termed them[55] — which stressed self-denial, the 'English Sunday' and 'joylessness', and which had always been opposed to popular amusements.

Blatchford himself also played a role in generating support for the Palace. Before establishing the *Clarion* in 1891 he contributed a column to the *Sunday Chronicle*, and here he shared Hulton's attitude to the venture. As early as 1889 he anticipated the problems the Palace would encounter, writing:

> I'm afraid music halls are not as pure as I should like to see them, though I don't believe they are as vile as they are painted. But I don't think I said they were pure. I only said that the good music hall was better than the bad one, and that the proper way to improve the general tone of our public entertainment was not the refusing of one licence out of 400, but the making of such places so clean, so cheap, so public, and so attractive that decent men might take their wives there.[56]

In 1892 Blatchford used the *Clarion* to stress these points more forcefully. That summer, after Scott had been fined for staging a play illegally,

Blatchford visited a number of the smaller halls in the city in order to compare them with the Palace. He was soon convinced, as was his colleague, A. M. Thompson, that socialists should support the Palace. Thompson wrote that it was unfair to deny the Palace a licence when licences were granted to 'unhealthy singing rooms, screened by their obscurity from the eyes of public morality'. If licences were to be denied, then they should be denied to those 'drinking-dens . . . where vile inflammatory poisons are . . . dealt out to the accompaniment of obscene songs and filthy conversation'.[57]

It is ironic — and also revealing — that activists in the socialist movement should throw their support behind the Palace, and hence, by implication, behind an industry that was attempting to remake working-class culture and reduce the space available for the development of autonomous forms of working-class expression. On the one hand, Blatchford spoke out against 'commercial tyranny', and against the profit motive and a drink industry that kept the worker in bondage. But, on the other, he rejected the teetotal Puritanism of many of his comrades, such as Burns, and believed that the right to decent recreation was as important as the right to decent housing, health and improved conditions of labour. The Palace may have been a capitalist venture, but it was one that treated workers as respectable consumers, capable of differentiating wholesome from disreputable pastimes. The kind of worker the directors claimed visited the Palace was the kind Blatchford wanted for the socialist movement. Rather than pose a threat to the moral fabric of society, the Palace — and in time the whole industry of which it was but one small part — managed to convince some of the most ardent critics of capitalism of its own worthiness.

The Palace and the state

Throughout the nineteenth century numerous individuals were eager to reform popular culture through sober programmes of rational recreation. Those programmes were manifested in many different kinds of activity. But what united them all was an emphasis on supervision: no longer would the working class be able to take its pleasures away from the benevolent — and often not so benevolent — gaze of those who believed they knew best what the working class *should* desire. But by the 1890s, as we have seen, and as A. M. Thompson noted, philanthropic schemes of recreational reform were in disarray, rejected by those who preferred the conveniences and glamorous pleasures offered by the halls and other forms of emerging 'mass' entertainment. They succeeded, where reformers failed, in bringing many popular pleasures into full public view. Stressing this achievement, the Palace's directors claimed that capital was the best guarantee of morality. Moreover, in making this claim they convinced some critics to support the Palace. None the less, Manchester's ruling élite more often than not rejected the Palace's rhetoric. Thus, in the 1890s — a decade of crisis for philanthropy and voluntary associations in general — reformers began to turn to the state, hoping that it might succeed, where philanthropic efforts had failed — and commercial efforts could not hope to succeed — in promoting a more moral popular culture.

Although the state had always exercised a degree of control over places of entertainment through its licensing powers, its methods of control became more elaborate in the 1890s. In that decade the directors of the Palace faced a new phenomenon — a municipality that changed the rules behind their backs, granting them a drama licence on the understanding that they would not apply for a drink licence. Moreover, after confronting the authorities in Manchester, Edwardes became embroiled in a similar battle in London. In 1894, Mrs Ormiston Chant, the Mary Whitehouse of her day, opposed the renewal of the Empire's licence, claiming that the hall was used by prostitutes to solicit business. Eventually the London County Council renewed the licence, but only after the management promised to abolish the promenade and refrain from serving alcohol in the auditorium. During the hearings, Chant claimed that she did not oppose amusement, but that she wanted 'to see those things in the right hands'.[58] What was at issue here was not merely the right of the authorities to grant a licence, but their power to supervise large places of public entertainment at all times. Capitalism had drawn a form of amusement into full public view but now the state stepped in to regulate it.

Once the role of the state in monitoring entertainment had been accepted, it was but a small step to suggest that the state might assume responsibility for its provision. Socialists, even while supporting the Palace, claimed that the best guarantee of truly edifying entertainment was state or municipal control. The Fabians were particularly eager to put forward such policies, which formed an integral part of the 'municipal socialism' of the 1890s. As one socialist wrote, complaining of the 'greasiness' of most music hall performances, 'give it to them good, ensuring its quality in the only possible way, by state ownership or control, with provision for a constant readjustment to people's improving tastes'.[59] Some individuals believed that even if the state did not operate its own halls it should make better provision for their regulation. One critic in Manchester agreed. Suspicious of the entertainment offered by the Palace, but also tired of the moral homilies espoused by its critics, he asked: 'Ought we not to have some department of the State which might deal with public amusement or recreation as we have to deal with education?'[60]

Thus the battle over the Palace gave rise to a debate about how to control an emerging leisure industry. In Manchester many of the Palace's supporters suggested that control should reside with elected representatives, not with appointed magistrates. The *Clarion* staff agreed with this. But what if elected bodies were influenced by well-organised pressure groups, such as those concerned with 'moral purity'? After Mrs Ormiston Chant once spoke at Stockport, A. M. Thompson complained: 'If you think that we men are going to elect you women to . . . decree whether we shall go to a music hall or not . . . you are . . . likely to be disen-Chant-ed.'[61] State control, then, was

a double-edged sword. While it promised popular supervision of entertainment, it could also result in puritanical attempts to suppress it. While
the *Guardian* claimed that the council was merely protecting Manchester
morality against the unprincipled dealings of London profiteers, the
Chronicle saw things rather differently: 'Shall the moral scruples of a small
but wealthy minority of the public', the paper asked, 'be allowed to deprive
a number of . . . citizens of the right to buy a drink within the walls of the
Palace?'[62] For those who shared these sentiments the threat posed by
the Palace was not as great as that posed by the revival of forms of puritanism they believed had been tried and found wanting in the seventeenth
century.[63]

Many workers shared the *Chronicle's* alarm at the growing interference of
the state with their 'legitimate' pleasures. As one of them claimed, 'we are in
great danger of only being allowed such amusements as our self-constituted
morality keepers think proper to give us'.[64] The *Advertiser* agreed, suggesting
to its working-class readers that their social superiors had demonstrated
their belief that workers were 'incapable of exercising reasonable and proper
self-restraint'.[65] Thus the battle over the Palace drove a large number of
workers to attack the state in its regulating capacity. But in so doing it had
driven them into the arms of the leisure industry, an industry that in
encouraging the development of a new mass audience for its products was
destroying the bonds that had once existed between work, the community
and popular culture.[66]

In its early days music hall attendance was largely determined by the social
calendar of work and leisure in a given neighbourhood. But in the 1890s the
Palace tended to break down these connections. Its audience was more geographically dispersed than was that of the Victorian music hall in the 1860s,
and, in addition, it was determined more by income levels and status aspirations than by the structure of local trades. Thus the increasing presence of
the state was attacked not by a community of workers but by an audience
which was constituted as a community only in so far as it was a creation of a
new breed of music hall entrepreneurs.

In terms of the political consequences of working-class opposition to Manchester's 'municipal puritanism', the battle over the Palace worked to sever
the ties between workers and Liberal politics. In so doing it assisted the
growth of Tory populism. When, for example, the Palace applied for a drink
licence in September 1891 it was opposed by 29 Liberals and Liberal
Unionists and only 11 Conservatives. In its favour were a mere 4 Liberals
and Liberal Unionists — one of whom was a worker — and 14 Conservatives.[67] Clearly, the opposition of nonconformist politics to forms of entertainment many workers were coming to desire allowed the new conservatism
of the late nineteenth century to make at least some working-class converts
in Lancashire. If *Cleopatra* wedded workers to a world of jingoism, patriotism
and heroism, then working-class rejection of Liberal morality suggested that
Toryism, populism and the new world of commercial entertainment often
went hand in hand.

Notes

(Place of publication is London unless stated otherwise.)

1. Andrew Wilson, 'Music Halls', *Contemporary Review*, vol. 78, 1900, pp. 134–41.
2. Peter Bailey, 'Custom, Capital and Culture in the Victorian Music Hall' in Robert Storch (ed.), *Popular Culture and Custom in Nineteenth-Century England*, 1982, p. 202.
3. Ian Watson, *Song and Democratic Culture in Britain*, 1983, pp. 18–19.
4. Walter Tomlinson, *Bye-Ways of Manchester Life*, Manchester, 1887, p. 73. See also George E. Wewiora, 'Manchester Music Hall Audiences in the 1880s', *Manchester Review*, vol. 12, 1973, pp. 124–8.
5. *Manchester Evening News (MEN)*, 24 March 1891. See also *Manchester Examiner and Times (MET)*, 25 March 1891. On the earlier large halls, see *Free Lance*, 25 January and 8 February 1868; see also Charles Coborn, *'The Man Who Broke the Bank'. Memories of the Stage and Music Hall*, 1928, pp. 98–100.
6. Ernest A. E. Woodrow, 'Manchester Palace of Varieties', *American Architect and Building News*, vol. 49, 1895, pp. 35–7.
7. Palace Theatre, *Souvenir*, Manchester, 1913, pp. 3, 5.
8. See *Public General Acts*: 51 & 52 Victoria, 'Chap. 41: An Act to ammend the laws relating to Local Government in England and Wales . . .', parts I/3, II/35; 53 & 54 Victoria, 'Chap. 59: An Act to ammend the Public Health Acts . . .', part IV, section 51/1 and 2. See also 'Regulation of the Music Halls', a clipping in a Manchester Central Library (MCL) scrapbook, 'Newspaper Clippings, 1907–13, Stage'; *Era*, 30 October 1891.
9. See *The Fiery Cross to Rouse the Ratepayers to Rescue the New Councils from the Threatened Grip of the Brewers and Publicans*, Manchester, 1894.
10. See D. F. Cheshire, *Music Hall in Britain*, Newton Abbot, 1974, p. 93. At one of the hearings, the defence for the Palace claimed that the Comedy Theatre had both a drama and music licence — see *Era*, 9 April 1892.
11. Manchester Palace of Varieties Ltd, 'Minute Book of Directors' Meetings, 1889–1893' (MCL archives, M359) ('Minutes'), 23 May, 7 and 28 October 1890.
12. *Manchester Evening Mail (MEM)* and *MEN*, 17 February 1891; *Manchester Courier and Lancashire General Advertiser (MCLGA)* and *MET*, 18 February 1891; *Era* and *Manchester City News* (MCN), 21 February 1891.
13. 'Minutes', 25 February 1891; *MEM*, 16 March 1891; *MET*, 23 March 1891.
14. *Sunday Chronicle (SC)*, 29 March 1891. For the March 1891 hearings, see *MEM* and *MEN*, 24 March 1891; *MCLGA* and *MET*, 25 March 1891; *Era*, 28 March 1891.
15. *MCLGA*, 16 May 1891; *Era*, 23 May 1891.
16. *MEM* and *MEN*, 28 August and 24 September 1891; *MCLGA* and *Manchester Guardian (MG)*, 29 August and 25 September 1891; *MCN*, 29 August and 26 September 1891; *SC*, 6 September 1891; *Era*, 3 October 1891.
17. 'Minutes', 28 April and 14 November 1891; 11 February and 3 June 1892.
18. *MEN*, 31 March and 6 April 1892; *Era* and *MCN*, 2 and 9 April 1892.
19. *MCLGA*, 28 October 1892; 2 December 1892; *Era*, 29 October 1892; 3 December 1892.
20. *MEN*, 3 May 1898; *Era* and *MCN*, 7 May 1898.
21. *MCLGA*, 25 August 1900. See also *MCLGA*, 3 August 1900; *MCN*, 4 and 25 August 1900.

22. *MEM*, 28 August 1891.
23. *MET*, 18 February 1891. For the Empire's balance sheet, see *MG*, 26 August 1892. For Palace figures, see *Era*, 27 August 1892; 'Minutes', 20 May and 23 September 1892.
24. For shareholders' reports, see *MCLGA*, 30 August 1892; *Era*, 27 August and 3 September 1892; 4 July 1896.
25. *Era*, 4 March 1899; *MG*, 10 and 17 June 1904; *Magnet*, 18 June 1904.
26. Brian Harrison, *Drink and the Victorians*, Pittsburgh, 1971, pp. 95, 198, 315, 324.
27. *MG*, 9 September 1892. The material in Tables 7.1 and 7.2 is derived from the findings in this article in *MG*.
28. *MG*, 29 August 1891.
29. Quoted in a letter, *MCLGA*, 19 September 1891.
30. Editorial, *MCN*, 9 April 1892.
31. Letter, *MCLGA*, 8 April 1892.
32. *MG*, 25 October 1892; 29 August 1891. On an earlier date similar sentiments had been expressed in Bradford — see James Burnley, *Phases of Bradford Life*, 1871, p. 54.
33. *MCLGA*, 18 and 24 February, 24 March 1891; *MEN*, 24 March 1891; *MET*, 25 March 1891. On Edwardes's career , see Ursula H. Bloom, *Curtain Calls for the Guv'nor. A Biography of George Edwardes*, 1954.
34. Letter, *MET*, 23 March 1891. For the Bishop's thoughts, see *MG*, 25 August 1891.
35. *MET*, 25 March 1891.
36. Alan J. Kidd, 'Charity Organisation and the Unemployed in Manchester *c.* 1870–1914', *Social History*, vol. 9, 1984, p. 47. See also John Seed, 'Unitarianism, Political Economy and the Antinomies of Liberal Culture in Manchester, 1830–1850', *Social History*, vol. 7, 1982, pp. 1–25.
37. John Seed and Janet Wolff, 'Class Culture in Nineteenth Century Manchester', *Theory, Culture and Society*, vol. 2, 1984, p. 51.
38. *MEM*, 17 February 1891; *MET*, 18 February 1891.
39. *MG*, 26 August 1891.
40. Clement Scott, 'The Modern Music Hall', *Contemporary Review*, vol. 56, 1889, p. 684. For comments on *Cleopatra*, see *MET*, 18 February 1891; *MEN*, 16 May 1891. For the idea of opening the Palace with a religious concert, see 'Minutes', 23 February 1891.
41. Penelope Summerfield, 'The Effingham Arms and the Empire: Deliberate Selection in the Evolution of Music Hall in London' in Eileen and Stephen Yeo (eds), *Popular Culture and Class Conflict, 1590–1914*, Hassocks, 1981, pp. 223–4.
42. *MET*, 25 March 1891.
43. Ibid.
44. 'Minutes', 28 April 1891. See also the programmes printed in 'Manchester Amusements and Souvenir of the Stage' (MCL). On audiences, see Bob Dickinson, 'In the Audience', *Oral History*, vol. 11, 1983, pp. 52–61. For the pricing structure of football matches, see Tony Mason, *Association Football and English Society 1863–1915*, Brighton, 1980, pp. 148–50.
45. For the smaller halls in Manchester, see C. E. B. Russell and E. T. Campagnac, 'Poor People's Music Halls in Lancashire', *Economic Review*, vol. 10, 1900, pp. 290–1. For the large, Manchester halls of the 1860s, see Dagmar Höher's article, Chapter 4, this volume.

46. *SC*, 17 May 1891. On music hall and mass culture, see in particular Martha Vicinus, *The Industrial Muse*, New York, 1974, esp. pp. 238–9.

47. 'Minutes', 17 January and 23 February 1891; *MEN*, 17 February 1891; *MET*, 18 February 1891; *MCLGA*, 1 April 1892; *MCN*, 2 April 1892.

48. The shareholders' register (MCL archives) lists 320 shareholders with 70,640 shares in August 1895. At first, shares appear to have been sold in £5 denominations, but dividend reports that indicate a divident of 5%, or 1s., would suggest that at least by 1895 shares cost £1, sold in multiples of five (see *Era*, 27 August 1892; 4 July 1896). For the Palace's claim that half its shareholders resided in Manchester, see *MET*, 18 February 1891. For shareholders in football clubs, see Mason, *Football*, pp. 38–42.

49. Letter, *MG*, 5 April 1892.

50. *MCN*, 21 March 1891. For a summary of Rowley's work, see Chris Waters, 'Socialism and the Politics of Popular Culture in Britain, 1884–1914', unpublished PhD thesis, Harvard University, 1985, pp. 220–5.

51. *Era*, 12 October 1889.

52. *MCLGA*, 20 March 1891. See also 21 February and 23 March 1891. The *SC* was most consistent in advancing this argument — see 15 and 29 March, 27 September 1891.

53. John Burns, *Music and Musicians*, Manchester, n.d., p. 1.

54. *Clarion*, 27 November 1903. Socialists in Bradford felt likewise — see *Bradford Labour Echo*, 28 January 1899.

55. William Morris and E. Belfort Bax, *Socialism: Its Growth and Outcome*, 1893, p. 26. See also E. Belfort Bax, *Outspoken Essays on Social Subjects*, 1897.

56. *SC*, 13 October 1889. See also *SC*, 8 March 1891.

57. *Clarion*, 27 August 1892. For Blatchford's visit to the halls, see 3 September 1892. On another occasion, however, readers of the *Clarion* were urged to send money to the Manchester, Salford and District Temperance Union to help that organisation defray the costs of opposing the licence — see *Clarion*, 9 January 1892.

58. Mrs Ormiston Chant, *Why We Attacked the Empire*, 1895, p. 19. See also Cheshire, *Music Hall*, pp. 38–42. For the LCC and the halls, see S. Pennybacker, Chapter 6, this volume.

59. P. P. Howe, 'The Municipalisation of Music Halls', *Socialist Review*, vol. 5, 1910, p. 425.

60. *MET*, 23 March 1891.

61. *SC*, 27 October 1889.

62. *SC*, 30 August 1891. Just as the proprietor of the *Chronicle* owned stock in the company and sided with the Palace, so C. P. Scott of the *MG* was a magistrate who voted against the Palace and aired his views in that paper.

63. *MEN*, 25 March 1891. See also *MET*, 19 February 1891; *MCLGA*, 19 and 25 February 1891; 8 April 1897.

64. *MET*, 19 February 1891. See also *MCLGA*, 26 February and 20 March 1891.

65. *MCLGA*, 25 September 1891.

66. See Dagmar Höher's article, Chapter 4, this volume, for a discussion of audiences. While I agree with her assessment of audience patterns in the 1860s and 1870s, evidence from the Palace tends to suggest that subtle, but significant, changes had taken place by the end of the century. As we have seen, observers often pointed to the distances individuals travelled in order to attend performances at the Palace when they wanted to contrast the Palace with the earlier halls.

67. *MCN*, 3 October 1891. On popular conservatism and cultural politics in Lancashire, see Patrick Joyce, *Work, Society and Politics*, Hassocks, 1980, *passim*.

Index